CW00828589

WALKING THE CORBETTS

VOLUME 2: NORTH OF THE GREAT GLEN

About the Author

Since taking early retirement from his career as a physics and sports teacher, Brian Johnson has found time for three through-hikes of the Pacific Crest Trail, a 2700-mile round-Britain walk, three hikes across the Pyrenees from the Atlantic to the Mediterranean, a hike along the Via de la Plata from Seville to Santiago, a single summer 'compleation' of the Munros (Scotland's 3000ft mountains) and has now reclimbed all the Corbetts while researching this guide. He has also completed a 2200-mile cycle tour of Spain and France and done multi-week canoe tours in Sweden, France, Spain and Portugal.

In his younger days, Brian's main sport was orienteering. He competed at a high level and coached both Bishop Wordsworth's School and South-West Junior Orienteering Squads. He also surveyed and drew many orienteering maps. He has walked and climbed extensively in summer and winter conditions in Britain, the Alps, the Pyrenees and California, often leading school groups.

As a fanatical sportsman and games player, Brian competed to a high level in cricket, hockey, bridge and chess. His crowning achievement was winning the 1995/96 World Amateur Chess Championships.

Other Cicerone guides by the author

The Pacific Crest Trail
Walking the Corbetts Volume 1: South of the Great Glen

WALKING THE CORBETTS

VOLUME 2: NORTH OF THE GREAT GLEN

by Brian Johnson

2 POLICE SQUARE, MILNTHORPE, CUMBRIA LA7 7PY
www.cicerone.co.uk

© Brian Johnson 2013
First edition 2013
ISBN: 978 1 85284 653 4

Printed in China on behalf of Latitude Press Ltd.

A catalogue record for this book is available from the British Library.
All photographs are by the author unless otherwise stated.

Route mapping by Lovell Johns www.lovelljohns.com
Contains Ordnance Survey data © Crown copyright and
database right 2013. NASA relief data courtesy of ESRI

Advice to Readers

While every effort is made by our authors to ensure the accuracy of
guidebooks as they go to print, changes can occur during the lifetime of an
edition. If we know of any, there will be an Updates tab on this book's page
on the Cicerone website (www.cicerone.co.uk), so please check before
planning your trip. We also advise that you check information about such
things as transport, accommodation and shops locally. Even rights of way
can be altered over time. We are always grateful for information about
any discrepancies between a guidebook and the facts on the ground, sent
by email to info@cicerone.co.uk or by post to Cicerone, 2 Police Square,
Milnthorpe LA7 7PY, United Kingdom.

Front cover: Creag a'Chumhaing buttress on Meall Gorm, Applecross (Route 56)

CONTENTS

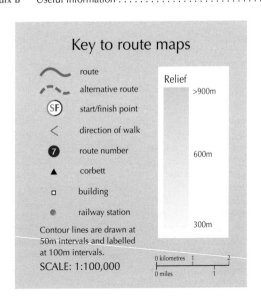

Key to route maps

~ route

- - - alternative route

(SF) start/finish point

< direction of walk

7 route number

▲ corbett

□ building

● railway station

Contour lines are drawn at 50m intervals and labelled at 100m intervals.

SCALE: 1:100,000

Relief

>900m

600m

300m

0 kilometres 1   2

0 miles   1

FOREWORD BY
LORD HAWORTH OF FISHERFIELD

Sweeping generalisations are best avoided, unless they contain an essential truth. Here is a sweeping generalisation which does just that – the best Corbetts are to be found north of the Great Glen.

This second volume of *Walking the Corbetts* covers Morvern, Sunart, Ardgour and Moidart where no Munros are to be found; but steep and dramatic Corbetts abound. Garbh Bheinn of Ardgour is one of the finest mountains in the Western Highlands and is as rough as its name implies. Sgurr Dhomhnuill, pointed and shapely, is the highest peak hereabouts. Sgurr Ghiubsachain, best seen from the Glenfinnan Monument, throws down a steep and inviting ridge to the edge of Loch Shiel; and the views from Beinn Resipol are among the finest on the western seaboard. Further north, in the area from Loch Eil to Glen Shiel, the long undulating ridge of Streap is a joy; Ben Aden is every bit as rocky and rough as the toughest Munros in the Rough Bounds of Knoydart and vies with Sgurr a' Choire Bheithe as the least accessible. The latter was for many years regarded as a candidate as a possible undiscovered Munro. Now measured definitively with a huge degree of accuracy it remains, tantalisingly, at 913m – just missing the magic height for a Munro.

However, surveyors supported by the Munro Society have recently discovered a new Corbett. Beinn a' Chlaidheimh, in the Fisherfield Forest, has been found to be lacking vital inches and has returned to the fold of the Corbetts, having previously been promoted to a Munro. Are there more Munros to be demoted or Corbetts to be promoted to Munro status? Almost certainly not. As this volume goes to press all the marginal Munros and Corbetts have been surveyed to an accuracy of ±5cm, and there should be no more surprises.

Further north, superlatives abound when describing the hills of Torridon, Coigach and Assynt. Beinn Dearg and Boasbheinn, on the edges of Flowerdale, represent considerable challenges to get up and down; but the rewards are more than worth the effort. Beinn Airigh Charr and Beinn Dearg Mor, of Fisherfield, are my two favourite Corbetts – the former for the view from the summit and the latter for the view of the mountain from Shenavall. In the east of the northern hills, attention needs to be drawn to lonely Carn Ban, one of the most remote. The great hills of Assynt, mostly Corbetts, provide stunning views of Suilven and Stac Pollaidh, neither of which are themselves high enough to be in this list but which

Liathach from Beinn Damh, Glen Torridon (Route 57)

dominate the surrounding landscape like medieval castellated fortifications. And before we reach the north coast, we have the shining quartzite of majestic Foinaven, the double-header of Cranstackie and Beinn Spionnaidh and last but certainly not least the multi-topped gem of Ben Loyal – all hills which never disappoint.

And, finally, this volume includes the islands of Rum, Mull, Skye and Harris – with another half a dozen precious pearls.

The southern hills are perfectly fine; but these are the real deals. And more often than not, you will have them to yourself. Go there.

Lord Haworth was the first member of the House of Lords to compleat (*sic*) the Munros, many of which he climbed with former Labour Party leader John Smith and Chris Smith, the only member of the House of Commons to have compleated the Munros. Although a Lancastrian, his love of the hills of Scotland led him to take the title of Lord Haworth of Fisherfield when elevated to the peerage in 2004. The Fisherfield Forest in Wester Ross contains some of the most remote and dramatic Munros and Corbetts, including A' Mhaighdean and Beinn Dearg Mor. He is a member of the Munro Society and has sponsored some surveys to measure the height of 'dubious' Munros and Corbetts, including the one which resulted in Beinn a' Chlaidheimh being relegated to Corbett status.

PREFACE

Connoisseurs of the Scottish Highlands will know that north-west Scotland has some of the most magnificent mountain and coastal scenery in the world.

North of the Great Glen the sea-lochs cut deep into the western seaboard, giving fjord-like scenery, and islands of the Inner and Outer Hebrides have a magic of their own. This side of the Great Glen most of the mountains are rocky and rise steeply from a rough and wild landscape dotted with sparkling lochs and lochans. Along the western seaboard there are far more Corbetts than Munros and most of these are magnificent mountains. In fact, there are no Munros at all in the wild Ardgour or Moidart, nor on the islands of Harris and Rum, and in the far north and west few of the spectacular isolated peaks composed of Torridonian sandstone reach Munro status.

A list of the 50 best walks on the Corbetts would contain at least 45 from north of the Great Glen!

You will find that most of the peaks in Volume 2 of this guide are tougher and more committing than the peaks described in Volume 1 and many could be daunting for the inexperienced walker in bad weather.

This guide is aimed at the walker who wants the most interesting route on the mountain, but even the peak bagger looking for the shortest way up might get more out of his 'tick' by following the routes suggested here.

Brian Johnson

Mountain Warning

Mountain walking can be a dangerous activity carrying a risk of personal injury or death. It should be undertaken only by those with a full understanding of the risks and with the training and experience to evaluate them. While every care and effort has been taken in the preparation of this guide, the user should be aware that conditions can be highly variable and can change quickly, materially affecting the seriousness of a mountain walk. Therefore, except for any liability which cannot be excluded by law, neither Cicerone nor the author accept liability for damage of any nature (including damage to property, personal injury or death) arising directly or indirectly from the information in this book.

To call out the Mountain Rescue, ring 999 or the international emergency number 112: this will connect you via any available network. Once connected to the emergency operator, ask for the police.

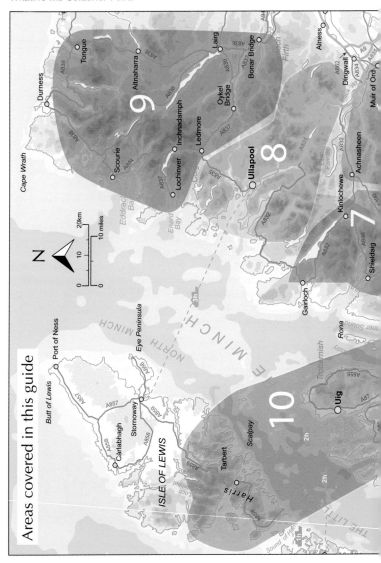

Areas covered in this guide

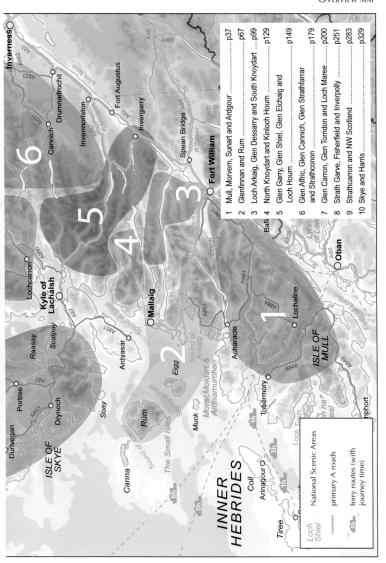

Loch
Shiel

National Scenic Areas

primary A roads

ferry routes (with
journey time)

INNER
HEBRIDES

13

Glen Barisdale, Knoydart (Route 31)

INTRODUCTION

Scottish Peaks over 3000ft (914.4m) became known as 'Munros' after they were listed by Sir Hugh Munro in 1891. The Scottish Mountaineering Club (SMC) published the list and 'Munro-bagging' soon became a popular sport. By 2010 over 4000 people were recorded as having 'compleated' all the Munros, although there are many more unrecorded compleatists, too.

In 1930 John Rooke Corbett, a district valuer from Bristol, became the fourth person and first Sassenach (Englishman) to compleat the Munros, but he didn't stop there. He went on to climb all Scotland's hills and mountains over 2000ft (610m) and drew up a list of mountains between 2500ft (762.0m) and 3000ft (914.4m) with a drop of at least 500ft (152.4m) on all sides. When Corbett died in 1949, his sister passed his list on to the SMC, who published it alongside the Munro tables.

Corbett's original list has been adjusted as the accuracy of maps has improved, and this has meant the addition of about 20 Corbetts and the deletion of others. Also mentioned in the route descriptions are 'Grahams', which are mountains between 2000 and 2499ft.

Volume 2 covers the Corbetts north of the Great Glen, including the western seaboard and the islands of Mull, Rum, Skye and Harris. South of the Great Glen it is the Munros which attract most attention, but along the western seaboard and in the far north it is often the Corbetts or even the lowly Grahams which dominate the landscape, with isolated rocky peaks rising steeply above the sea and inland lochs, in a wilderness of heather and bog dotted with sparkling lochs and lochans. There are few Munros here, but there are spectacular Corbetts all the way from Ardgour to Cape Wrath, including those in Ardgour, Knoydart, Applecross, Torridon and Fisherfield. The far north-west provides some of the most magnificent mountain scenery in the world and it is difficult to beat the magical islands of Mull, Rum, Skye and Harris.

Is it a Corbett?

Since the lists of Munros, Corbetts or Grahams were first published there have been many revisions as more accurate OS maps have been produced. Accurate surveys, sponsored by the Munro Society, have probably settled all doubts at the boundary between Munros and Corbetts, but there are still likely to be a number of promotions or demotions between Corbett and Graham status.

The problem is highlighted in the case of a peak which appeared

Loch Beinn Dearg, Fisherfield Forest (Route 72)

in the first draft of this guide but has now been excluded; Beinn Talaidh on Mull. When the OS 1:50,000 maps were first published, Beinn Talaidh was listed at 762m, the minimum height for a Corbett. Later editions listed Beinn Talaidh at 761m and it was relegated to Graham status. However, the latest OS 1:50,000 map shows Beinn Talaidh as a confusing 761(763)m. The OS seem to be doing this when the trig point is not the highest point on a summit. John Barnard and Graham Jackson in 2009, using sophisticated GPS equipment, measured the highest point as 761.7 ±0.1m and this height has now been accepted, missing the requirement for a Corbett by about 30cm (1ft). Barnard and Jackson believe the 763m may

be a mistake by the OS measuring to the top of the large 'prehistoric tumulus' which is nearby. Incidentally, the author's measurements gave a reading of 766m which is the same reading as he got for nearby Dun da Ghaoithe which is listed at 766m!

The OS only claim an accuracy of ±3.3m for spot heights on their maps derived from aerial photography.

GEOLOGY

Much of the early pioneering work in geological theory was based on investigations on the rock formations of NW Scotland. This is recognised in the UNESCO-endorsed award of Geopark status to the North-West Highlands. Geopark designation is intended to encourage geotourism, and a number of excellent visitor centres as well as roadside information boards have been developed to encourage this. This Geopark area is undoubtedly the most scenically attractive area in the UK.

The North-West Highlands contain rock formations which span over 3000 million years of earth history and include some of the oldest rocks in the world. Along the west coast, the oldest rock in the region, Lewisian gneiss, creates a landscape of low hills and scattered lochans. Rising from this gneiss landscape are huge masses of Torridonian sandstone, capped by quartzite, which form the distinctive mountains Cul Mor, Suilven, Canisp and Quinag within the Geopark as well as the mountains of Fisherfield, Torridon and Applecross further south-west.

Lewisian gneiss: Most of the Outer Hebrides and the North West Highlands Geopark have a bedrock formed from Lewisian gneiss. These are among the oldest rocks in the world, having been formed up to 3 billion years ago. About 2900–2700 million years ago north-west Scotland, together with parts of Greenland and North America, made up the ancient continent of Laurentia, which was being built up as igneous rock deep in the earth's crust and then metamorphosed at very high temperatures. These rocks, with irregular light and dark layers, were intruded by later basaltic dykes and granite magma.

Geological timeline

YEARS AGO	Event
3000 million	Formation of Lewisian gneiss
1000 million 800 million	Formation of Torridonian sandstone in the west and Moine schist in the east
550 million 500 million	Formation of basal quartzite, pipe rock, Salterella grit, fucoid beds and Durness limestone
	A major mountain chain created and eroded away. Moine Thrust pushes Moine schists north-west over younger rocks
400 million	No evidence of geological activity in this region
200 million	Opening of the Atlantic Ocean begins
140 million	Sea level much higher than today and thick layers of chalk limestone laid down
65 million	Most of chalk eroded away and volcanic activity along the west coast
2 million	Ice ages alternate with warmer periods
10,000	Peat develops during wet periods
Today	

Cliffs above Allt Slochd a' Mhogha on Sgurr Coire Choinnichean, Knoydart (Route 33)

Torridonian sandstone: Many of the most spectacular mountains in north-west Scotland are composed of Torridonian sandstone, a coarse-grained purplish-red sandstone. Sediments were laid down upon the gneiss by broad, shallow rivers, where the water flowed in many small channels separated by sand-bars. These sand grains and pebbles would have come from an eroding mountain range whose roots are now on the other side of the Atlantic. Deposition over 200 million years was followed by uplift and tilting downwards to the west. By 540 million years ago, erosion had formed a near-horizontal surface.

Moine schists: At the same time as the Torridonian sandstone was being laid down in the west, silt was being laid down in the east. The silt was pushed down into the earth's crust and passed through a series of metamorphic processes, with the individual mineral grains in the schist being drawn out into flaky scales by heat and pressure, with the result that the schist splits easily into flakes or slabs. The gentler mountains in the north-east of Scotland are mainly composed of these Moine schists.

Basal quartzite, pipe rock, fucoid beds, Salterella grit and Durness limestone: Eventually, after a long period of erosion, the remains of the Torridonian sandstone in this part of Laurentia sank beneath a shallow sea. A thin sequence of sandstones, silt-stones and limestones were formed in the coastal sand-bars, tidal flats and in the sea. Clean quartz sand was deposited on top of the Torridonian sandstone and a pure sandstone composed of rounded grains of quartz, cemented by further quartz between the grains was formed. This sandstone had completely different properties and is the rock we now know as basal quartzite, a white rock which is resistant to weathering and erosion. Life was developing in these waters and there is a layer of quartzite called 'pipe rock' where there are pipe-like burrows of fossil worms. As animals with shells developed, their fossilised remains resulted in the sediments becoming richer in 'lime' and in the formation of the Durness limestone.

The remarkable thing about these rocks is that the fossils are identical to those found in the Appalachian Mountains in the US but distinct from those of the same age in the rest of Britain. It is now clear that 500 million years ago Scotland, Scandinavia, Greenland and north-east America were one continent and that they were on the opposite sides of a now vanished Lapetus Ocean to the rest of Europe. This was the first conclusive evidence for continental drift.

About 430 million years ago there were intrusions of magma creating sills of crystalline rock parallel to the bedding plane, dykes cutting the bedding plane as well as plutons (irregular masses).

Between 430 and 420 million years ago a vast mountain range was being built up to the south-east as the Lapetus Ocean had closed and the 'European plate' was moving north-west and colliding with Laurentia. The

An Teallach from Sail Mhor, Fisherfield Forest (Route 74)

Lewisian gneiss 2900–1100 million years old

most dramatic effect on Scotland was the pushing of a large slab of the old Moine schists over the younger rocks of north-west Scotland. This is known as the Moine Thrust.

Eventually, Scotland collided with England and fused to form one land mass before quiet conditions returned. There is no evidence in the rock record of any activity in north-west Scotland but this was a period of the build-up of sediment forming sandstone, coal, limestone, chalk and other sedimentary rocks in the remainder of Britain.

Around 60 million years ago the continent split apart, with Europe and Africa separating from America, as the Atlantic Ocean began to develop and there was volcanic activity along Scotland's western edge.

During this time the climate cooled and by 2 million years ago the Ice Age began to affect the whole planet. Scotland would have been buried under ice and would have looked like Greenland today. It was during this time that today's landscape developed, with massive glaciers carving out the U-shaped valleys which are such a feature of the Highlands today. Glaciers would also have carved out the corries and transported boulders long distances to scatter them over the landscape.

As in Greenland, the highest peaks would have stuck out of the ice and so wouldn't have been smoothed by the ice, but left jagged and angular. The white cap of resistant quartzite on many of the Torridonian sandstone peaks would have helped protect them from erosion, leaving the spectacular peaks we see today. As the

Torridonian sandstone 1000–750 million years old

Basal quartzite 570–550 million years old

glaciers and icefields melted there would have been enormous flows of meltwater flowing beneath and out of the glaciers, cutting out gullies and gorges.

It wasn't until about 11,000 years ago that the last of the glaciers finally left Scotland and peat bogs began to build up in the warmer wet conditions. Peat forms when plant material is inhibited from decaying fully by acidic and anaerobic conditions, usually in marshy areas. Peat bogs grow only at the rate of about 1mm per year.

For more information see www.scottishgeology.com or www. northwest-highlands-geopark.org.uk.

The walks in this guide have not been designed for the peak-bagger, but primarily for the walker who wants an interesting day out on some of the less well-known but most spectacular peaks in Scotland.

Some people think the Corbetts are something to do in your declining years after you have 'compleated' the Munros. If you take this attitude you will miss out on many of the most spectacular and rewarding mountains in Scotland. It is true that as you get older you may appreciate the shorter walks offered by some of the Corbetts, but many of the Corbetts are very remote from road access and will still give a demanding hike. What is more, between many of the peaks listed as Munros, there is little drop, so you can often climb several in one day. By contrast, the requirement for a 500ft drop on all sides between listed Corbetts means that there are few occasions where Corbetts can be linked together. It is also surprising how few Corbetts can sensibly be combined with climbing a Munro.

This two-volume guide suggests 185 day-hikes to climb the 221 Corbetts. All the routes were walked by the author when preparing this guide. Suggestions are also made for alternative routes, but these have not always been checked by the author. This volume covers 109 Corbetts in 90 routes.

There are some areas, such as Knoydart, where the Corbetts are so

Glacial moraine hummocks in Choire a' Cheud-Chnoic, Torridon (Route 59)

remote that walking them in a day will be too much for the average walker and backpacking possibilities are considered.

WHEN TO GO

You will find people hiking in the Scottish Highlands throughout the year but this guidebook assumes that the Corbetts are being walked when they are free of snow. The mountains can be at their best in the winter, but weather and snow and ice conditions mean this won't be the time for the inexperienced walker. For the experienced walker, winter in the Scottish Highlands can be magnificent. In the middle of winter there will be less than eight hours of daylight and climbing Corbetts could be a better option than climbing the Munros.

The spring in Scotland is often drier and sunnier than the summer and many consider April and May to be the best months for being in the Highlands. June, July and August are the warmest months, with the added advantage of the long daylight hours. The biggest problem with the Scottish Highlands in summer are the swarms of midges that can torment the walker, especially in the early morning and on still evenings. This is not too much of a problem for the day-hiker, but it means that this isn't the ideal time of year for backpacking and wilderness camping.

September and October are generally relatively dry and you won't have too much problem with midges. A combination of autumn storms and short daylight in November and December means that you are likely to be on your own in the mountains.

THE TERRAIN

Many newcomers to Scotland underestimate the conditions they will encounter when walking in the Scottish mountains. The mountains in this guidebook may be under 1000m high, but you will usually be starting your walk from near sea level and you will spend most of the time above the tree-line, which means you will get spectacular views but will be exposed to wind, rain and sun.

Hikers from Europe and the US may be accustomed to walking on well-maintained paths and trails. Climbing the Corbetts you will frequently find the only paths are sheep or deer tracks. There are usually good tracks in the glens, maintained by the owners of the shooting estates, but higher up it is only on the most popular Corbetts that you will find well-maintained paths. Deep heather or boggy grass can make for hard walking on the approach to the mountain and steep rocky slopes protect many of the ridges. Unless there are lots of crags, the going is usually relatively easy on the ridges as a combination of wind and Arctic conditions in winter keeps the vegetation down to a minimum, although on some peaks you will have to cope with peat hags or boulderfields. Most of the peaks in the north-west are rocky and easy scrambling is required on a few of them. However, in good visibility it is possible to avoid the crags on most of the Corbetts.

Walkers on the 801m subsidiary summit of Baosbheinn (Route 63)

WEATHER

The main feature of the Scottish weather is its changeability and you should be prepared for anything. Sometimes it can seem as if you get all four seasons in one day. Don't be surprised if you set out on a warm summer's day and find it cold and windy on the summit ridge.

The north-west of Scotland has a reputation as the wettest part of Britain, with the prevailing wind bringing cloud and storms in from the Atlantic Ocean, and showery weather is common, but you may be lucky enough to get long periods of sunny weather. For instance in 2007 and 2012, when England suffered two of the wettest summers on record, north-west Scotland was largely dry and sunny and even approaching drought conditions.

There can be rain any month of the year, even in February when you may find it raining rather than snowing at 3000ft! Although there may be deep snow on the Corbetts in winter, the wind will tend blow the bulk of the snow off the peaks into the glens. Since the weather in Scotland is relatively mild for such a northerly country, the snow can melt very quickly in the glens and even on the peaks. If there is significant snow, only those with experience of winter mountaineering should attempt the steeper peaks because of the risk of cornices above the gullies and avalanche on the slopes.

It is the wind that is the most dangerous aspect of Scottish weather. If it is windy down in the glens, it could be too windy to stand up on an exposed peak. Even in summer, with the temperature well above freezing,

Storm approaching the Bealach Bhearnais, Glen Carron (Route 53)

Gleann Chorainn, Bac an Eich, Strathconon (Route 49)

a combination of wind and rain can lead to hypothermia unless you are properly equipped. In winter, wind can cause spindrift in the snow, creating a whiteout, even if it isn't actually snowing. Apart from the risks of hypothermia and the difficulty of walking into a blizzard, this will also make navigation very difficult.

Mist is a feature of the weather that can cause problems for the inexperienced. If you hit a spell of cloudy weather your options can be very limited if you aren't prepared for walking in the mist. Many of the Corbetts are rarely climbed and paths haven't developed, so navigation in mist can be very demanding.

ACCESS

Scotland has a system of law based as much on common law as statute law, and trespass has never been a criminal offence in Scotland. Although in the 19th century landowners were very protective of their rights of privacy, access for walkers and climbers gradually became accepted through the 20th century and free access to the mountains became enshrined in the Land Reform (Scotland) Act 2003. This act gives some of the best access rights in the world and the public have access to most land (including hills, woods and pastureland) for recreation, provided they act responsibly (see box).

THE SCOTTISH OUTDOOR ACCESS CODE

The Highlands are the home of Scotland's diverse wildlife and enjoyed by the people who live and work there as well as visitors. You can exercise access rights responsibly if you:

- Respect people's privacy and peace of mind. When close to a house or garden, keep a sensible distance from the house, use a path or track if there is one and take extra care at night.
- Help land managers and others to work safely and effectively. Do not hinder land-management operations and follow advice from land managers. Respect requests for reasonable limitations on when and where you can go.
- Care for your environment. Do not disturb wildlife, leave the environment as you find it and follow a path or track if there is one.
- Keep your dog under proper control. Do not take it through fields of calves and lambs, and dispose of dog dirt.

Deer stalking

If you're planning to walk in the Scottish hills from 1 July to 20 October, you should take reasonable steps to find out where deer stalking is taking place. As well as providing income, regular culling ensures that there is enough grazing for the herd and other animals, and that the fragile upland habitat is not damaged.

Red deer beside Loch More

The Hillphones service provides information to enable hillwalkers and climbers to find out where red deer stalking is taking place during the stalking season, and to plan routes avoiding stalking operations. For more information go to www.snh.org.uk/hillphones.

Grouse shooting

The grouse-shooting season runs from 12 August to 10 December, with most shoots taking place during the earlier part of the season. Be alert to the possibility of shooting taking place on grouse moors and take account of advice on alternative routes. Avoid crossing land where a shoot is taking place until it is safe to do so.

Low-ground shooting

Low-ground shooting can take several forms. Pheasant and partridge shooting takes place during the autumn and winter in woods and forests, and on neighbouring land. Avoid crossing land when shooting is taking place. Avoid game bird rearing pens and keep your dog under close control or on a short lead when close to a pen.

Fishing

Access rights do not extend to fishing and the regulations are complex so you need to know the regulations before doing any fishing.

Cycling

Access rights extend to cycling. Cycling on hard surfaces, such as wide paths and tracks, causes few problems. On narrow paths, cyclists should give way to walkers and horse riders. Take care not to alarm farm animals, horses and wildlife.

If you are cycling off-path, you should avoid going onto wet, boggy or soft ground, and avoid churning up the surface. Effectively when climbing the Corbetts this means that you can use your bicycle on the estate roads and tracks to access the mountain, but the paths and off-path sections are likely to be too wet to be able to cycle without causing damage.

Wild camping

Access rights extend to wild camping. This type of camping is lightweight, done in small numbers and only for two or three nights in any one place. Avoid causing problems for local people and land managers: do not camp

in enclosed fields of crops or farm animals and keep well away from buildings, roads or historic structures. Take extra care to avoid disturbing deer stalking or grouse shooting. If you wish to camp close to a house or building, seek the owner's permission.

Leave no trace by:
- taking away all your litter
- removing all traces of your tent pitch and of any open fire
- not causing any pollution

These rights do not extend to those using motorised transport.

Lighting fires

Wherever possible, use a stove rather than an open fire. If you do wish to light an open fire, keep it small, under control and supervised. Never light an open fire during prolonged dry periods or in areas such as forests, woods, farmland or on peaty ground, or near to buildings or in cultural heritage sites where damage can be easily caused.

Human waste

If you need to urinate, do so at least 30m from open water or rivers and streams. If you need to defecate, do so as far away as possible from buildings, from open water, rivers and streams. Bury faeces in a shallow hole and replace the turf.

Dogs and dog walking

Access rights apply to people walking dogs provided that their dog is kept under proper control.

Ptarmigan on Beinn Bhan

Your main responsibilities are:
- Ground-nesting birds: During the breeding season (April–July) keep your dog on a short lead or under close control in areas such as moorland, grasslands, loch shores and the seashore to avoid disturbing birds that nest on the ground.
- Farm animals: Never let your dog worry or attack farm animals. Don't take your dog into fields with young farm animals.
- Public places: Keep your dog under close control and avoid causing concern to others, especially those who fear dogs.
- Dog waste: Pick up and dispose of carefully.

Fuller details can be found at www.outdooraccess-scotland.com.

Roadside camping
There is no legal right to roadside camping from a car. At one time it was common practice and this led to pollution problems in popular areas such as Glen Coe. You will find people camping beside the road, particularly in remote glens, but you should realise that you have no right to do so. You should obey any prohibition signs and you must leave if requested to do so by the landowner. Take particular care not to cause any form of pollution.

Motorhomes are a good base if you are walking in Scotland and there is rarely any difficulty finding somewhere to park. Caravans are much less flexible and should use caravan sites. Many of the single-track roads with passing places that are still common in the Highlands are not really suitable for caravans.

Roadside camping is legal under the access laws if you are walking or cycling.

MOUNTAIN BOTHIES

The Mountain Bothies Association (MBA) is a charity that maintains about 100 bothies in Scotland. These are shelters, usually old crofts, which are unlocked and available for anyone to use. Almost all of the bothies are in remote areas and are only accessible on foot or possibly by bicycle. The MBA itself does not own any of the bothies; they are usually remote buildings that the landowner allows walkers to use.

When going to a bothy, it is important to assume that there will be no facilities. No tap, no sink, no toilets, no beds, no lights, and even if there is a fireplace, perhaps nothing to burn. Bothies may have a simple sleeping platform, but if busy you might find that the only place to sleep is on a stone floor. Carry out all your rubbish, as you would do if you were camping, and aim to leave the bothy tidier than you find it.

If you intend to make regular use of bothies you should join the MBA to contribute towards the costs of running the organisation. The MBA organises working parties to maintain and tidy up the bothies and they would welcome volunteers to help with this task. For more details on using bothies, consult the MBA's excellent website: www.mountainbothies.org.uk.

NAVIGATION

The 1:100,000 maps in this guide are good for planning purposes and will give you a general idea of the route, but they don't give enough detail for accurate navigation in difficult conditions. For this reason it is essential that you carry the relevant maps.

The Ordnance Survey (OS) 1:50,000 maps, available in paper form or for GPS devices, are very good and should be all you need to follow the recommended routes. In popular areas updated OS 1:25,000 maps are available but not really necessary. Probably the best maps are the Harvey maps (mainly 1:40,000) but they don't have full coverage of the Scottish Highlands.

The contour lines on all of these maps are remarkably accurate and should be seen as your main navigational tool. Inexperienced walkers going out in good visibility should learn to relate contours to the ground so they are better prepared if they get caught out in mist.

You should always carry a good compass (those produced for orienteering by Silva and Suunto are probably the best). In good visibility it should be sufficient to orientate the map using the compass, so that north on the map lines up with north on the ground. At present, magnetic north is near enough to grid north not to have to adjust for magnetic variation. Learn to take bearings from a map and follow them using the compass in clear conditions, before you find yourself having to navigate in mist.

The most difficult thing in navigation is knowing how far you have travelled, which can be important when navigating in mist on Scottish hills. In extreme conditions it may be necessary to pace-count to measure distance – practise this skill in good conditions, so that you are prepared.

Probably the most common navigational error is to head in the wrong direction when starting to descend so it is a good habit to always check your compass when leaving a mountain summit, even in clear conditions.

GPS

If you are experienced at using map and compass, a GPS unit is not essential for navigating the Corbetts. However, even experienced mountain navigators will find they can make navigation easier in mist and the less experienced might find that using a GPS unit allows them to navigate safely in poor visibility.

SAFETY

The most important thing is not how to deal with accidents, it's how to prevent them. There are three main tips for reducing your chance of a mountain accident by about 90%:

- Learn to navigate!
- Learn to navigate better!
- Learn to navigate even better!

The 90% figure is not a made-up statistic. Research done about 40 years ago suggested that poor navigation was a major contributory factor in about 90% of Mountain Rescue incidents in the Scottish Highlands.

Three more tips should account for the other 10% of accidents:

- Make sure you have a good tread to your walking shoes or boots. Don't wear shoes with a worn tread.
- Use two walking poles – this greatly increases safety on steep grass slopes and during any difficult river crossings.
- Always have waterproofs, hat and gloves in your pack, whatever the weather.

Finally, if you are intending to do any walking in winter you should take some training in walking in snow-covered mountains. There are excellent courses at Glenmore Lodge National Outdoor Training Centre (See Appendix B for details).

AREAS IN THIS GUIDE

1 Mull, Morvern, Sunart and Ardgour

The southern section of this guide contains some of the most magnificent, rugged, rocky mountains in Scotland, with the scenic value being enhanced by the fjord-like Loch Shiel, Loch Eil, Loch Linnhe and Loch Sunart that surround the area. Despite the fabulous scenery, this sparsely populated wilderness is rarely visited, possibly because there aren't any Munros in the area. Ardgour (Ard Ghobhar) means 'height of the goats', and you can still see feral goats and it is an area where you are likely to see golden eagles.

The Isle of Mull has been included in this section because it can be convenient to access it across the Sound of Mull from Lochaline to Fishnish. The scenery on Mull is magnificent, but for many visitors it is the wildlife (including the spectacular white-tailed eagle) which attracts them to the island.

2 Glenfinnan and Rum

This section covers the peaks either side of the A830, the 'Road to the Isles', which links Fort William to Mallaig. The road and the spectacular railway attract a lot of tourists, but the mountains are rarely frequented, again possibly because of the absence of Munros. Centred round the tiny village of Glenfinnan at the head of Loch Shiel, included are the peaks of Moidart, the north of Ardgour and those just north of Glenfinnan. This is an area of magnificent rocky peaks which would be demanding for the inexperienced walker in bad weather.

The island of Rum has been included in Section 2 as it is accessed by ferry from Mallaig at the end of the 'Road to the Isles'. Most of Rum is a National Nature Reserve managed by Scottish Natural Heritage. The walking throughout this rocky island is magnificent. The island is a haven for a variety of birds and animals. Rum is where the white-tailed eagle was first reintroduced to Scotland and the island is the breeding ground for about one third of the world's population of Manx shearwater.

While you are at Mallaig you could also take a ferry to Inverie to climb the Corbetts in Knoydart which are featured in Sections 3 and 4 or a ferry to Skye to climb the two Corbetts on that island.

3 Glen Loy, Loch Arkaig, Glen Dessarry and South Knoydart

This section includes all the Corbetts that can be accessed from the minor road between Fort William and Loch

SE face of Garbh Bheinn, towering over Loch Linnhe (Route 6)

Liathach from Beinn Dearg, Wester Ross (Route 58)

Arkaig, including those that can be climbed from the roadhead at the western end the loch. There is a big contrast between the relatively gentle Corbetts in Glen Loy and overlooking Loch Arkaig and the remote, rough and rocky mountains in Glen Dessarry and Knoydart to the west of Loch Arkaig. There is neither accommodation nor campsites in this section so most visitors will be staying in or around Fort William.

Glen Dessarry is one of the access routes to the wild Knoydart peninsular. Ben Aden in Knoydart is too remote to contemplate as a day-hike from any access point and the suggestion is to access Knoydart along Glen Dessarry and stay at Sourlies Bothy on Loch Nevis to climb Ben Aden and Beinn Bhuidhe. This access could also be used, as an alternative to Kinloch Hourn, to access the remaining

Corbetts in Knoydart, described in Section 4.

4 North Knoydart and Kinloch Hourn
This section includes the Corbetts that can be accessed from the small settlement of Kinloch Hourn at the eastern end of the long sea loch, Loch Hourn. Sections 3 and 4 cover an area known as na Garbh-Chriochan (the Rough Bounds), because of its harsh terrain and remoteness, and this is a good description of Knoydart which is sometimes referred to as 'Britain's last wilderness'. Fortunately it has good stalker's paths to enable easy access through the rough terrain.

The distances from Loch Arkaig, Loch Hourn or from the village of Inverie mean that it isn't really feasible to day-hike some of these Corbetts. Sgurr a' Choire-bheithe is climbed from the remote Barisdale

Bothy and other Corbetts from Inverie which can be accessed by ferry from Mallaig (see Section 2), by walking in from Sourlies Bothy (see Section 3) or by walking in from Barisdale Bothy as described in Section 4. Although Ben Aden and Beinn Bhuidhe have been included in Section 3 they could also be accessed from Barisdale or Inverie. The author recommends backpacking these peaks.

5 Glen Garry, Glen Shiel, Glen Elchaig and Loch Hourn

This section includes all the Corbetts that can be accessed from the A87 which links Invergarry to the Kyle of Lochalsh and Skye. This area is best known for the 16 Munros which line magnificent Glen Shiel and Loch Cluanie, including the Five Sisters which tower above Shiel Bridge. The Corbetts in Glen Shiel provide excellent viewpoints for these superb Munros. Also included are the remote peaks to the west of the massive Munro Carn Eige which would be best climbed on a backpacking trip and the isolated Corbetts above Arnisdale which provide magnificent views across Loch Hourn to the Knoydart Peninsula.

6 Glen Affric, Glen Cannich, Glen Strathfarrar and Strathconon

Glen Affric, Glen Cannich, Glen Strathfarrar and Strathconon are the four big glens which drain eastwards reaching the sea at Beauly Firth or Cromarty Firth, either side of the Black Isle. The long easy ridges bordering

the glens provide excellent backpacking terrain and this would be the best way of climbing both the Munros and Corbetts in the area. The Munros tend to be concentrated at the head of these glens with the Corbetts further to the east. Many of the Munros are very remote but access to the Corbetts is easier for day-hikers.

7 Glen Carron, Glen Torridon and Loch Maree

This section includes the spectacular peaks of Applecross and Torridon as well as the gentler peaks along Glen Carron and the isolated peaks in the Letterewe Forest to the north of Loch Maree.

Torridon is best known for the Munros Liathach and Beinn Eighe but the Corbetts in the area are every bit as dramatic, providing some of the best mountain scenery in Britain. The towering peaks are composed of Torridonian sandstone, often with a white quartzite cap, sitting on a base of Lewisian gneiss

Many of these peaks are steep and rocky and could be dangerous for the inexperienced walker in poor weather conditions.

8 Strath Garve, Fisherfield and Inverpolly

This is a rather mixed section with some rather uninteresting Corbetts along the A835 to the south-east, but some of the most dramatic mountains in Scotland to the north-west; the boundary being the line of the

Moine Thrust, north-west of which the Torridonian sandstone peaks of Fisherfield and Inverpolly stand as 'inselbergs' above a heather wilderness scattered with numerous lochs and lochans. Also in this region is the majestic Munro An Teallach, but the finest mountains are possibly the Grahams, Suilven and Stac Pollaidh. Quite a lot of driving will be needed if you use Ullapool as a base for all these routes, but this is a region with very little accommodation and few official campsites. The peaks in the Fisherfield Forest are rather remote for a day-hike so the suggestion is to stay at Shenavall Bothy or to backpack these magnificent mountains.

9 Strathcarron and north-west Scotland

North-west Scotland provides some of the most stunning scenery in the world with Torridonian sandstone peaks rising starkly out of a wild moorland dotted with innumerable lochs and lochans finished off with views of a magnificent wild and scenic coastline. In an area with few Munros, it's the Corbetts which dominate the landscape. There is no obvious base for this widespread section with most of the tiny population being scattered among small coastal villages whose economy is now based mainly around tourism. The magnificent scenery makes this prime backpacking terrain.

Also included in this section are the two Corbetts in Strathcarron at the head of the Dornoch Firth. These don't fit naturally into any section but might be climbed on the drive north to the other peaks.

10 Skye and Harris

Skye is best known to walkers for the 'Black Cuillin' which provide some of the most dramatic and challenging mountain terrain in Scotland. Neither of the Corbetts in Skye is in the Black Cuillin, but Garbh-bheinn with some easy scrambling gives a taster of the delights of the Cuillin ridge. In complete contrast is Glamaig in the 'Red Cuillin', whose rounded hills are composed of granite with many long screes slopes on their flanks.

Harris (from the old Norse meaning 'high land') is the southern and more mountainous end of Lewis and Harris, the largest of the islands in the Outer Hebrides. Lewis has an incredibly diverse landscape, ranging from the dramatic, rocky landscape of the east coast and west coast with miles of golden sandy beaches with a backdrop of the mountains in the interior. While visiting Harris you should climb the three magnificent Grahams as well as the lone Corbett, An Cliseam.

USING THIS GUIDE

Walking the Corbetts is divided into two volumes:

- Volume 1 covers the Corbetts south of the Great Glen (which runs from Fort William to Inverness) and includes the islands of Arran and Jura.

Sgurr Mhic Bharraich across Loch Duich from Sgurr an Airgid, Kintail (Route 41)

• Volume 2 covers the Corbetts north of the Great Glen and includes the islands of Mull, Rum, Skye and Harris.

Other guides number and organise the Corbetts as they appear in the SMC lists. This organisation was actually designed for the Munros and is illogical for the Corbetts. There are Corbetts in many areas where there are no Munros, and in other areas adjacent Corbetts are listed in different sections of the tables. For instance, Beinn Chuirn, Beinn Bhreac-liath and Beinn Odhar are all within 5km of Tyndrum but appear in three different sections of the SMC lists.

In this guide the Corbetts have been divided into 21 sections, 11 in Volume 1 and 10 in Volume 2. Each section could be climbed in a 1–2 week holiday. Corbetts have been

arranged based on road access, so that it could be possible to climb the Corbetts in each section on a single trip.

Maps to take

The 1:100,000 maps in this guide should be sufficient to give you a feel for the route, but they are not intended for detailed navigation, particularly in bad weather. You should always carry the relevant OS Landranger (1:50,000) maps suggested for the route, either as a paper copy or loaded onto a GPS device. The Harvey maps at 1:40,000 are excellent alternatives to the OS maps, but they don't cover all of Scotland.

Route descriptions

For each Corbett a single ascent is described. Information about distance, amount of ascent, route

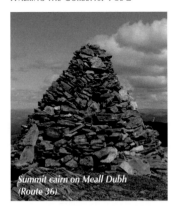

Summit cairn on Meall Dubh (Route 36)

difficulty, time needed to complete the route, summits reached, maps required and access to the start of the route is given in the information box at the start of each description. In some cases alternative routes are also suggested, and these are marked on the route maps with a dashed orange line. The route maps are at 1:100,000 scale and based on Ordnance Survey data. Information about bases and local facilities is given in the introduction to each section.

Distances and ascents

Distances and the amount of climb are quoted to the nearest kilometre (or mile) and 10m (or 100ft) of ascent.

Timings

All timings are those measured by the author's GPS device as he checked the routes. This device stops recording walking time whenever the walker stops, even for a few seconds, so the total time required to complete a walk will be considerably longer than that given in the guide. You should make an allowance for refreshments stops, taking photos and your own pace and fitness.

Grid references

All grid references are 10-figure references taken from the author's GPS device, but rounded up or down to the nearest 10m. A full grid reference with the letters indicating the grid square is given in the information box at the start, but letters are only used in the grid references in the route description if the route crosses into a different grid square.

Heights

Where spot heights are given on the route maps these figures are used in the route description. All other heights were measurements from the author's GPS device quoted to the nearest 5m. GPS does not measure height as accurately as it does horizontal position and it is possible that some of these readings are as much as 10m out. For Corbetts (but not for other summits) the height is also given in feet; note that this is not the conversion of the metric height, but is the height given on the OS 1 inch: 1 mile map, most of which are derived from surveys in the 1950s.

1 MULL, MORVERN, SUNART AND ARDGOUR

Aircraft debris on Maol Odhar (Route 2)

Mull, Morvern, Sunart and Ardgour: Bases and facilities

Base for Route 1: Craignure, Mull

Craignure is a small village with a ferry terminal, shop, cafés and a variety of accommodation.

Tourist information: VisitScotland, The Pier, Craignure, Isle of Mull, PA65 6AY Tel: 01680 812 377

The Craignure Inn, originally an 18th-century drover's inn, has retained much of its original character. Mull used to have an extensive network of drover's inns, with sheep being driven across the island to be shipped to Lismore and then on to mainland Scotland. The Craignure Inn features in the book *Kidnapped* by RL Stevenson, where it is referred to as the Inn of Torosay. Tel: 01680 812 305 www.craignure-inn.co.uk

Isle of Mull Hotel Tel: 01680 812 544 www.crerarhotels.com

Shieling Holidays operate a camping and caravan site along with a cottage and self-catering accommodation in the form of 'shielings' which are carpeted 'cottage tents', some of which are now serviced with full kitchens and bathrooms and constant hot water. Tel: 01680 812 496 www.shielingholidays.co.uk

Base for Routes 2–8: Strontian

Strontian is a village with shops, a tourist information office and a variety of accommodation.

Tourist information: VisitScotland, Strontian, Acharacle, Argyll, PH36 4HZ Tel: 01967 402 382

The Strontian Hotel Tel: 01967 402 029 www.thestrontianhotel.co.uk

Ben View Hotel and the Strontian Holiday Cottages Tel: 01967 402 333 www.benviewhotel.co.uk

Bluebell Croft self-catering accommodation Tel: 01967 402 226 www.bluebellcroft.co.uk

The Ariundle Centre has a craft workshop, tearoom, restaurant and bunkhouse. Tel: 01967 402 279 www.ariundlecentre.co.uk

Glenview Caravan and Camping Park Tel: 01967 402 123

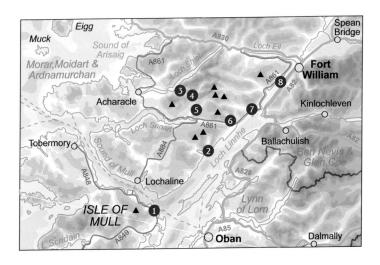

Local facilities for Routes 2 and 6–8: Corran

The Inn at Ardgour is at the W slipway of the Corran Ferry. It would be possible to stay at the Corran Ferry Inn or Corran Bunkhouse on the E of the Corran Narrows and use the Corran Ferry which sails every 30min to access Ardgour.

The Inn at Ardgour Tel: 01855 841225 www.ardgour.biz

Corran Bunkhouse Tel: 01855 821 000 www.corranbunkhouse.co.uk

The Corran Ferry Inn was for sale at the time of writing.

Access to Mull

Caledonian MacBrayne operates two car ferry routes to Mull:

Oban to Craignure with about 6 sailings/day for a 45min crossing

Lochaline to Fishnish with about 10 sailings/day for a 15min crossing.

Tel: 0800 066 5000 (UK only) www.calmac.co.uk

Lochaline has the ferry terminal, shop, snack bar and the Lochaline Hotel.

Lochaline Hotel Tel: 01967 421 657 www.lochalinehotel.co.uk

While on Mull you might like to visit the Island of Iona and take a boat trip to Staffa. Iona, a small island off the west coast of Mull, was a centre of Irish monasticism for four centuries and is today renowned for its tranquillity and natural beauty. Staffa is a remarkable little island off the west coast of Mull, best known for the famous Fingal's Cave with the same structure of the basalt columns which are found in the Giant's Causeway in Northern Ireland.

ROUTE 1

Dun da Ghaoithe FORT OF THE TWO WINDS

Start	Scallastle Forestry Commission car park (NM 71260 37530)
Distance	16km (10 miles)
Total ascent	890m (2900ft)
Difficulty	The suggested ascent route up the E ridge is steep at the top and crosses a couple of rock bands which will be awkward to climb. It would be unwise to climb the E ridge in poor visibility when it would be difficult to see the weaknesses through the crags. The author would not want to descend this ridge because of the steepness and the difficulty of finding a route through the crags from above. Inexperienced or timid walkers, or experienced walkers in poor weather, should traverse to the N ridge and climb that ridge. Take care with the descent route in poor visibility as it is very steep on the left-hand side and there are crags to the S.
Time	4hr 50min
Summits	Dun da Ghaoithe (766m, 2512ft), Mainnir nam Fiadh (754m)
Maps	OS Landranger 49
Access	From Craignure head NW along the A849 and turn left to Scallastle Forestry Commission car park which is just before the Isle of Mull Hotel.
Note	If you prefer not to climb the top of the steep E ridge you could veer off to the right and contour to cross the Allt an Dubh-choire burn and climb to the N ridge which is easier. The main alternative is to climb and descend by the recommended decent route.

Dun da Ghaoithe is an attractive hill rising above Craignure at the junction of Loch Linnhe, the Firth of Lorn and the Sound of Mull. The steep N-facing slopes with bands of rock on Mainnir nam Fiadh are particularly impressive.

The **white-tailed eagle**, commonly known as the sea eagle, is the largest and heaviest bird of prey in the British Isles, with a wingspan of 2.5m. Its diet includes fish, birds, carrion and small mammals.

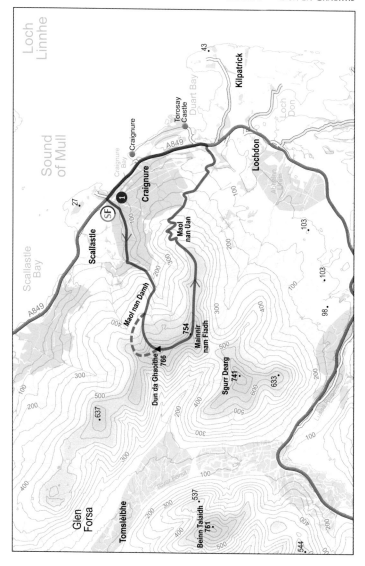

Loch Linnhe

Sound of Mull

Scallastle Bay

Glen Forsa

43·
Kilpatrick
Duart Bay
Torosay Castle
Craignure
Craignure Bay
Craignure
A849
Loch Don
Lochdon
·100
SF
1
·27
100
Scallastle
Maol nan Uan
·103
·103
98·
200
Maol nan Damh
300
200
300
400
754
766
Dun da Ghaoithe
Mainnir nam Fiadh
400
500
600
500
Sgurr Dearg 741
633·
200
·637
300
500
200
400
100
Tomslèibhe
Beinn Talaidh ·537 761
544·
300
400
500
200
100

41

Scallastle River in Coire Mor, Dun da Ghaoithe

Until the late 19th century the white-tailed eagle was common in the N and W of Scotland. However, persecution during Victorian times led to the eagle being exterminated as a British breeding species by 1916. A re-introduction programme on the island of Rum from 1975–1985 has been so successful that the population has spread, and by 2011 15 pairs were nesting around Mull's coastline. The white-tailed eagle attracts thousands of tourists to Mull each year and facilities have been developed to help them see the birds, generating millions of pounds for the local economy. www.white-tailed-sea-eagle.co.uk

Follow the track from the car park, ignoring a left-hand turn, until you reach the Scallastle River (55m, 69610 37160) with its impressive waterfalls. Cross the bridge, turn left and continue until the track recrosses the burn (110m, 69530 36720). Leave the track just before the bridge turning right up a faint, boggy path along the right-hand side of the burn to a gate in the deer fence (45min, 155m, 69370 36470). Continue up rough pasture along the right-hand side of the burn. When you reach a small tributary on the right (270m, 68760 36190), by two large erratic boulders, head NW up the hillside onto the Maol nan Damh ridge and gradually veer WSW towards Dun da Ghaoithe. After crossing some easy rock bands, the ridge steepens and reaches a short but difficult rock band, which can be easily crossed at a small gap (at 650m, 67430 36420). The final 100m of climb is up a mixture of scree and grass to reach the top rock band. The author climbed this in bad weather and found it uncomfortably steep and slippery. It is the sort of broken crag which probably has an easy way through, but only if you can see it clearly from below. After passing through this rock band it is easy going to the summit of **Dun da Ghaoithe** (2hr 30min, 766m, 67260 36210).

The summit is a big rockpile which is probably an ancient burial mound. Head S, veering SSE, to a saddle (700m) and up to the trig point and another rockpile on the summit of **Mainnir nam Fiadh** (2hr 50min, 754m, 67660 35340). ▶

Head ESE, veering E, down a narrow ridge. Be careful in mist as it would be easy to head down a ridge going off SE. The ridge broadens to reach a good track by the top communications mast (3hr 15min, 550m, 69190 35190). Follow the track, turning left by the lower communications masts (425m, 70290 35840) on **Maol nan Uan** and down to Achnacroish Farm where the track becomes a tarmac road which is followed down to the **A849** (4hr 15min, 20m, 72670 34950). Turn left and it is now a 3km road walk through **Craignure** and back to the Scallastle car park (4hr 50min).

The author's GPS measurements suggest there is actually very little difference in height between Mainnir nam Fiadh and Dun da Ghaoithe.

ROUTE 2

Fuar Bheinn COLD MOUNTAIN
and Creach Bheinn MOUNTAIN OF SPOIL

Start	Glen Galmadale (NM 86660 53090)
Distance	15km (10 miles)
Total ascent	1480m (4900ft)
Difficulty	The ridge, which is mainly grass with scattered crags, is relatively easy. However, the initial ascent and final descent are rough and steep, and accurate navigation will be needed in mist to avoid the dangerous crags which face Glen Galmadale.
Time	6hr 35min
Summits	Beinn na Cille (652m, Graham), Fuar Bheinn (766m, 2511ft), Creach Bheinn (853m, 2798ft), Maol Odhar (794m), Meall nan Each (591m)
Maps	OS Landranger 49
Access	From Strontian, follow the A861 E, then the B8043 S along Loch Linnhe. There is a parking area just E of the Glengalmadale River just E of Kingairloch.
Note	It would be possible to save a little time by ascending to the saddle between Beinn na Cille and Fuar Bheinn from Glen Galmadale and descending from Maol Odhar or the saddle between Maol Odhar and Creach Bheinn.

Fuar Bheinn and Creach Bheinn are the two Corbetts on the impressive ridge which surrounds Glen Galmadale overlooking Loch Linnhe on the E side of Morvern. There are plenty of crags facing Glen Galmadale, but the most spectacular terrain is on the N slope of Creach Bheinn.

On 5 May 1964 a USAF McDonnell F101C Voodoo **fighter-bomber** was on a training flight from its base at RAF Bentwaters in Suffolk. While flying over the Scottish highlands at 28,000ft, the fighter exploded in mid-air, giving the pilot no opportunity to eject,

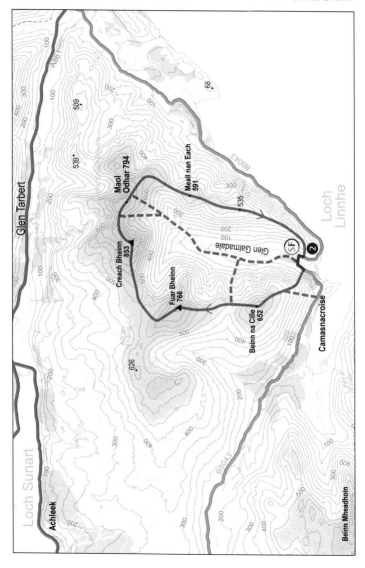

*Loch Linnhe from
Beinn na Cille*

and wreckage was strewn over Maol Odhar. On operations the Voodoo carried nuclear-tipped air-to-air missiles and was capable of carrying a thermo-nuclear bomb, giving rise to media speculation that the crash was caused by the explosion of nuclear warheads, but this was denied.

Follow the road across the bridge and SW to the forestry (86370 52920) before heading up a steep faint path along the forest edge. At the top of the forest it is best to veer well to the left to avoid the worst of the crags on the steep slope. When you reach the S ridge of Beinn na Cille turn right up the ridge. If you are doing the route in reverse and descending Beinn na Cille it would be easier to continue S to the **B8043**. Head easily to the summit of **Beinn na Cille** (1hr 30min, 652m, 85430 54190), then descend just left of N to a saddle (460m, 85310 54940) and climb N to the summit cairn on **Fuar Bheinn**, which appears to be on the highest of several tops (2hr 40min, 766m, 85350 56330).

There are crags on the direct route to the saddle between Fuar Bheinn and Creach Bheinn. Head roughly NW until clear of the crags, then veer NNE to the broad saddle (540m, 85390 57410). Head just left of E up grass and scattered crags to the summit of **Creach Bheinn** (3hr 55min, 853m, 87070 57640). The summit is marked by a rock wall surrounding the remains of the trig point marked on the OS map.

The descent is NE, veering E, over fairly rocky terrain to a saddle (715m, 87720 58030) from where it would be possible to descend S. Our route continues easily up to the summit of **Maol Odhar** (4hr 30min, 794m, 88140 57950). Continue down the ridge, SE veering E, looking out for aircraft remains. After about 400m, head SE down grassy slopes, gradually veering SW, to a broad saddle (510m, 88470 56500) and then on to the summit of **Meall nan Each** (5hr 10min, 591m, 88340 56120).

Continue SSW over several minor tops to **Peak 535** (87990 54865) from where a faint path leads down the Druim na Maodalaich ridge. Near the bottom of the ridge head W down steep rough slopes to the B8043 (86700 52900) and turn right back to the parking area (6hr 35min).

ROUTE 3

Beinn Resipol HOMESTEAD MOUNTAIN (OLD NORSE)

Start	Loch Doilet (NM 79510 67970)
Distance	13km (8 miles)
Total ascent	900m (3000ft)
Difficulty	Beinn Resipol is possibly the easiest peak in this section of the guide. There is some rough, boggy terrain but this is mainly crossed on paths. The rocky outcrops on the grassy summit ridge are scattered enough to pose few problems. Care would be needed with navigation on descent in mist.
Time	4hr 20min
Summits	Beinn Resipol (845m, 2775ft)
Maps	OS Landranger 40
Access	From Strontian follow the minor road N towards Polloch. The maximum gradient on this narrow road is 20% so it is not recommended for large vehicles or caravans. There is a parking area at the W end of Loch Doilet where a forestry track, signed to Strontian, goes off left.
Note	The E ridge of Beinn Resipol could also be approached up the 'coffin road' from Strontian. The main alternative route is the W ridge, starting from Resipole on the A861. This route is shorter but steeper. If transport could be arranged a traverse from Resipole to Strontian or Loch Doilet would be the best way to climb the mountain.

Beinn Resipol is an isolated peak standing between Loch Shiel and Loch Sunart to the W of Ardgour. As well as providing fine views of the mountains of Ardgour, it is a good viewpoint for the islands of the Inner Hebrides.

In the 7th century St Finan had a cell on the beautiful little island of **Eilean Fhianain** (St Finan's Isle) on Loch Shiel. Early chapels would have been built of wood, but a stone chapel was built about 1500, the ruins of which can be seen today. The island was the burying place of the Clan Ranald until the end of the 16th century and the suggested route up

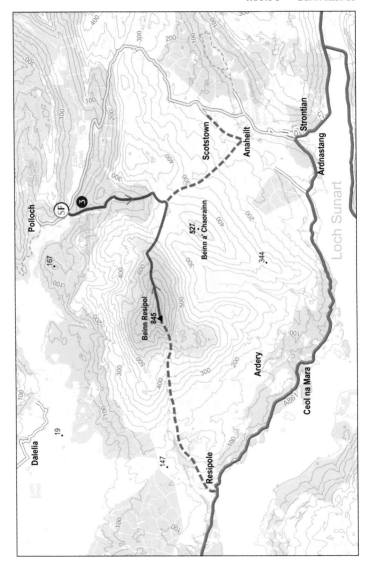

E ridge of Beinn Resipol

Beinn Resipol uses the remains of the old 'coffin road' from Strontian to Polloch. Large cairns at the high point of the path on the NE ridge of Beinn a' Chaorainn mark resting places as coffins were carried across the mountain. In the 18th and 19th century the path was used to access the Corrantee lead mine.

Head up the good track which becomes a maintained path that takes a different line up the Allt Coire an t-Suidhe than shown on the OS map. When the maintained path ends (35min, 220m, 79800 66170), continue up a boggy path which passes old mine buildings and forks right across a small burn at an indistinct junction. Pass more mine buildings and immediately turn right across a bigger burn to reach a deer fence at the edge of the forest (310m, 80010 65750). Cross the fence (at the time of writing the stile is broken, but there is a gap in the broken gate) and follow the path SW until a small cairn at a sharp left-hand bend, just before the top of the ridge (1hr, 385m, 79630 65350).

The 'coffin road' continues left, but we head W along a very faint, often boggy path. If you lose the path head roughly WNW to reach the broad E ridge of **Beinn Resipol** (at about 550m, 78450 65850). Turn left up the gradually narrowing ridge. The upper part of the ridge has many rocky knolls which can be climbed or bypassed on their right. There is a large cairn and ruined trig point on the rocky knoll (2hr 35min, 845m, 76650 65460) which is at the W end of the summit ridge.

Return by the same route to the 'coffin road' (3hr 40min) and back to the parking area (4hr 20min).

ROUTE 4

Carn na Nathrach CAIRN OF THE ADDERS

Start	Loch Doilet (NM 81530 67320)
Distance	17km (11 miles)
Total ascent	960m (3200ft)
Difficulty	Although Beinn Mheadhoin is a rocky ridge, any difficulties can be avoided. There is a short steep climb through the forest, after which faint paths take the walker easily through the rough lower slopes to the grassy ridge. Other routes on the mountain will be much tougher. Care would be needed with navigation in mist.
Time	5hr 30min
Summits	Carn na Nathrach (786m, 2579ft)
Maps	OS Landranger 40
Access	From Strontian follow the minor road N towards Polloch. The maximum gradient on this narrow road is over 20% so it is not recommended for large vehicles or caravans. There is a forestry road on the right, signed to Ardgour, at Kinlochan just before Loch Doilet, at the bottom of the steep descent. Continue 350m along the 'main' road to a parking area (NM 81530 67320).
Note	It would be possible to cycle the first 4km of the route. If you look at the map you might be tempted to combine Carn na Nathrach and Sgurr Dhomhnuill but a closer look at the terrain will probably make you forget the idea. The other easy approach to the mountain is from Glen Scaddle to the E. A traverse from Loch Doilet to Inverscaddle Bay would provide a good walk if transport could be arranged at either end.

Carn na Nathrach is the highest top on the long ridge of Beinn Mheadhoin. This steep rocky peak in the centre of Ardgour is surrounded by other rocky Corbetts. The recommended approach from the W starts through an area where there are major forestry operations, but the long, gentle W ridge soon takes the walker above the forests into the rocky wilderness.

In 1790, the element **Strontium** was discovered by Adair Crawford in the ores taken from the lead mines above the village of Strontian (Sron an t-Sithein). Strontium is a silver metal which was used in large quantities in the production of sugar from sugar beet. It was also used to provide the bright red colours required by flares and fireworks and more recently to prevent the emission of X-rays from television tubes.

Return to the forestry road, signed to Ardgour, turn left and ignore side turns. After crossing the **River Hurich**, turn right and follow the left-hand side of the river past farm buildings to reach another bridge (83700 68170). After crossing the river, immediately turn left and cross a burn to reach a track junction. Fork right and climb the ridge until you reach a small cairn (45min, 120m, 84340 68310) where the track levels out after a switchback.

Turn left up a rough path which takes you up the steep slope through the forest, soon reaching the open ridge. The lower slopes of the ridge are rough, but the path makes progress relatively easy. Further up, the ridge becomes broader, grassy and rockier with many knolls which could make navigation awkward in mist. Continue to a new deer fence (605m, 87000 69660). This fence was still being completed when the author checked the route and there was no stile so the fence had to be climbed. The buttress, just after the fence, can easily be bypassed on its right. Continue up the broad, knobbly ridge to the cairn on a prominent knoll on **Carn na Nathrach** (3hr 10min, 786m, 88630 69870).

Return by the same route to the forest road (4hr 50min) and the parking area (5hr 30 min).

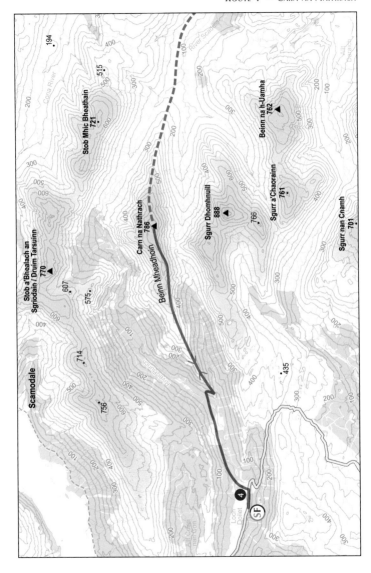

ROUTE 5
Sgurr Dhomhnuill DONALD'S PEAK

Start	Ariundle National Nature Reserve car park (NM 82570 63300)
Distance	18km (11 miles)
Total ascent	910m (3000ft)
Difficulty	There is some rough boggy pasture to cross. The route is relatively easy in good weather, but the mountain is very rocky and in bad visibility it would be difficult to find the easy route described. The featured route is much easier than the alternative routes suggested below.
Time	5hr 10min
Summits	Sgurr Dhomhnuill (888m, 2914ft)
Maps	OS Landranger 40
Access	From the N of Strontian, take the minor road signed to Ariundle and park in the National Nature Reserve car park at the head of the public road.
Note	It would be possible to descend the S ridge, climbing Sgurr na h-Ighinn and descending its W ridge, Druim Leac a' Sgiathain. The shortest approach to Sgurr Dhomhnuill is from the W, starting at the high point on the road from Strontian to Polloch. The main difficulty on this route, which traverses the Druim Garbh ridge, is the ascent of the rocky NW ridge of Sgurr Dhomhnuill which is fairly continuous scrambling. These ridges could be combined by starting at Ariundle and climbing Druim Garbh from the lead mines and descending the Druim Leac a' Sgiathain ridge.

Sgurr Dhomhnuill is the highest peak in Ardgour and as such makes a good viewpoint. In common with other Ardgour peaks it is a rocky mountain with many crags and slabs limiting access to the mountain. The attractive approach through the Ariundle National Nature Reserve, one of the finest oak woodlands in Scotland, is the shortest of the easy routes up the mountain.

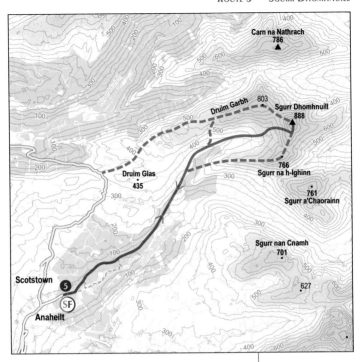

Mining in this area dates back to 1722, when Sir Alexander Murray discovered galena (lead sulphide) in the surrounding hills. Strontian was established in 1724 to provide homes for some of the 600 miners who worked in the mines in their heyday. Ariundle Woods provided timber for pit props and wood to make charcoal for the local lead smelters. Lead was required in large quantities for shot during the Napoleonic wars and, ironically, French prisoners of war were employed in the lead mines. You will see plenty of evidence of the lead mining industry on the route up Sgurr Dhomhnuill and the remains of charcoal burning platforms can still be seen in the woods.

Sgurr Dhomhnuill

Head up the good track through the Ariundle Nature Reserve, ignoring any side turns, to a fork immediately after a gate through the deer fence at the top of the nature reserve (120m, 84890 64850). Fork left, following the old miner's track, which soon becomes an excellent path, eventually leaving the forest and passing through an area of old lead mines. Continue until the good miner's path ends (1hr 10min, 280m, 86240 66700).

The summit is topped by a massive cairn with a depression in the middle which looks as if it could have been an old burial mound. There is little left of the nearby trig point.

Continue along an intermittent, boggy path up the left-hand side of the unnamed burn heading for the obvious saddle between the Druim Garbh ridge and Sgurr Dhomhnuill. When the burn splits (565m, 88400 67850) a short distance below the saddle you can see a grassy 'valley' leading ESE to a pass high on the S ridge of Sgurr Dhomhnuill. Head for this saddle (765m, 88940 67610) and climb easily up grass slopes between the crags to the summit of **Sgurr Dhomhnuill** (2hr 55min, 888m, 88960 67880). ◄

Return by the same route to the end of the miner's track (4hr 5min) and the car park (5hr 10min).

ROUTE 6

Garbh Bheinn ROUGH MOUNTAIN

Start	Abhainn Coire an Iubhair (NM 92850 59730)
Distance	12km (8 miles)
Total ascent	1310m (4300ft)
Difficulty	The rough path up the SE ridge of Garbh Bheinn has occasional rocksteps and slabs to climb. The suggested route is only for experienced mountaineers in good weather. It involves finding the only feasible route through the steep crags down the N face of Garbh Bheinn; a route which is not obvious from above and would be very difficult to follow in bad visibility. Most walkers will want to return by the ascent route rather than follow the suggested traverse of Beinn Bheag and Druim an Iubhair. This is one of the most difficult mountains on the Scottish mainland to explore and not a mountain on which inexperienced walkers should take any chances.
Time	6hr 25min
Summits	Gharbh Choire Bhig (823m), Garbh Bheinn (885m, 2903ft), Beinn Bheag (736m, Graham), Sgurr Mhic Eacharna (650m, Graham)
Maps	OS Landranger 40 and 49
Access	Follow the A861 E from Strontian and park beside the old road bridge across the Abhainn Coire an Iubhair, about 600m before the junction with the B8043.
Note	Walkers should think of returning down the SE ridge as the normal descent route. Another possibility is descending steeply NE from the saddle between Garbh Bheinn and Garbh Coire Bhig. There is a bit of a rough path down the corrie, but the author has not tested this route and it looks rather unpleasant when viewed from across the glen.

Garbh Bheinn is a magnificent mountain. Steep crags protect the mountain on all sides and it is a mecca for rock climbers and scramblers as well as walkers. It appears to be impregnable from most directions and the SE ridge is the only relatively easy approach. There are good views across Loch Linnhe towards Glen Coe.

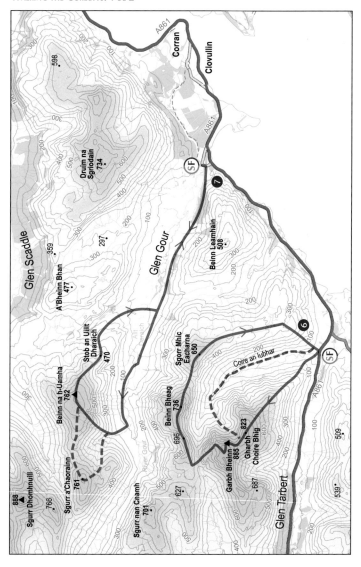

Glen Scaddle

598

Druim na
Sgriodain
734

Corran

Clovullin

A861

A861

SF

7

Beinn Leamhain
508

Glen Gour

359
297

A'Bheinn Bhan
477

Allt
Breisach

200

300

6

SF

Stob an Uillt
Dharaich
470

Sgorr Mhic
Eacharna
650

Coire an Iubhar

Beinn na h-Uamha
762

Beinn Bheag
736

Sgurr a'Chaorainn
761

696

Garbh Bheinn
885

Gharbh
Choire Bhig
823

509

888
Sgurr Dhomhnuill

766

Sgurr nan Cnamh
701

River Gour

627

687

539

Glen Tarbert

Garbh Bheinn provides some of the best **rock climbing and scrambling** in Scotland. Details of the scrambles can be found in the Cicerone guide *Scrambles in Lochaber* by Noel Williams. Pinnacle Ridge, a difficult scramble, and the Great Ridge, an easy rock climb (described in Dan Bailey's guide to *Scotland's Mountain Ridges* (Cicerone)), are fine routes on the NE face of Garbh Bheinn in Garbh Choire Mhoir.

Cross the bridge and follow a rough path up the SE ridge of Gharbh Choire Bhig. This path, which is occasionally boggy and sometimes indistinct, especially where it climbs rocksteps or crosses rocky slabs, takes you to the summit of **Gharbh Choire Bhig** (1hr 40min, 823m, 90820 61710). Follow the path steeply down to a saddle (750m, 90440 61930). The path up Garbh Bheinn continues NW, to avoid the cliffs on its SE face, before turning NE to the summit cairn on **Garbh Bheinn** (2hr 15min, 885m, 90440 62200).

In bad weather, or if you have any doubts about your ability to navigate through, and descend, very difficult terrain, you should descend by the ascent route. The featured route heads WNW to a small pond on a shallow saddle (845m, 90140 62320). Turn sharp right (NE veering ENE) down grass slopes to reach a gully (775m, 90370 62520) just before you reach the N ridge of Garbh Bheinn. Descend carefully, on grass beside the boulderfield, NW down the gully and keep to the right of the burn that appears further down the mountain. Aim for the obvious grassy saddle on the ridge on your right, then go about 50m left (E) to the top of a gully, marked by a small (easily missed?) cairn (690m, 90140 62820). Descend the gully, bypassing difficulties on the left, to the saddle separating Garbh Bheinn and Beinn Bheag (2hr 45min, 535m, 90050 63070).

You will now be traversing the rocky ridges of Beinn Bheag and Sgorr Mhic Eacharna. Although rocky the going is generally easy. Head NW until the slope eases, then head NE, veering E, over two tops (690m, 90240

N face of Garbh Bheinn

63320 and 696m, 90670 63450) and on to the highest summit on the **Beinn Bheag ridge** (3hr 50min, 736m, 91470 63520).

Descend roughly ESE to a saddle (485m, 92230 63220) and over a minor top (625m, 92620 63140) to the summit of **Sgorr Mhic Eacharna** (4hr 55min, 650m, 92870 63030). Continue SSE down the grassy Druim an Iubhair ridge, avoiding a few crags, before veering SW towards the bottom, back to the parking area (6hr 25min).

ROUTE 7

Beinn na h-Uamha HILL OF THE CAVES

Start	Sallachan (NM 97840 62930)
Distance	18km (11 miles)
Total ascent	850m (2800ft)
Difficulty	There is rough boggy terrain to cross on the lower slopes of Beinn na h-Uamha, which is well protected by crags on the steep upper slopes. Accurate navigation is needed in descent and it is not recommended for the inexperienced in bad weather or poor visibility. The River Gour must be forded twice, which won't be a problem in normal conditions but could be if the river is in flood.
Time	6hr
Summits	Beinn na h-Uamha (762m, 2499ft)
Maps	OS Landranger 40
Access	From Strontian head E along the A861 and turn left along a minor road to Sallachan about 4km W of the Corran Ferry at Ardgour. There is limited parking just after the bridge over the River Gour.
Note	You could combine Beinn na h-Uamha with the Graham Sgurr a' Chaorainn, to the W.

Beinn na h-Uamha is a rocky hill between Glen Gour and Glen Scaddle set among the rocky peaks of Ardgour. It appeared on the 1 inch:1 mile OS maps at 2499ft, but appears as 762m on the 1:50,000 map and was promoted to Corbett status in 1981. Its twin peak, Sgurr a' Chaorainn, is shown as 761m on the latest OS map. The recommended ascent up Glen Gour is through a deep glacial valley with much bare rock on the steep valley sides.

There has been a **car ferry** crossing the Corran Narrows of Loch Linnhe since 1934. Prior to that, the ferry was a rowing boat, later replaced by a motor launch. In those days a lot of cattle and sheep were brought from the Ardnamurchan Peninsula to

Beinn na h-Uamha over Loch nan Gabhar

the market in Fort William and were taken across the Narrows in a large rowing boat. Horses were expected to swim behind the boat (see www. ambaile.org.uk for more on Highland history and culture).

See map in Route 6.

Cross the bridge and turn right along the track, signed to Strontian, up the left-hand side of the **River Gour**. Pass Loch nan Gabhar and fork right at a junction. Eventually the track deteriorates and veers right, down to the River Gour (1hr 20min, 55m, 92550 64770). Cross the river, on stepping stones when the water level is low. The grassy, often boggy, track continues up the glen. If you lose the track just continue up the glen until you reach the burn draining the corrie between Beinn na h-Uamha and Sgurr a' Chaorainn (2hr, 155m, 90910 64980). Head N up the burn, staying above the edge of the gully through which the burn flows, until you reach the foot of the rocky SW ridge of Beinn na h-Uamha (235m, 90720 65360). Head NNE up the ridge, either up the rock slabs or steep grass slopes, veering right as the gradient eases on the approach to the knobbly summit plateau. The summit cairn of **Beinn na h-Uamha** is on a knoll at the far end of the plateau (3hr 35min, 762m, 91710 66410). ▶

Great care is needed in descending the E ridge. Initially head ESE down easy grass slopes, dodging round crags on the ridge. Veer SSE at a knoll (92600 66040) to another knoll, **Stob an Uillt Dharaich** (470m, 92720 65730), surrounded by crags. Wind your way down steep grass slopes between these crags, initially heading roughly ENE and veering SE when below the main crags, eventually reaching the Allt an t-Sluichd burn which is followed to the River Gour (5hr, 20m, 94140 64440). Ford the river and head S across boggy ground back to the track in **Glen Gour**. Turn left back to the parking area (6hr).

There is about 200m of descent between Beinn na h-Uamha and its twin peak Sgurr a' Chaorainn so it is possible that both of them, either of them or neither of them is actually a Corbett!

ROUTE 8

Stob Coire a' Chearcaill PEAK OF THE ROUNDED CORRIE

Start	Stronchreggan (NN 07130 72520)
Distance	14km (9 miles)
Total ascent	870m (2900ft)
Difficulty	Once the paths in Gleann Sron a' Chreagain are left behind, there is tough going on rough pasture and heather moorland on the lower slopes.
Time	4hr 40min
Summits	Stob Coire a' Chearcaill (770m, 2525ft)
Maps	OS Landranger 41
Access	Follow the A861 E from Strontian and continue up the shore of Loch Linnhe and Loch Eil to Stronchreggan where the A861 crosses the Abhainn Sron a' Chreagain at a sharp bend. There is limited parking in a layby 100m further E. For those without vehicles there is a ferry for pedestrians and cyclists from Fort William to Camusnagaul, which is about 4km NE of the start point of this route.
Note	If the rivers are in flood it would be sensible to climb and descend by the suggested descent route.

Stob Coire a' Chearcaill is an isolated peak in the NE of Ardgour. There are impressive crags in the E-facing Coire a' Chearcaill and good views across Loch Eil to Ben Nevis.

In 2010 Moidart and Ardgour was classified as a Special Protection Area for its population of **golden eagles**. Golden eagles require large areas of open ground over which to hunt, and Ardgour is ideal for them because there is little human disturbance and an abundance of crags suitable for nesting. They feed mainly on live prey, favouring rabbit, hare, ptarmigan and grouse, but also pine marten, squirrel, fox, water voles, ducks and seabirds. They also feed regularly on the carcasses of sheep and deer.

Stob Coire a'
Chearcaill

Head 100m W to the Abhainn Sron a' Chreagain and follow the track along the right-hand side of the burn. When the track appears to end (30min, 150m, 05040 73050), you should be able to see a continuation further up the

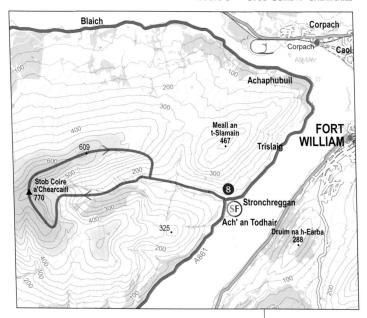

glen and there may be a vehicle track through the grass heading SW down to it. Follow this track, if visible, to the track which continues alongside the burn. Unless someone has driven an off-road vehicle up the track recently, it will end again and you should continue along a boggy animal track to just above a junction in the burn (55min, 170m, 03880 72670). Unless the burn is in flood, it will be easy to cross here. Climb the ridge on your left up to the deer fence, turn right and follow it until it turns sharp left as it crosses a burn (1hr 40min, 475m, 02630 72460).

Follow the fence left for another 250m. When it veers left (475m, 02680 72230), leave the fence and head S towards a shallow saddle (570m, 02680 71810) on the ridge ahead. On reaching the ridge, turn right (W veering NW) to a top (745m, 02060 72060) and continue NW to the large summit cairn, with nearby trig point, on **Stob Coire a' Chearcaill** (2hr 45min, 770m, 01690 72670).

Head N, gradually veering to ENE and eventually E, down the NE ridge. When you are sure that you are past the crags on the S face of the ridge (at about 440m, 04800 73800) head SE, gradually veering S down rough grass slopes. You will have to cross a barbed wire fence. There is an easy crossing point just right of a burn (185m, 05120 73250) roughly N of the track end. Descend to the track (4hr 10min) and turn left back to the parking area (4hr 40min).

2 GLENFINNAN AND RUM

Rum and Eigg across the Sound of Arisaig (Route 16)

Glenfinnan and Rum: Bases and facilities

Base for Routes 9–15: Glenfinnan

Glenfinnan is just a tiny village with two hotels, a bunkhouse, café, but no shop or campsite.

The Princes House Hotel Tel: 01397 722 246 www.glenfinnan.co.uk

Glenfinnan House Hotel Tel: 01397 722 235 www.glenfinnanhouse.com

Glenfinnan Station has been converted into a railway museum. A dining car has been converted into a café and a sleeping car has been converted into a bunkhouse. Open June–mid October, but may open outside this period by advanced request. Tel: 01397 722 295

www.glenfinnanstationmuseum.co.uk

The National Trust for Scotland Visitor Centre which caters for visitors to the Glenfinnan monument has a snack-bar. www.nts.org.uk/Property/Glenfinnan-Monument

Alternative base for Routes 9–15: Fort William

As there are so few facilities at Glenfinnan, many walkers climb these mountains from a base in Fort William, which is the premier tourist resort in the W Highlands and has all facilities for walkers and climbers.

Tourist information: VisitScotland, 15 High Street, Fort William, PH33 6DH Tel: 01397 701 801

Glen Nevis SYHA, Fort William, PH33 6SY Tel: 01397 702 336

Linnhe Lochside Holidays is a large complex on the A830 on the N side of Loch Eil just outside Fort William with chalets, static caravans and a camping and caravan site. Tel: 01397 772 376
www.linnhe-lochside-holidays.co.uk

Local facilities for Route 9: Lochailort Inn and Glenuig Inn

Lochailort Inn is an old droving inn. Tel: 01687 470 208
www.lochailortinn.co.uk

Glenuig Inn on the Sound of Arisaig has both traditional hotel facilities and bunkhouse accommodation. Tel: 01687 470 219 www.glenuig.com

Base for Route 16: Kinloch, Rum

Only the locals are allowed to take cars to Rum and it is not feasible to climb the Corbetts on a day trip so you will need to stay on the island. Assuming you are staying for longer than is needed to climb the Corbetts, it might be worth taking a bicycle for use around the bay and on the dirt road to Harris, which has recently been resurfaced.

Rum has hostel accommodation, a basic campsite, camping cabins and a caravan. There is also a bothy which would be a suitable base for climbing the Corbetts and wild camping is permitted on the island. An excellent website gives full information on the island, including accommodation details: www.isleofrum.com

There are likely to be big changes in the accommodation during the life of this guide with the possible closure of the facilities at the castle, to be replaced by new facilities including a B&B, so check the website to see the latest situation. The facilities tend to get full in high season and booking is advisable.

Kinloch Castle Hostel has dormitory accommodation as well as a few double bedrooms. Breakfast, packed lunches and evening meals are available. Evening meals are also available to non-residents. Tel: 01687 462 037

There is a basic camping area 10min walk from the ferry by the shore of Loch Scresort, with water, toilets and hot showers. There are two 'camping cabins' as well as two open shelters on the campsite.

At the head of Loch Scresort there is a small well-stocked store (with post office), a community hall with a teashop and other facilities, including internet access.

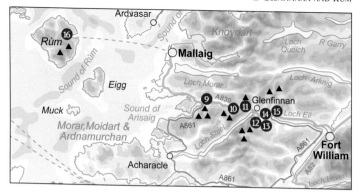

Access to Rum

Caledonian MacBrayne runs the ferry service from Mallaig to the 'Small Isles': Eigg, Muck, Rum and Canna. Crossing time varies as on some of these sailings you go to or from Rum via other islands. In 2012 the timetable was as follows:

Summer
- Mallaig to Rum: Mon 10.15am, Wed 10.15am, Fri 12.40pm and Sat 7.30pm
- Rum to Mallaig: Mon 3.20pm, Wed 4.05pm, Fri 4.35pm and Sat 7.40pm.

Winter
- Mallaig to Rum: Mon, Tue, Thur and Sat at 10.20am
- Rum to Mallaig: Mon 2.20pm, Tue and Thur 2.25pm and Sat 11.50am. Tel: 0800 066 5000 (UK only) www.calmac.co.uk

Arisaig Marine Ltd runs 'Island and Wildlife' cruises from Arisaig to the Small Isles. Although they primarily organise round trips, they will take passengers on one-way trips if space is available. Operating a much smaller boat, they can be fully booked and are more liable to disruption from the weather. In 2012 they operated sailings from 30 April to 21 September.

- Arisaig to Rum: Tue, Thur and Sat at 11.00am
- Rum to Arisaig: Tue 3.30pm, Thur 3.45pm and Sat 3.30pm Tel: 01687 450 224 www.arisaig.co.uk

ROUTE 9

Sgurr na Ba Glaise PEAK OF THE GREY COW, *Rois-Bheinn*
MOUNTAIN OF SHOWERS *and An Stac* THE STACK

Start	Inverailort (NM 76470 81710)
Distance	16km (10 miles)
Total ascent	1610m (5300ft)
Difficulty	There is a great deal of rock on the ridges of these grassy mountains, but the going is surprisingly easy as any difficulties can be bypassed, provided you have good visibility. These are not mountains for the inexperienced in bad weather when finding the easy route down steep, craggy ridges will be difficult. There is easy, but boggy terrain to cross on the lower slopes of the mountains.
Time	7hr 40min
Summits	Beinn Coire nan Gall (787m), Druim Fiaclach (869m), Sgurr na Ba Glaise (874m, 2817ft), Rois-Bheinn (882m, 2887ft), An Stac (814m, 2550ft).
Maps	OS Landranger 40
Access	From Glenfinnan follow the A830 W to Lochailort, turn left along the A861 and after 600m there is limited parking by a minor road signed to Glen Shian. At the time of writing it looked as if a large factory was going to be built here to service the fishing industry, but this shouldn't affect the route.
Note	If the walk is too long for you it would be possible to miss out Druim Fiaclach and climb the steep grass slopes up Coire a' Bhuiridh to the Bealach an Fhiona pass between Sgurr na Ba Glaise and Rois-Bheinn or the pass to the S of An Stac; however, this would miss out the dramatic ridge between Druim Fiaclach and Sgurr na Ba Glaise.

This group of rocky Corbetts in the N of Moidart provides an excellent ridge walk round the head of Coire a' Bhuiridh. Rois-Bheinn is the most westerly Corbett on the mainland and provides magnificent views towards the islands of Rum and Eig. The recommended route includes Druim Fiaclach, which just fails to reach Corbett status because the drop between it and Sgurr na Ba Glaise is only about 410ft. Druim Fiaclach used to be listed as the Corbett rather than Sgurr na Ba Glaise as it was shown as higher (2852ft compared with 2817ft) on the OS 1 inch:1 mile maps.

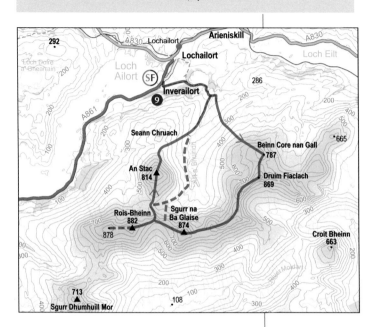

Inverailort House was requisitioned by the War Office at the end of May 1940 and the house became a training centre for irregular forces, with trainees being taught how to work behind enemy lines, hand-to-hand combat, sabotage, use of explosives and survival techniques. Special Operations Executive (SOE) training was centred on nearby Arisaig House. In August 1942 the army was replaced by the Royal Navy; the house became HMS Lochailort, used for training naval cadets and ratings to become officers on the small craft used by Combined Operations. The Royal Navy moved out in January 1945.

Don't follow the road to Glenshian Lodge, but head S along a tarmac farm road. Turn left along a grass track, signed Druim Fiaclach, immediately before the cottages. Pass through three sets of gates, passing the remains of outbuildings erected by the army in the war, and keep straight on along a faint boggy path which goes to the right of the wooded Tom Odhar knoll. The old stalker's path improves as you climb to cross a couple of vehicle tracks before joining another track, marked by a small cairn (120m, 77700 81430). A little higher, fork left along a vehicle track which drops down to a bridge over the gorge of the **Allt a' Bhuiridh** (35min, 125m, 77890 81340).

Climb roughly SE up the grassy slopes of Beinn Coire nan Gall. There are some boggy vehicle tracks on the slope, but they don't tend to head in the right direction and are best ignored. Eventually reach the summit of

An Stac from Beinn Coire nan Gall

Beinn Coire nan Gall (2hr 25min, 787m, 79220 79770). Head SSW to a small lochan (245m, 79130 79600) and climb easily up grass slopes between crags on the N ridge of **Druim Fiaclach** to reach the cairn on a rocky rib (2hr 50min, 869m, 79150 79170).

Follow the SW ridge of Druim Fiaclach, which has steep crags on either side, veering S to Bealach an Fhalaisg Dhuibh (745m, 78520 78560). Climb S to a small lochan then veer WSW, veering W, over a minor top and to the cairn on the summit of **Sgurr na Ba Glaise** (4hr, 874m, 77020 77750).

Head W, veering WNW, to the Bealach an Fhiona (701m, 76420 77980) and head W, soon picking up a wall which takes you all the way to the E summit of **Rois-Bheinn**. This summit has a very small cairn which includes concrete from the remains of the trig point shown on the OS map (4hr 45min, 882m, 75610 77830). If you have surplus energy you could continue along the wall to the W summit of Rois-Bheinn, which has better views out to sea. ▸

The W summit is about 3m lower than the E summit, but it is topped by a massive cairn which takes it to about the same height!

Whether or not you visit the W summit you should now retrace your steps down the wall and follow it as it veers left down steep rocky slopes. The wall disintegrates into a line of fence posts and you should continue down between the fence posts and a second wall. When the wall and fence posts rejoin, on a slight rise, turn right down to the saddle S of An Stac (5hr 15min, 565m, 76190 78500). Pick a route up the S ridge. In good visibility it should be possible to climb up grass slopes avoiding the many crags to reach the small cairn on a rock outcrop on the summit of **An Stac** (5hr 55min, 814m, 76300 79270).

You now need to wind your way carefully down grassy rakes through the crags on the steep rocky N ridge of An Stac to reach a broad saddle (485m, 76500 80000). It would be possible to continue over Seann Chruach, but it's quicker to descend ENE down grass slopes to a vehicle track (at about 250m, 77200 80300) running down the glen. Turn left following the boggy track to the top of the stalker's path (120m, 77700 81420), which is followed back to the parking area (7hr 40min).

ROUTE 10

Beinn Odhar Bheag LITTLE DUN-COLOURED MOUNTAIN *and*
Beinn Mhic Cedidh MacCEDIDH'S MOUNTAIN

Start	5km W of Glenfinnan (NM 85650 81330)
Distance	13km (8 miles)
Total ascent	1310m (4300ft)
Difficulty	All the ridges on this route are rocky and although there are grassy ways through the crags, route-finding would be difficult in mist. The ridge between Beinn Odhar Mhor and Beinn Odhar Bheag is complex and would be particularly difficult in poor visibility. There is some rough grassland to climb on the ascent and boggy terrain on the descent.
Time	6hr
Summits	Beinn Odhar Mhor (870m), Beinn Odhar Bheag (882m, 2895ft), Beinn Mhic Cedidh (783m, 2350ft ring contour)
Maps	OS Landranger 40
Access	Park in a large layby about 5km W of Glenfinnan on the A830 where the railway comes alongside the road on a sweeping right-hand bend.

Beinn Odhar Bheag and Beinn Mhic Cedidh are rocky peaks in the NE corner of Moidart just W of Glenfinnan. As well as interesting ridges, there are good views in all directions. Beinn Odhar Mhor is the dominant mountain when viewed from Glenfinnan, but it is about 10m lower than its twin summit, Beinn Odhar Bheag. Beinn Mhic Cedidh was shown about 200ft lower on the 1 inch:1 mile OS maps and was only promoted to Corbett status when the 1:50,000 OS maps were published.

The **West Highland Line**, which runs 164 miles from Glasgow to Mallaig, is arguably the most scenic railway line in Britain. There are at least three passenger trains in each direction every day. During the summer, a steam locomotive 'The Jacobite' provides a daily return service between Fort William

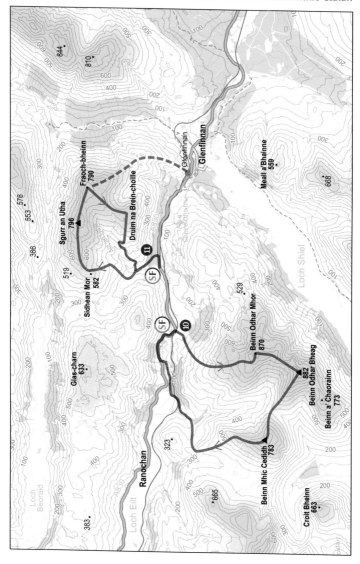

and Mallaig. It was The Jacobite that was the 'Hogwarts Express' in the *Harry Potter* films. **www. westcoastrailways.co.uk**

Cross the bridge over the Allt Lon a' Mhuidhe, then carefully cross the railway line and follow a faint boggy path SSW, veering WSW. When the path fades away continue WSW up a rocky spur, gradually veering left up the N ridge of Beinn Odhar Mhor to reach a small bog, marked as a lochan on the OS map (580m, 84670 80090). Continue roughly SSE to the summit of **Beinn Odhar Mhor**, which is marked by a cairn and the remains of a trig point (2hr 5min, 870m, 85150 79090).

The complex ridge to Beinn Odhar Bheag could be very confusing in mist and great care would be needed. Head S (to about 820m, 85100 78530) then veer SW and back S again to reach the low point (760m, 84910 78200). The easy route is obvious in good visibility, but in mist you don't want to get involved with the crags on the right of the ridge. Head a little left from the low point then head SW up a grassy rake to reach the summit of **Beinn Odhar Bheag** (2hr 45min, 882m, 84660 77860).

Head roughly NW down the ridge; this appears to be an easy grass slope from above but care is needed bypassing bands of hidden crags. Continue down to a rocky saddle (490m, 83680 78680) and then ascend the easy E ridge to a small cairn on the summit of **Beinn Mhic Cedidh** (4hr 5min, 783m, 82840 78810).

Take care descending the rocky N ridge of Beinn Mhic Cedidh. It is necessary to weave around to find a grassy way through the crags. At about 600m (82900 79640) head NNW down the easy grassy slope on your left, reaching the NNW ridge, which is followed to a saddle with the remnants of an old track (5hr, 255m, 82570 80880). Turn right along this sometimes boggy and indistinct vehicle track, which leads down to a bridge (80m, 83450 81020) over the gorge of the Allt a' Choire Bhuidhe. Turn left after crossing the bridge and follow the still boggy track as it veers right alongside the railway. It passes under the railway (83960 81300), down to the E

end of **Loch Eilt** and E along damp meadows. Eventually the track fords the Allt Lon a' Mhuidhe and climbs to the **A830** by a sign for a bend in the road (84910 81680). Turn right and walk along the grass verge to the parking area (6hr).

S ridge, Beinn Odhar Mhor

ROUTE 11

Sgurr an Utha PEAK OF THE UDDER

Start	Allt an Utha (NM 87320 81690)
Distance	10km (6 miles)
Total ascent	760m (2500ft)
Difficulty	There is some rough, possibly boggy grassland on the lower slopes of the mountain but otherwise the going is easy, provided the visibility is good enough to pick the best route through the multitude of crags that cover all the ridges. The descent ridges are very ill defined and could test navigational skills, even in good weather.
Time	3hr 40min
Summits	Sgurr an Utha (796m, 2610ft), Fraoch-bheinn (790m)
Maps	OS Landranger 40
Access	There is a parking area on the A830 just W of the Allt an Utha, which is at the end of the forestry about 2km W of Glenfinnan.
Note	For those using the train rather than a car it would make sense to climb the SE ridge of Fraoch-bheinn from Glenfinnan. In mist, navigation would probably be easier if you reverse the route.

Sgurr na Utha is the grass-covered rocky peak to the NW of Glenfinnan. The featured route provides an interesting traverse of the rocky ridges surrounding the Allt an Utha.

Glenfinnan boasts the best known **railway viaduct** in the world. Built between 1897 and 1901, the 390m viaduct has 21 supporting arches 30m high. It is featured in the film *Harry Potter and the Chamber of Secrets* when the 'Hogwarts Express' train steams across it.

See map in Route 11.

Head E along the **A830**, cross the **Allt an Utha** and, after 200m, turn left up a good track into the forest. The track soon leaves the forest and continues up the E bank of the Allt an Utha to a track junction (20min, 200m, 87290 82380) which is not shown on the OS 1:50,000 map. The main track turns sharp right but we keep straight on and 50m later cross a bridge over the Allt an Utha. Ignore the

Allt an Utha rushes down from the slopes of Sgurr na Utha

faint boggy path shown on older OS maps, but instead pick a route roughly NE up the ridge, through the crags to the left of the burn. If you keep left of the Allt an Utha and its tributaries you will eventually reach an old fence line on the W ridge of Sgurr na Utha at Sidhean Mor (1hr 20min, 570m, 87250 83780). On the climb, try and get a picture in your mind of the terrain on the W ridge of Druim na Brein-choille across the glen, as you will want to hit the top end of the track in descent and it will be invisible from above. Turn right and follow the fence line up the rocky ridge. When the fence veers left (N) just before the final climb to **Sgurr na Utha**, you should continue E to the summit cairn on a rocky knoll (2hr 5min, 796m, 88510 83970).

Head just S of E to a low point (725m) and on to the summit of **Fraoch-bheinn**. This summit has many tops and it is not immediately clear which is the highest. The author's measurements suggest the W top (89310 83765) is only a couple of metres lower than Sgurr na Utha and is considerably higher than the E top (2hr 30min, 790m, 89460 83700), which is shown as the summit on the OS maps.

The descent could be confusing, even in good visibility. Head roughly SW, veering SSW, to the multi-topped summit of **Druim na Brein-choille** (about 620m, 88800 82600) and then head W. You are aiming for the top of the track, which isn't visible until you are right on top of it (3hr 10min, 430m, 88010 82680). Turn sharp right down the track and follow it all the way back to the A830 and the parking area (3hr 40min).

ROUTE 12

Stob a' Bhealach an Sgriodain

PEAK OF THE PASS OF THE SCREES

Start	Callop River (NM 92410 79210)
Distance	21km (13 miles)
Total ascent	1180m (3900ft)
Difficulty	The ridges are rocky, but any difficulties can easily be bypassed. The Cona River and the Allt Coire na Leacaich must be crossed twice. These crossings will probably involve getting the feet wet, but they should be crossable except in extreme conditions.
Time	7hr 30min
Summits	Stob a' Bhealach an Sgriodain (770m, 2520ft), Meall Mor (759m)
Maps	OS Landranger 40
Access	Turn S down a forestry road from the A830, about 2.5km E of Glenfinnan and 400m W of the railway bridge. Cross the bridge over the Callop River and park in the car park on the right.
Note	Looking at the map it might be thought desirable to approach the remote Stob a' Bhealach an Sgriodain from the W up the forest roads in Glen Hurich. However, there is no easy way out of the forest. The main alternative is the easy but long approach up Cona Glen from the E.

Stob a' Bhealach an Sgriodain is a remote peak at the head of Cona Glen. It is not named on the OS map but it seems to be the normal practice to name it after the pass to the W of the summit over which a path used to go from Glenfinnan to Glen Hurich.

On 19 August 1745 **Charles Edward Stuart** landed in a small rowing boat at the N end of Loch Shiel. Gathering 200 MacDonalds, 1000 men of the Clan Cameron and 300 MacDonnells in support of rebellion, Bonnie Prince Charlie climbed the hill

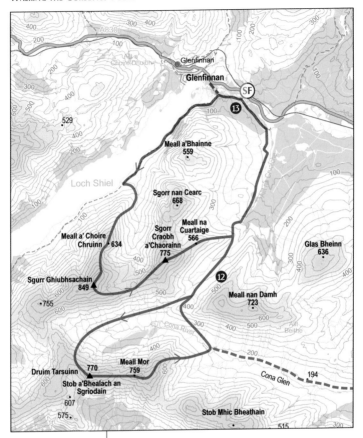

behind today's National Trust for Scotland Visitor Centre and raised his standard.

His army reached Derby on 6 December 1745 then retreated, not knowing that the Hanoverian court of George II was packing its belongings onto ships in the Thames in preparation for flight. Had Charles advanced British history and the history of the Highlands could have been very different.

Less than eight months later the rebellion ended in bloody failure at Culloden and in its aftermath the Highland way of life that had existed for hundreds of years was swept away.

Head S along the estate road, turning right and left at Callop Cottage and continuing along the good track until just before it ends at a small dam. Turn right up a faint path (30min, 145m, 91860 77070), which soon becomes much clearer. Cross the Allt Coire na Leacaich burn, pass through a gate in the deer fence, cross the E ridge of Meall na Cuartaige and head up the **Allt na Cruaiche** burn to the pass between Sgorr Craobh a' Chaorainn and Meall nan Damh. Reach a path junction as the path starts descending (1hr 40min, 365m, 89750 74570).

Fork right. The path shown on the OS map has largely disappeared but, with a bit of imagination, you can follow its course as it traverses WSW, dropping slightly, to the **Cona River** (2hr 15min, 300m, 88050 73970). Ford the river, and head SW to reach a small burn. Follow

Storms in Cona Glen

the right bank of this burn up to an obvious grassy gully which leads easily to Bealach an Sgriodain (655m, 87170 73040). Climb easily SE up the rocky ridge of **Stob a' Bhealach an Sgriodain**. There are two sets of old fence posts to aid navigation in poor visibility. The summit is marked by a tiny cairn on a rock outcrop (3hr 40min, 770m, 87470 72730).

Head E along the knobbly ridge to a saddle (660m, 88290 72810) and up to the multi-topped summit of **Meall Mor**. The highest point is probably the first top that you reach (4hr 20min, 759m, 88700 72750). Continue E another 350m then leave the fence line and veer down the NE ridge of Meall Mor. To have an easy ascent on grass you will want to veer E further down the ridge, rather than continue down the NE branch of the ridge. Continue down to the Cona River by a small island on a bend (5hr 25min, 200m, 90820 73290).

This should be a safe place to ford the river, even when it is running strongly. Turn left along the track on the far bank, forking right as you start the ascent to get back to the junction just below the pass between Sgorr Craobh a' Chaorainn and Meall nan Damh (6hr, 365m, 89760 74570). Return to the car park by the outward route (7hr 30min).

ROUTE 13

Sgurr Ghiubhsachain PEAK OF THE FIR TREES *and*
Sgorr Craobh a' Chaorainn PEAK OF THE MOUNTAIN ASH

Start	Callop River (NM 92410 79210)
Distance	17km (10 miles)
Total ascent	1220m (4000ft)
Difficulty	There is a lot of rock on the ridges traversed by this route. While it is possible to thread a way through the crags in good visibility, this would be a demanding expedition in bad weather when it could be dangerous for the inexperienced.
Time	6hr 45min
Summits	Meall a' Choire Chruinn (634m), Sgurr Ghiubhsachain (849m, 2784ft), Sgorr Craobh a' Chaorainn (775m, 2543ft)
Maps	OS Landranger 40
Access	Parking as for Route 12
Note	If you arrive at Glenfinnan by train you can join the route by taking the footpath from the Glenfinnan Visitor Centre to Loch Shiel.

Sgurr Ghiubhsachain is the prominent rocky peak on the left looking down Loch Shiel from Glenfinnan. The traverse of Sgurr Ghiubhsachain and Sgorr Craobh a' Chaorainn, the peaks at the head of Coire Ghiubhsachain, provides a magnificent walk.

Loch Shiel is one of the largest freshwater lochs in Scotland, stretching 28km from Glenfinnan to Acharacle. Although very narrow, it is exceptionally deep, more than 100m in several places, having been carved out by glaciers during the last ice age. In summer, 'Eagle-Watch Cruises' are run from the Glenfinnan House Hotel. The birds you may see include golden eagles, black and red throated divers, goosander, plover, whimbrel and curlew.

Sgurr Ghiubhsachain

See map in Route 12.

This is the scar left behind in burying a pipeline and hopefully this will return to nature during the life of this guide.

Follow the forestry road NW along the River Callop to Loch Shiel and along the S shore of the loch until Guesachan Cottage and the bridge over the Allt Coire Ghiubhsachain burn (1hr 5min, 15m, 88390 77820). Cross the burn and turn left up a good track. Before reaching the generator hut turn right up a messy 'track'. ◄ Continue up the 'track' until you reach an inspection cover for the pipeline (115m, 88790 77500). Having bypassed the crags at the lower end of the ridge, turn right up the ridge. Higher up you will find a faint path which will help you weave a route, up grass slopes, between the crags to the multi-topped summit of **Meall a' Choire Chruinn** (2hr 35min, 634m, 87970 76350).

Descend SW to a complex saddle (595m) and find a route through the big crags on the N ridge of Sgurr Ghiubhsachain to reach the N top. If you were doing the route in reverse, finding a safe descent route in mist would not be easy. Head SSW to the large cairn on the summit of **Sgurr Ghiubhsachain** (3hr 30min, 849m, 87560 75120).

There is now an awkward steep descent, initially SE, down a craggy slope. Don't veer left otherwise you will get mixed up with dangerous crags. Once the slope eases there is easy going E to a broad saddle (595m, 88520 74980) containing a peat bog rather than the lochan shown on the OS map. Climb easily ENE, veering NE, to the summit buttress of **Sgorr Craobh a' Chaorainn** which is climbed on its right-hand edge to reach the summit cairn (4hr 50min, 775m, 89560 75780).

Take care on the initial descent ENE down the rocky ridge. The going eases as you reach a broad saddle and climb easily to the summit of **Meall na Cuartaige** (566m, 90570 76280). Descend E, veering ENE, down the ridge until you reach an old stalker's path (6hr, 260m, 91580 76570). Turn left, pass through a gate in the deer fence and down to a good track (100m, 91830 77010). Head down the track, turning right and left at Callop Cottage, and back to the car park (6hr 45min).

ROUTE 14

Streap CLIMBER'S HILL

Start	Craigag car park, Fassfern Estate (NM 92990 79860)
Distance	18km (11 miles)
Total ascent	1510m (5000ft)
Difficulty	The multitude of crags on the ridges are easily bypassed in good visibility, but would require skilful route-finding in mist. The final approach to Streap is along an easy knife-edge ridge that could be dangerous in strong winds. There is rough grass on the lower slopes, which is hard going. This route is not recommended for the inexperienced in bad weather.
Time	7hr 20min
Summits	Beinn an Tuim (810m), Meall an Uillt Chaoil (844m), Stob Coire nan Cearc (887m), Streap (909m, 2988ft), Streap Comhlaidh (898m)
Maps	OS Landranger 40
Access	Park at the Fassfern Estate Craigag car park, which is just E of the point where the A830 passes under the railway about 3.5km E of Glenfinnan.
Note	It would be quicker to ascend and descend by the descent route, but the climb up Streap Comhlaidh would be a long grind.

Streap is the highest point on the fine rock and grass ridge which stretches from Glenfinnan to the W end of Loch Arkaig. The recommended traverse climbs four other peaks over 2500ft, but with insufficient drop to qualify for Corbett status. There are magnificent views from the ridge. The popular Gleann Dubh Lighe Bothy which could be used as a base for climbing Streap and Braigh nan Uamhachan was destroyed by fire in 2011, but it is intended that it should be rebuilt.

By 1815 the Jacobite threat had receded sufficiently into history to allow the erection of a **monument** at Glenfinnan to mark the raising of the standard. Paid for by Alexander MacDonald of Glenaladale,

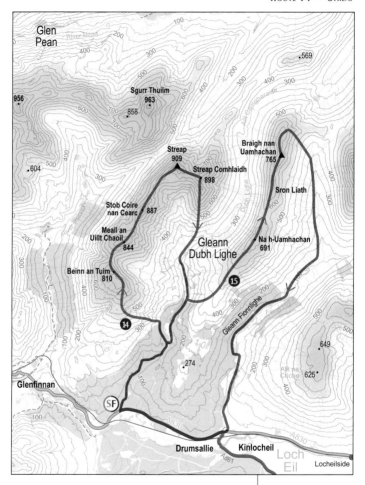

the stone tower is surmounted by a statue of a
kilted highlander, not the Prince himself as is often
assumed. If you look carefully, you can see that the
tower leans slightly to one side – the monument is
actually sinking at a rate of about 0.4mm a year.

Streap Comhlaidh
from Streap

Return to the **A830**, turn left and almost immediately turn left up the forestry track which heads up the left bank of the Dubh Lighe burn. Continue to a junction (140m, 94380 81710) where you keep straight on (left) along a grassy forest track to the edge of the forest (40min, 175m, 94200 82170). Climb the gate and turn left up the fence. When the fence veers left, head roughly WNW picking a route between the crags, up a steep rough grass slope. At about 400m the gradient and the going eases and you continue to a shallow saddle on the S ridge of **Beinn an Tuim** (590m, 93100 82680). Turn right (N) up the undefined ridge to the S top of Beinn an Tuim and then NW to the N summit (2hr 30min, 810m, 92850 83540). The cairn may be on the highest top, but the highest point could be another nearby top (92930 83540). ▶

Descend carefully N down a steep rocky ridge. It is possible to descend on grass avoiding the crags to a low point (665m, 92920 83930). Climb easily to the tiny cairn on the summit of **Meall an Uillt Chaoil** (3hr 10min, 844m, 93190 84330) then descend ENE, veering NNE down an easy rocky ridge to Bealach Coire nan Cearc (745m, 93530 84800). The crags on the ascent of **Stob Coire nan Cearc** are best bypassed on the right to reach the summit (3hr 50min, 887m, 93760 85200). Descend NW to a low point (795m, 93990 85660) after which the ridge starts to narrow into an easy knife-edge ridge as you climb to the summit of **Streap** at the NE end of the ridge (4hr 30min, 909m, 94670 86360).

There is a faint path and some old fence posts to aid navigation on the next section of the route. Descend steeply SE, veering ESE to a saddle (820m, 95050 86110) and climb to the grassy summit of **Streap Comhlaidh** (4hr 55min, 898m, 95290 86050).

Head SSE, veering S, down the steep grass slopes of the S ridge of Streap Comhlaidh. There are a few crags to avoid, but the main problem is the tussocky grass lower down the ridge. Continue down until you reach an old track (at about 270m, 95290 84520). Turn right along this grassy track, which is boggy and indistinct in places, to reach the main burn draining the S face of Streap. Ford this burn and continue along the track to a bridge over the **Dubh Lighe** burn (6hr 10min, 190m, 94760 83730). ▶ After crossing the bridge the track improves and is followed past Gleann Dubh Lighe Bothy to another bridge across the Dubh Lighe. Cross the bridge and climb to a junction. Turn left back to the A830 and the car park (7hr 20min).

Beinn an Tuim has the feel of a separate Corbett, but the author's measurements agree with the OS map that there is only a 490ft drop between it and Meall an Uillt Chaoil.

There is a superb swimming hole under this bridge.

ROUTE 15

Braigh nan Uamhachan BRAE OF THE CAVES

Start	Craigag car park, Fassfern Estate (NM 92990 79860)
Distance	23km (15 miles)
Total ascent	1100m (3600ft)
Difficulty	Braigh nan Uamhachan is a grassy mountain. The suggested route is relatively easy, the main problem being the tussocky, possibly boggy grass on the lower slopes of the mountain.
Time	6hr 40min
Summits	Braigh nan Uamhachan (765m, 2513ft)
Maps	OS Landranger 40
Access	Parking as for Route 14
Note	The quickest route would be to descend by the ascent route. Time could also be saved by cycling the good forest track up Gleann Dubh Lighe.

Braigh nan Uamhachan is the highest point on a long ridge stretching N from the W end of Loch Eil and it is actually the SW ridge of the Munro Gaor Bheinn (Gulvain). The suggested route gives a fine but easy ridge walk followed by a descent down the remote Choire Reidh and Gleann Fionn Lighe.

Thomas Telford, destined to become the greatest civil engineer in Scottish history, was born the son of a shepherd on 9 August 1757. He started out as an apprentice stonemason but later became an engineer. In 1801 he made a survey of roads across Scotland, which revealed a road network that barely existed N and W of the Great Glen, and over the next 20 years Telford was responsible for the construction of over 920 miles of road and 120 bridges in the Highlands.

See map in Route 14.

Return to the **A830**, turn left and almost immediately turn left up the forestry track which heads up the left bank of the Dubh Lighe burn. Continue to a junction (140m, 94380 81710) where you turn sharp right to a bridge across the **Dubh Lighe**. The track veers left, passing Gleann Dubh Lighe Bothy. Continue to the edge of the forest (55min, 165m, 94900 82880). Climb up steep grass slopes on the right, staying to the left of the deer fence. It's easiest to follow animal tracks alongside the fence. Follow the fence to reach the SW ridge of Na h-Uamhachan (1hr 35min, 485m, 95900 82980).

Turn left up the easy grass ridge, crossing Na h-Uamhachan (691m, 96680 84290). An old fence line joins from the right as you descend to a saddle (585m, 97030 85030) and the fence line becomes a wall as you climb **Sron Liath** (700m). There is a short descent then leave the wall as it heads off left on the final climb to **Braigh nan Uamhachan** (3hr 15min, 765m, 97530 86650). The highest point is the first small cairn.

Continue along the ridge, which becomes very narrow, until it steepens (730m, 97600 87250). Turn down the ridge to the E until you can see a grassy gully (660m, 97770 87280) heading to the right (ESE). This gully leads you easily down to the Allt a' Choire Reidh, which you follow, taking advantage of animal tracks, until you reach the good track running down **Gleann Fionnlighe** (4hr 45min, 110m, 98600 83900). Turn right, following the track as

Braigh nan Uamhachan

it crosses the **Fionn Lighe** burn (65m 96310 81290) and down to the old road. Turn right and left to reach the A830 (6hr, 95990 79340). Unless you've arranged transport you will now need to turn right and walk 3km along the grass verge back to the car park (6hr 40min).

ROUTE 16

Ainshval ROCKY RIDGE HILL *and Askival* SPEAR HILL

Start	Ferry terminal, Rum (NM 41100 99130)
Distance	21km (13 miles)
Total ascent	1890m (6200ft)
Difficulty	This is probably the most demanding walk in this guide. There is plenty of easy scrambling on small rocksteps along all the ridges and, if you fail to find the easiest route, you could find some yourself confronted with much more difficult scrambling. Finding a safe descent avoiding the crags on Sgurr nan Gillean at the end of a long day is not straightforward. When the burns are in flood the return route from Dibidil will be difficult. This is not a route to do in poor visibility or in bad weather.
Time	9hr 45min
Summits	Hallival (723m), Askival (812m, 2663ft), Trollaval (702m, Graham), Ainshval (781m, 2552ft), Sgurr nan Gillean (764m)
Maps	OS Landranger 39
Access	See Section 2 introduction.
Note	It is possible to shorten the traverse by contouring around Hallival and Trollaval and missing out Sgurr nan Gillean by returning to Bealach an Fhuarain after climbing Ainshval and descending down Glen Dibidil. If you want to climb Askival and Ainshval separately, you could climb Askival by the recommended ascent route, descending by the same route, probably traversing Hallival instead of climbing it again. Ainshval could be climbed from Dibidil Bothy, with or without Sgurr nan Gillean. Based on the 2012 ferry timetable, it would just about be possible to climb one Corbett on a Saturday day trip from Mallaig.

The Cuillins of Rum provide one of the most magnificent mountain traverses in Scotland and it is strongly recommended that you should attempt the full traverse of the main ridge. There are five fine rocky mountains on the ridge with Hallival, Sgurr nan Gillean and the Graham Trollaval, in addition to the two Corbetts. The Cuillins of Rum can be compared with the mountains of Arran. However, on Rum paths are only starting to develop, the burns are not bridged and route-finding skills are required to avoid the difficulties on the ridges.

Rum is perhaps most famous for its colony of **Manx shearwaters**. Over 60,000 pairs of this black and white pigeon-sized bird nest in burrows near the summits of the island's highest mountains. After spending the winter off the E coast of S America the shearwaters return in late March to reclaim their burrows, under the cover of darkness to avoid predators such as golden eagles. Each pair of shearwaters lays a single egg in May and the chick is fed by the parents until early September when it is abandoned and it must find its own way to the sea on a dark September night.

Head W along the shore from the new ferry terminal and past the old pier. Immediately after this is the National Nature Reserve Visitor Centre (40640 99080), which is well worth visiting, water point, toilets, showers, camping cabins, open shelters and the campsite. Continue along the shore to the 'White House' and along the middle track towards Kinloch Castle. ▶ About 100m before the castle, a path goes left over a stile, signed to Rum Cuillin. (If you are coming from Kinloch you should take the track along the S side of the castle, signed to Coire Dubh, turn left opposite the hostel entrance, then turn left along a path to join the described route.) Continue along the right-hand side of the Allt Slugan a' Choilich, ignoring turns, to reach open hillside. A small path leads to a water catchment dam (50min, 185m, 39320 98280). Continue up the path to the remains of an old dam at the lip of Corrie Dubh (1hr 5min, 280m, 38920 97830).

Guided tours are available for the magnificent Edwardian Kinloch Castle.

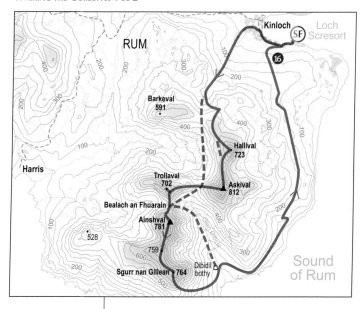

Follow a faint path left from here, veering right then left before it gradually fades as it reaches a shallow saddle on the N ridge of Hallival (1hr 25min, 410m, 39230 97370). Turn right (SW) up the ridge, crossing a shallow saddle (505m) and shortly afterwards veering left (SSE to SE) up the ridge, which is mainly grassy with crags and boulders. ◄ The ascent is easy with a couple of easy rocksteps. Reach the large cairn on the summit of **Hallival** (2hr 20min, 723m, 39540 96250).

The descent SSW involves more easy scrambling – with careful route-finding needed to avoid the main difficulties – to reach a saddle (2hr 40min, 600m, 39430 95970). The route continues along a narrow grassy ridge which leads to the foot of the Askival Pinnacle (685m, 39360 95510). The direct ascent of the pinnacle is a moderate rock climb (Grade 4 scramble), but it can easily be avoided by following a small path below the crags to the left and then picking a route back to the ridge (possibly at

Note the Manx shearwater burrows on the ridge.

about 760m, 39360 95320 but you may prefer to contour further along the E face and then climb the E ridge to avoid more of the scrambling) to reach the trig point (3hr 20min, 812m, 39320 95210).

Descend the W ridge of **Askival**. Again your route-finding skills will be tested if you are to avoid awkward scrambling and boulderfields. If in doubt, it is probably best to bypass difficulties on the left. You will reach the Bealach an Oir (3hr 50min, 460m, 38560 95260). It would be possible to return to Kinloch from here by heading roughly N across Atlantic Corrie to Bealach Bairc-mheall and back down Corrie Dubh. If you need to save time en route to Ainshval you could contour roughly WSW round to Bealach an Fhuarain. The ascent, roughly W, up **Trollaval** is easy, as any difficulties on the rocky ridge can be avoided on the right to reach the E top (702m, 37800 95140). The maps and some other accounts seem to suggest this is the summit, but the W top is about 1m higher. The route to the W top is an easy, but exposed, scramble (4hr 30min, 702m, 37740 95190).

Return to the E top and descend the S ridge of Trollaval. Again route-finding skills are needed to avoid the difficulties. It's probably easier to descend roughly SE to start with then veer S to reach the **Bealach an Fhuarain** (4hr 50min, 510m, 37900 94820). The buttress ahead of you is a rock

Askival

climb, but it is easily avoided by following a small path to the right and then climbing the boulderfield to reach the ridge above the buttress (610m, 37930 94610). A path is developing up the ridge, avoiding any difficulties by staying left of the ridge-line to reach the summit cairn on **Ainshval** (5hr 20min, 781m, 37850 94320).

The easiest descent would be to return to the Bealach an Fhuarain and then descend down **Glen Dibidil.** The featured route continues down the grassy S ridge of Ainshval to a saddle (680m, 37810 93820) and then easily up the rocky N ridge of the N top of **Sgurr nan Gillean** (759m, 37710 93590). Head SSE down the grassy ridge to a saddle (705m) and climb easily to the summit cairn (6hr, 764m, 38020 93040).

Great care is needed in the descent of Sgurr nan Gillean as it is much better protected by crags than is indicated on the OS map. There are a few large cairns indicating the route, but they are too far apart to be of much use in mist. Head S, aiming for a flattish area (490m, 38060 92480) at the foot of some big crags on the ridge. There are big crags (not marked on the OS 1:50,000 map) on the direct line, so you need to stay slightly right of the direct line. The gradient eases now and you should head just N of E to reach **Dibidil Bothy**, which is maintained by the Mountain Bothies Association (7hr 5min, 30m, 39320 92730).

Follow the path NNE from the bothy to cross the Dibidil River. This is very easy at normal water flows, but if it has been raining you may have to head upstream to find a safe crossing place. In wet conditions, other burns you have to cross on the return to Kinloch will also be difficult. You now follow the old path back to Kinloch, initially climbing to a saddle and continuing to climb very gently. Cross a burn above a waterfall (100m, 40930 94310) and then climb more steeply to a high point (8hr 25min, 225m, 41360 96430) and continue, crossing two more significant burns, before descending to the main estate track (9hr 35min, 10m, 40440 99110). Turn right (turn left for the castle and Kinloch) back to the ferry terminal (9hr 45min).

3 GLEN LOY, LOCH ARKAIG, GLEN DESSARRY AND SOUTH KNOYDART

Glen Loy, Loch Arkaig, Glen Dessarry and South Knoydart: Bases and facilities

The only facilities in this section are at the small community of Gairlochy, centred on the locks of the Caledonian Canal, which has several B&Bs and the Gairlochy Holiday Park. However, most walkers will be based in or around Fort William. More adventurous walkers may prefer to use A' Chuil Bothy in Glen Dessarry or the remote Sourlies Bothy in Knoydart.

Base for Routes 17–24: Gairlochy

There are several B&Bs and the Gairlochy Holiday Park, which has self-catering holiday caravans and chalets as well as pitches for touring caravans and tents. Tel: 01397 712 711 www.theghp.co.uk

Alternative base for Routes 17–24: Fort William

See Section 2 for details of facilities in Fort William

Alternative base for Routes 20–24: Glen Dessarry

A' Chuil Bothy, Glen Dessarry (NM 94420 92420)

Base for Routes 26 and 27: Sourlies Bothy

Sourlies Bothy (NM 86890 95060)

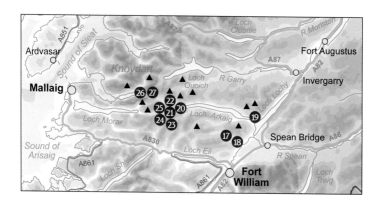

ROUTE 17

Meall a' Phubuill HILL OF THE TENT

Start	Achnanellan, Glen Loy (NN 09320 84730)
Distance	15km (9 miles)
Total ascent	850m (2800ft)
Difficulty	Although the route is pathless once the glen is left behind, the walking is generally fairly easy.
Time	4hr 30min
Summits	Meall a' Phubuill (774m, 2533ft), Druim Gleann Laoigh (698m)
Maps	OS Landranger 41
Access	From Fort William take the A830 towards Mallaig then, at Banavie, turn right along the B8004 towards Gairlochy and turn left up Glen Loy (from Gairlochy head SW down the B8004 and turn right up Glen Loy). There is limited parking at the end of the public road at Achnanellan.
Note	Meall a' Phubuill could also be climbed from Fassfern on Loch Eil to the S. Routes 17 and 18 could be combined by traversing from Meall a' Phubuill to Beinn Bhan.

Meall a' Phubuill and Beinn Bhan are the highest points on the long ridge which stretches 20km from Kinlocheil, on Loch Eil, to Loch Lochy. The section of the ridge joining these Corbetts forms the N wall of Glen Loy.

The route follows the remains of the **old pony track** which went up Glen Loy, past Glensulaig Bothy and down to Loch Eil. In Gleann Suileag there is a collection of 14 raised platforms for charcoal-burning and the track would once have been busy with ponies carrying huge loads of charcoal down to Loch Eil. Charcoal burning was the principal reason for the destruction of the Caledonian Forest in this area.

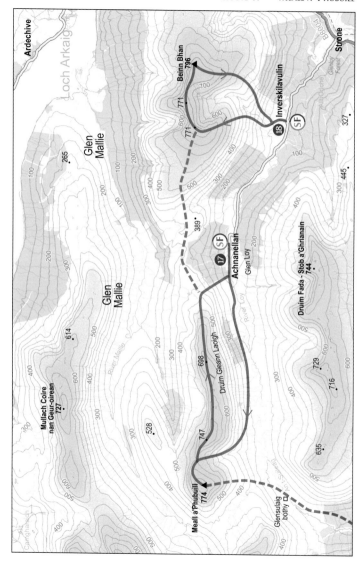

Meall a' Phubuill from upper Glen Loy

Follow the road past Achnanellan and continue along a good track until it ends (235m, 06450 84340). Continue up **Glen Loy** along the path, which is very faint in places. Soon after reaching a shieling beyond the high point of the pass, the path becomes impossible to follow (1hr 15min, 260m, 04350 84030). Head diagonally right (NW) towards the unnamed burn draining the corrie to the E of Meall a' Phubuill. Reach the burn near the top of a waterslide and follow it up to its source just below the pass, then continue N to the pass (2hr 10min, 645m, 03630 85560). Head W, veering SW, up the ridge to the summit cairn on **Meall a' Phubuill** (2hr 30min, 774m, 02940 85410).

Return to the pass where you pick up an old fence line and/or dilapidated wall which leads to **Peak 747**, down to another pass (640m) and up to the summit cairn on **Druim Gleann Laoigh** (698m, 06200 85340). Continue down the E ridge until the intermittent wall finally ends above the forest (4hr, 395m, 08110 85620). Head right, downhill, to the forest and follow the forest edge down to the track up **Glen Loy**. Turn left along the track past Achnanellan to the parking area (4hr 30min).

ROUTE 18

Beinn Bhan WHITE MOUNTAIN

Start	Inverskilavulin (NN 12580 83120)
Distance	8km (5 miles)
Total ascent	780m (2600ft)
Difficulty	The ascent is easy. In descent, care would be needed with navigation in mist. There is a little rough heather to cross.
Time	2hr 50min
Summits	Beinn Bhan (796m, 2612ft)
Maps	OS Landranger 41
Access	Head up Glen Loy, as described in access to Route 17, and continue until the road crosses the River Roy at Inverskilavulin. There is limited parking in the gateway immediately before the bridge.
Note	It would be easy to combine Routes 17 and 18 by traversing from Meall a' Phubuill to Beinn Bhan.

Beinn Bhan is a prominent hill to the SW of Loch Lochy. The recommended route traverses the ridge at the head of Coire Mhuilinn. There are dramatic waterfalls on the Allt Mhuilinn.

Loch Lochy forms part of the **Caledonian Canal.** Constructed in the early 19th century, the 62-mile canal follows the Great Glen, connecting Corpach near Fort William with Inverness. It provided much-needed employment to the Highland region as well as a safe passage for ships from the NE of Scotland to the SW, avoiding the dangerous waters around the N coast via Cape Wrath and the Pentland Firth.

Cross the bridge and head up the track to Inverskilavulin Estate. At the gate to the lodge follow the signed route left to the hill, along the deer fence and up the W side of the Allt Mhuilinn. At about 300m head up the ridge

See map in Route 17.

*River Loy below
Inverskilavulin*

and climb up a grassy slope to a cairn (1hr 25min, 765m, 12340 85500). Head along the easy ridge over a couple of tops (both 771m) following a line of old fence posts onto the summit plateau of **Beinn Bhan**. In mist just follow the fence posts to find the trig point and cairn that mark the summit (1hr 50min, 796m, 14060 85700).

Head WSW for about 200m then S, gradually veering SW to pick up the ridge just above the burn. At some point you will pick up a path which leads you down between a fence and the burn. When you reach the deer fence above the estate buildings, follow the signed route right, crossing the burn on a footbridge and turning left to return to the parking area (2hr 50 min).

ROUTE 19

Meall na h-Eilde HILL OF THE HINDS
and Geal Charn WHITE CAIRN

Start	Eas Chia-aig waterfall (NN 17690 88860)
Distance	18km (11 miles)
Total ascent	1170m (3900ft)
Difficulty	The going can be a bit boggy in places but is generally easy.
Time	5hr 50min
Summits	Meall na h-Eilde (838m, 2663ft), Meall Coire nan Saobhaidh (826m), Geal Charn (804m, 2636ft)
Maps	OS Landranger 34
Access	From Fort William follow the A82 E to Spean Bridge and left to the Commando Monument. Turn left down the B8004 to Gairlochy and right along the B8005 along Loch Lochy, veering left towards Loch Arkaig. Park in the large Eas Chia-aig waterfalls car park at the E end of Loch Arkaig.
Note	From Geal Charn, it is possible to descend E down Gleann Tarsuinn and back down Gleann Cia-aig. If you take this alternative, stay N of the Allt Tarsuinn to avoid having to cross it downstream. Since this route description was written, much of the forest on the E slopes of Gleann Cia-aig was clear-felled, following severe wind damage. The route is still to be re-instated so detail is uncertain on the early part of the route.

Meall na h-Eilde and Geal Charn are two Corbetts N of the E end of Loch Arkaig. The recommended approach is from the dramatic Eas Chia-aig waterfall which, being right by the road, is a popular tourist attraction. There is a big contrast between the grassy Meall na h-Eilde and the rough heather-covered moor of Geal Charn. Meall Coire nan Saobhaidh was formerly listed as the Corbett, rather than Meall na h-Eilde, as it appeared as 2695ft on the OS 1 inch to 1 mile map. The drop between them is only about 350ft so only one of them can have Corbett status.

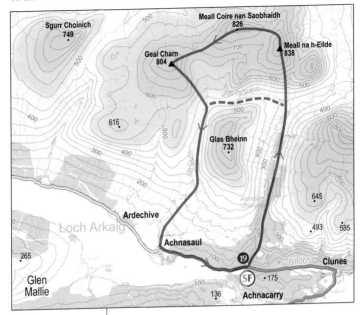

The **Clan Cameron Museum** at Achnacarry at the E end of Loch Arkaig is dedicated to the history of the Highlands and the Jacobite cause. The museum also includes artefacts, photographs and information about the commandos who trained at Achnacarry during World War II and there are references and exhibits relating to the clan regiment, the Queen's Own Cameron Highlanders. **www.clan-cameron.org**

Head up the maintained path from the top left-hand corner of the car park and follow the path up to a good forestry track. Turn left and keep going when the track changes to a maintained path taking you to a stile at the top of the forest (55min, 300m, 18570 92380). Cross the stile and continue up a possibly boggy path to the left of a new deer fence until you reach a bridge over the Allt Cam Bhealaich, the main tributary of the **Abhainn**

Chia-aig (305m, 18790 92820). Cross the bridge and continue about 100m up the Allt Cam Bhealaich to a small burn descending S from Bealach an Easain. Turn N up the left-hand side of this burn, veering away from the burn to climb the S ridge of **Meall na h-Eilde**. A line of old fence posts joins from the left just before you reach the summit cairn (2hr 20min, 838m, 18560 94620).

The fence is followed all the way to Geal Charn. Initially descend to the Bealach Choire a' Ghuirein (720m) and up to the summit of **Meall Coire nan Saobhaidh** (826m, 17470 95120). On the descent of the WSW ridge the terrain suddenly changes to heather moorland and there are peat hags on the broad Bealach Carn na h-Urchaire (645m, 16320 94620). Climb to the trig point on the summit of **Geal Charn** (3hr 35min, 804m, 15620 94250)

Leave the fence line and head roughly SE down the ridge. At some point (about 680m, 15900 93900) you need to veer left down to the **Allt Dubh**. There is no obvious line down from the ridge, but if you leave the ridge at this point the descent can be made down grass rather

Storm over Loch Arkaig

than heather slopes. When you reach the Allt Dubh, cross it and follow the burn into a marshy area where you pick up the top end of the descent path (4hr 15min, 425m, 16590 93060). Head S down the old stalker's path. If you lose the path you should be able to pick it up again at a communications mast. When you reach the lower slopes you pass through a gate and the path becomes a possibly boggy vehicle track which takes you down to the road (5hr 15min, 50m, 15290 89410). Turn left and follow the road back to the car park (5hr 50min).

ROUTE 20

Sgurr Mhurlagain PEAK OF THE INLET

Start	W end of Loch Arkaig (NM 98780 91580)
Distance	10km (6 miles)
Total ascent	900m (3000ft)
Difficulty	The ascent is easy, but a little boggy. Care is needed with navigation on the ill-defined ridge on the descent and on the final steep descent to the road.
Time	4hr
Summits	Sgurr Mhurlagain (880m, 2885ft)
Maps	OS Landranger 33
Access	From Fort William follow the route described in Route 19 to Loch Arkaig. Follow the narrow road, which is not suitable for large vehicles, to the roadhead at the W end of Loch Arkaig where there is limited parking. In long periods of wet weather you may find the road at the E end of Loch Arkaig flooded as the water level in the loch rises, and you may find yourself trapped on the wrong side of the flood.
Note	It would be possible to combine Sgurr Mhurlagain with Fraoch Bheinn (Route 21) by climbing the E ridge of Fraoch Bheinn after climbing Sgurr Mhurlagain.

Sgurr Mhurlagain is a grassy peak at the NW end of Loch Arkaig. There is a steep rocky N-facing corrie, but this is only visible from the summit.

Loch Arkaig from Sgurr Mhurlagain

Head W through the gate and fork right towards Glen Dessarry, continuing until you reach a cairn marking the start of an old stalker's path just before the Dearg Allt burn (15min, 80m, NM 97920 91610). You will see a sign ahead to a track up the W side of the burn, but this track is a bit of a boggy mess. Turn right up the stalker's path, which is indistinct in places but does take you easily through the rough grassland. Eventually this path joins the messy, boggy track (320m, NM 98650 92480) which is followed to the broad saddle between Sgurr Mhurlagain and Fraoch Bheinn (1hr 25min, 470m, NM 99650 93550). Head roughly E to the broad, grassy SW ridge of **Sgurr Mhurlagain** and follow it before turning right along the final narrow summit ridge to the small cairn (2hr 30min, 880m, NN 01270 94460).

Head back down the SW ridge. At about 600m you can either return by the ascent route or continue down the ridge until you can see a good route to the road down the slopes on the left (at about 450m, NM 99600 92900). Descend these grassy slopes, avoiding a few crags, to the road (at about NM 99300 91800). Turn right back to the parking area (4hr). ▶

The road along the north shore of Loch Arkaig was part of a grand scheme to connect Knoydart to the rest of the world, still unfinished 200-odd years after it was begun.

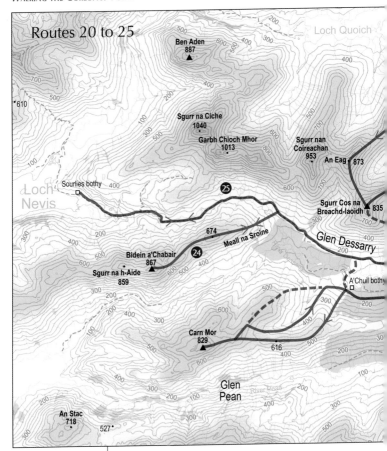

Routes 20 to 25

Loch Quoich

Ben Aden
887

*610

Sgurr na Ciche
1040

Garbh Chioch Mhor
1013

Sgurr nan
Coireachan
953   An Eag   873

Sourlies bothy

Loch
Nevis

25

Sgurr Cos na
Breachd-laoidh   835

674

Meall na Sroine

Glen Dessarry

24

Bidein a'Chabair
867

Sgurr na h-Aide
859

A'Chuil bothy

Carn Mor
829

616

Glen
Pean   River Pean

An Stac
718

527

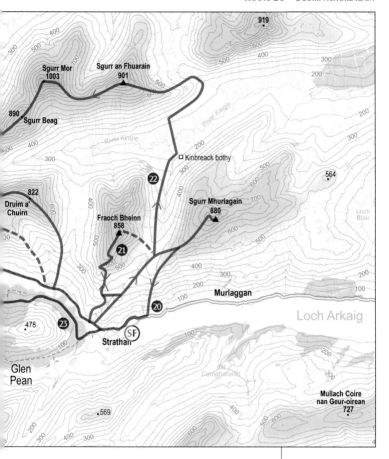

ROUTE 21

Fraoch Bheinn HEATHER MOUNTAIN

Start	W end of Loch Arkaig (NM 98780 91580)
Distance	8km (5 miles)
Total ascent	820m (2700ft)
Difficulty	Easy. A track leads through the rough grass lower down the mountain and then it is easy to weave up grass slopes through the crags higher up the ridge.
Time	3hr 10min
Summits	Fraoch Bheinn (858m, 2808ft)
Maps	OS Landranger 33
Access	Parking as for Route 20
Note	It would be possible to combine Fraoch Bheinn with Sgurr Mhurlagain (see Route 20).

Most of the interest in Fraoch Bheinn is in the rocky corrie and steep rocky ridges which overlook Glen Kingie to the N. However, most people climb the gentle S ridge which is featured in this route. Kinbreack Bothy could be used if you wanted to climb Fraoch Bheinn or Sgurr Mhurlagain from the N and this bothy would also be convenient for climbing Sgurr an Fhuarain (Route 22).

See map in Route 20.

Head W through the gate and fork right towards Glen Dessarry, continuing until you reach a track signed to Tomdoun just after the Dearg Allt burn (15min, 95m, 97830 91660). Turn right up the often boggy track until it takes you onto the ridge just below a ruined fence (335m, 98160 92440). Leave the track here and head easily up the ridge, weaving a route through the crags, continuing to the summit cairn on **Fraoch Bheinn** (1hr 55min, 858m, 98600 94010).

It is worth heading 500m along the ridge to the N top to view the crags on the N side of Fraoch Bheinn before returning to the parking area by the same route (3hr 10min).

ROUTE 22

Sgurr an Fhuarain PEAK OF THE SPRING *and Sgurr Cos na Breachd-laoigh* PEAK WITH THE CAVE OF THE SPECKLED CALF

Start	W end of Loch Arkaig (NM 98780 91580)
Distance	26km (16 miles)
Total ascent	2170m (7200ft)
Difficulty	The going on this route is generally easy. Apart from the length and amount of climb, the only problem would be the crossing of the River Kingie if it was in spate.
Time	9hr 20min
Summits	Sgurr an Fhuarain (901m, 2961ft), Sgurr Mor (1003m, Munro), Sgurr Beag (890m), An Eag (873m), Sgurr Cos na Breachd-laoigh (835m, 2600ft ring contour), Druim a' Chuirn (822m)
Maps	OS Landranger 33
Access	Parking as for Route 20
Note	If this route is too long for you the best option is to climb Sgurr an Fhuarain by the suggested ascent route and return by the same route. One option would be to use the Kinbreack Bothy. Sgurr Cos na Breachd-laoigh could then be climbed by its SE ridge, descending as in the recommended route.

Sgurr an Fhuarain is a remote peak to the S of Loch Quoich, from where it could be accessed by canoe. It is really just the E summit of the Munro Sgurr Mor and would normally be included in a backpacking trip involving the Munros to the S of Loch Quoich. Sgurr Cos na Breachd-laoigh, to the N of Glen Dessarry, was shown about 50m lower on the 1 inch:1 mile OS map and therefore Druim a' Chuirm was previously listed as the Corbett. Sgurr Beag and An Eag don't qualify as Corbetts because of insufficient drop from the Munros Sgurr Mor and Sgurr nan Coireachan respectively.

Glen Dessarry is still one of the wildest places in Scotland. The glen was in the possession of the McPhees of Lochaber from the 15th century until the lands were forfeited to the Government after the 1745 rising. The lawless reputation of the area led the Factor, Mungo Campbell, in 1758 to inform his superiors in Edinburgh that the McPhees and McMillans 'have ever been the most pestilent tribes in the Highlands'. Deserters from the military had long been made welcome in Glendessarry.

See map in Route 20.

Continue down the estate road, soon forking right, then, after crossing the Dearg Allt, turn right up a rough track signed to Tomdoun (15min, 90m, NM 97830 91660). This soon becomes a sometimes boggy grass track which does not follow the line shown on the OS maps. When the track breaks into several strands, take the one closest to the burn. The track crosses the burn and is rather indistinct in places by the time it reaches the broad saddle between Sgurr an Fhuarain and Sgurr Mhurlagain (1hr 20min, 460m, NM 99500 93720). Continue over the pass and downhill, crossing the Allt a' Chinn Bhric burn at **Kinbreack Bothy** (1hr 55min, 185m, NN 00170 96060).

Only in extremely dry conditions will you be able to cross without getting your feet wet. Greenshanks breed here.

Head down the burn to the **River Kingie**. ◄ The best place to cross, which should be safe even when water levels are high, is just right of the junction where the streambed is flat with small pebbles (175m, NN 00130 96400). Head N across the boggy moor to a good hill track (at about 2hr 10min, 210m, NN 00050 96990). Turn right and continue along the track until it crosses the Allt a' Choire Ghlais (2hr 35min, 325m, NN 00700 98280). Leave the track and head SW, veering W, up the E ridge of **Sgurr an Fhuarain**. This long grass ridge leads you easily to the trig point on the summit (4hr 10min, 901m, NM 98750 97970).

Here you pick up an old stalker's path which provides easy walking as you follow it over Sgurr Mor and Sgurr Beag. Descend the long grassy ridge W to a saddle (4hr 25min, 725m, NM 97600 97570) and follow the path as it goes right of the small crags on the ridge to reach the summit cairn on the Munro **Sgor Mor** (5hr 10min, 1003m, NM 96540 98030). The path veers left to a saddle with a cairn marking an escape route into

Glen Kingie (5hr 30min, 750m, NM 96250 97440). Keep straight on to the surprisingly cairnless summit of **Sgurr Beag** (5hr 45min, 890m, NM 95930 97090). The path switchbacks down the SW ridge of Sgurr Beag to a saddle. At the far end of the saddle there is a small cairn (6hr 10min, 670m, NM 95190 96400) marking the point where the stalker's path heads left down into Glen Kingie.

Leave the path here and head up the grassy NE ridge of **An Eag** to the summit cairn (6hr 40min, 873m, NM 94360 95860). Here you can pick up an old fence line which leads down the S ridge to a saddle (7hr, 654m, NM 94550 95040). Climb steeply up the NW ridge of **Sgurr Cos na Breachd-laoigh** following the old fence/wall line. When you reach a fence/wall line junction on the summit plateau continue a few metres to the small summit cairn (7hr 35min, 835m, NM 94880 94670).

Return to the fence line and follow it E to along a fairly narrow rocky ridge to Druim a' Chuirn. Leave the fence line when it passes just left of the E top (8hr, 815m,

Sgurr an Fhuarain

115

NM 96240 94960). Head roughly SE down an easy grass ridge with many erratic boulders and small, easily avoided crags. Eventually reach the path running down the glen of the Allt na Feithe (at about 8hr 35min, 250m, NM 97060 93360) and turn right down to the estate road (8hr 50min, 95m, NM 96880 92560). Turn left back to the parking area at the roadhead (9hr 20min).

ROUTE 23

Carn Mor BIG CAIRN

Start	W end of Loch Arkaig (NM 98780 91580)
Distance	21km (13 miles)
Total ascent	1100m (3700ft)
Difficulty	It is only the final part of the ascent that is significantly rocky and there are easy ways through the crags in good visibility but route-finding could be difficult in poor weather. There is rough grass, often boggy, on both ascent and descent.
Time	6hr 20min
Summits	Carn Mor (829m, 2718ft)
Maps	OS Landranger 33
Access	Parking as for Route 20
Note	It would be possible to climb the NE ridge of Carn Mor, over Meall nan Spardan, but crossing the Allt Coire an Eich could be difficult when it is in spate. For variety in descent you could cross the River Dessarry (there is a bridge) and return along the N side Glen Dessarry. It is possible to cycle as far as A' Chuil Bothy.

The remote Carn Mor is the highest point on the long ridge between Glen Dessarry and Glen Pean, which stretches from Loch Morar to Loch Arkaig. Carn Mor is at the boundary between relatively gentle grass-covered peaks to the E and rough rocky peaks to the W.

Glen Dessarry Estate is 15,000 acres of deer forest, with large herds of red deer, stretching from Loch Arkaig to the sea at Loch Nevis. Highland cattle and Iron Age pigs are farmed within large enclosures. The Iron Age pig is a hybrid between a male wild boar and a Tamworth sow that has been bred to recreate the type of pig that would have been kept over 2000 years ago. The estate is a good place for bird-watchers – golden eagles, ptarmigan, black grouse, woodcock, snipe and greenshank are just some of the birds you might see.

Head W through the gate and fork left to the bridge over the **River Dessarry**. Follow the good forestry track into the forest, forking right along the S flank of Glen Dessarry and continuing to the edge of the forest (1hr 5min, 145m, 94300 92320). Cross the burn, then head up the hill. A faint path is beginning to develop on the lower slopes of the steep, rough, grass slope to the right of the burn. Eventually reach the summit ridge of **Peak 616** (at about 565m, 93500 91320) and head roughly WSW to the summit (2hr 40min, 616m, 92560 91060).

Continue W down to the low point (540m, 91910 91110) and climb easily WNW on grassy rakes through the slabs on the E ridge of **Carn Mor**. Towards the top of the ridge, there are some big crags, which are best climbed up an obvious grassy rake that leads to a pond (805m, 90420 91060) on the summit plateau. You will need to veer left to the summit, which is a knoll close to the S edge of the knobbly plateau. This top, unlike a nearby top, only has a small cairn (3hr 50min, 829m, 90310 90930).

Return to the pond and descend the E ridge, veering left to the broad saddle between Carn Mor and Meall nan Spardan (640m, 91510 91540). Turn SE down the grass slopes into Coire an Eich and continue down the right bank of Allt Coire an Eich. When you are forced away from the burn by a steep, eroded slope (at about 270m, 93200 91940), it is best to contour onto the ridge on your right. You might pick up a boggy vehicle track which

See map in Route 20.

River Dessarry

leads easily down the grass slopes to the track a little W of the forest (5hr 10min, 115m, 94150 92580). Turn right, passing **A' Chuil Bothy**, and return to the parking area (6hr 20min) by the same route.

ROUTE 24

Bidein a' Chabair PEAK OF THE ANTLER

Start	W end of Loch Arkaig (NM 98780 91580)
Distance	23km (14 miles)
Total ascent	1220m (4000ft)
Difficulty	Bidein a' Chabair is well protected by steep rocky slopes. Route-finding abilities are required and it would not be a good mountain on which to be lost in poor visibility. There is some tough terrain on the lower slopes and some very easy scrambling to reach the summit. It is not a mountain for inexperienced walkers in poor weather.
Time	7hr 50min
Summits	Bidein a' Chabair (867m, 2750ft ring contour)
Maps	OS Landranger 33
Access	Parking as for Route 20
Note	It would be possible to cycle as far as Upper Glendessarry Cottage. It would also be possible to approach along the forest road through Glen Dessarry (see Route 23) and cyclists might prefer this as they could get their bikes a little nearer the foot of the mountain. It would be possible to climb Bidein a' Chabair from Sourlies Bothy, but the author has no knowledge of that route.

The 1 inch:1 mile OS map does not show Bidein a' Chabair at all! The summit is shown as Sgurr na h-Aide (2818ft) at the W end of a plateau 700m long enclosed by a 2750ft ring contour. Bidein a' Chabair (867m) is actually about 800m E of Sgurr na h-Aide (859m) on the ridge and separated from it by a 60m drop.

Evidence of **climate change** is obvious as you walk along Druim Coire nan Laogh, the E ridge of Bidein a' Chabair. The smooth rocks at over 2000ft bear witness to a big glacier flowing right over the ridge, with enough depth to grind down the hard rock.

*E ridge of Bidein a'
Chabair*

On either side of the ridge, steep rocky slopes drop down 2000ft into glens eroded away by enormous glaciers flowing down them.

See map in Route 20.

Head down the estate road, soon forking right, and continue past the newly rebuilt Glendessarry Lodge to just before the cottage at Upper Glendessarry (55min, 110m, 95200 93110) where the estate road ends. Turn right along the path signed to Inverie. This path, which is often rough or boggy, stays above the forest until just after it ends when an alternative route through the forest joins from the left (1hr 50min, 260m, 92340 94450).

Look across the glen for an obvious grassy line up the face of Meall na Sroine, to the right of the buttresses on the skyline ridge. Cross the burn and follow this line up rough grass to reach the ridge just above the buttresses (at about 2hr 25min, 435m, 91810 94080). Continue up the ridge, easily avoiding rock outcrops, to reach a minor top (600m, 91290 94020) and, after a short descent, to **Peak 674**, the main summit on the E ridge of Bidein a' Chabair (3hr 15min, 674m, 90640 93850). ◄

This summit, as is much of the ridge, is dominated by bare smoothed rock outcrops.

Continue roughly WSW along this ridge, going over or round numerous rocky knolls and eventually passing left of a lochan to reach the foot of the final climb (735m, 89290 93100). Head up the boulder-filled gully and keep going up a grassy line to the right of the ridge to reach the final summit buttress. Keep track of your route so you can retrace your steps on the descent. It is easiest to avoid the first part of this broken buttress on the left and then climb onto the ridge, with some easy scrambling being required to reach the small summit cairn on **Bidein a' Chabair** (4hr 20min, 867m, 88910 93050). The ridge W from here to Sgurr na h-Aide looks spectacular.

Return by the same route to the path (6hr 5min), estate road (7hr) and roadhead (7hr 50min).

ROUTE 25

Access route to Sourlies Bothy for
Routes 26 and 27

Start	W end of Loch Arkaig (NM 98780 91580)
Distance	14km (9 miles)
Total ascent	490m (1600ft) on walk in and 540m (1800ft) on walk out
Difficulty	This is a tough, rough path. It is actually considerably easier on the return journey as you are climbing the good stalker's path up Glen Finiskaig and descending the gentle boggy 'path' down Glen Dessarry.
Time	4hr 20min with heavy pack on walk in, 4hr on return.
Maps	OS Landranger 33
Access	Parking as for Route 20

Sourlies Bothy at the head of Loch Nevis is a small bothy, which can get crowded at peak times. The owner requests that groups of six or more don't use the bothy or camp nearby. During September or October the bothy is occasionally closed for use by the estate, so please check if you want to use it during that period. Tel: 01687 462 342

Head down the estate road, soon forking right, and continue past the newly rebuilt Glendessarry Lodge to just before the cottage at Upper Glendessarry (55min, 110m,

See map in Route 20.

Sourlies Bothy

95200 93110) where the estate road ends. Turn right along the path signed to Inverie. This path, which is often rough or boggy, stays above the forest. At the end of the forestry you will notice a vehicle track on your left which goes parallel to the old stalker's path that you are following. This track eventually joins the stalker's path, which by now is rather boggy and indistinct in places (at about 2hr 35min, 285m, 91540 94880). Shortly afterwards you need to follow the path which goes off left across a stream, ignoring the vehicle track which you can see crossing the ridge ahead. The path is not always clear as you approach the pass, which is marked by a large cairn (2hr 45min, 310m, 91100 94900).

Follow the path, which gradually becomes better defined, to the left of **Lochan a' Mhaim** and a second lochan. The path becomes vague below the second lochan, but its continuation can be seen across the burn. Cross the stream (at about 3hr 35min, 230m, 88870 94510) and then follow the path as it climbs a little and reaches a well-engineered stalker's path which descends to a bridge across the Allt Coire na Ciche. The path becomes vague again as you approach Loch Nevis – just choose the best animal track to get you to **Sourlies Bothy** (4hr 25min, 0m, 86750 95060).

ROUTE 26

Beinn Bhuidhe YELLOW HILL

Start	Sourlies Bothy (NM 86750 95060)
Distance	16km (10 miles)
Total ascent	1230m (4100ft)
Difficulty	This rough, rocky mountain would not be recommended for the inexperienced in bad weather or poor visibility.
Time	6hr 5min
Summits	Meall Bhasiter (718m), Beinn Bhuidhe (855m, 2803ft)
Maps	OS Landranger 33
Access	See Route 25
Note	The main alternative day-hike to climb Beinn Bhuidhe would be to start from Inverie, climb to Mam Meadail, follow the ridge W over Beinn Bhuidhe and continue over Sgurr Coire nan Gobhar before descending to Inverie. This would be a demanding walk. If you are camping rather than using the bothy it would be logical to camp beside the bridge over the River Carnach.

Beinn Bhuidhe is a remote peak in Knoydart, towering above the N shore of Loch Nevis. The shortest approach is from Inverie, but if you are going to climb Ben Aden from Sourlies Bothy, then it would make sense to spend an extra day climbing Beinn Bhuidhe.

Common and grey **seals** are seen regularly on the coastline of Knoydart where they feed off a wide variety of fish. Common seals are brown, tan or grey, with distinctive V-shaped nostrils. The pups, born in spring, are dark in colour and can swim as soon as they are born. The larger grey seal is distinguished by its straight head profile with nostrils that are well apart, and fewer spots on its body. Grey seal pups are born in autumn and are white and cannot swim for a month after birth.

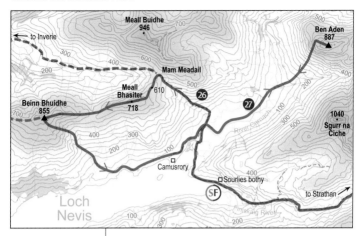

In 2012 there was a notice 'Bridge in dangerous condition. Use at own risk', and it will probably deteriorate further unless major repairs are done to it.

A path is marked on some editions of the OS 1:50,000 map linking Sourlies Bothy to the River Carnach. On careful inspection you will see that the path actually passes along the shore of Loch Nevis, below the high tide line! At low tide it is easy to walk along the sandy beach to reach the Carnach estuary. However, at high tide the low-level route is impassable, unless you have excellent rock climbing skills and a strong nerve. If the tide is in you need to climb diagonally right from Sourlies Bothy to reach a point above the cliffs (55m, 86410 95200) from where you drop down to the Carnach river estuary and follow the marshy shoreline to the suspension bridge over the **River Carnach** (35min, 5m, 86570 96460). ◀ The river would be safe to ford unless it was in flood.

Turn right after crossing the bridge, and after a few metres fork left up an old stalker's path, which passes the ruins of Carnoch, crosses a burn and then switchbacks easily up to the **Mam Meadail** (1hr 40min, 545m, 85340 97810) between Meall Buidhe and Meall Bhasiter. Turn sharp left (S) up a knobbly ridge. The going will be easy in good visibility as you can climb on grass avoiding the crags. The ridge gradually veers right over **Meall Bhasiter** (2hr 15min, 718m, 84630 97180).

A minor top with a big cairn (680m, 84200 97060) follows before reaching a low point at Mam Uchd (2hr 40min, 575m, 83510 96760). Continue W along the ridge. There is a buttress at about 750m which can be climbed up steep grass slopes on the left to reach a minor summit (3hr 15min, 802m, 82650 96830). Continue easily to the trig point on the summit of **Beinn Bhuidhe** (3hr 30min, 855m, 82180 96710).

The easiest way back to Carnoch would be to descend by the ascent route, but if you want some variety descend roughly ESE down grassy slopes into Coire an t-Sagairt, avoiding some crags. Descend down the right-hand side of the burn, crossing when you reach the bottom of the small gorge through which it flows (at about 4hr, 490m, 82910 96370) and then descending down the left bank. Once you get onto the lower slopes, you will encounter tough grass and bracken. You should veer left towards the pier (4hr 50min, 0m, 84350 95320) you can see below you on **Loch Nevis**. The author arrived at Loch Nevis about 1km W of the pier and found it was very hard going following the shore to the pier. From the pier a good track leads to **Camusrory House**. Follow a signed footpath left of the house and regain the track which leads you back to the bridge over the River Carnach (5hr 30min) and return to Sourlies Bothy (6hr 5min).

River Carnach

125

ROUTE 27

Ben Aden MOUNTAIN OF THE FACE

Start	Sourlies Bothy (NM 86750 95060)
Distance	14km (9 miles)
Total ascent	1020m (3400ft)
Difficulty	Ben Aden is extremely well guarded by crags. However, the suggested route avoids all the crags and there are no technical difficulties as long as you have good visibility and can thread your way through the weaknesses in the crags. This is not a mountain for the inexperienced to attempt except in good settled weather. Keep looking back as you climb the upper slopes through the crags as you will need to be able to find the route in descent.
Time	6hr 5min
Summits	Ben Aden (887m, 2905ft)
Maps	OS Landranger 33
Access	See Route 25
Note	Ben Aden is one of the most difficult mountains in Scotland to climb on a day-hike. The main option would be to climb the 550m Mam Meadail from Inverie, descending to sea level at Carnoch and then climbing the route described here before returning back over Mam Meadail. This route would be a very tough proposition.

Ben Aden, on the E edge of Knoydart, is the N summit of the Munro Sgurr na Ciche and the endpoint of the long complex ridge to the S of Loch Quoich. The suggested route approaching from Loch Arkaig along Glen Dessarry and Glen Finiskaig, using Sourlies Bothy or camping beside the Carnach River, may not be the easiest route, but it takes you through some fantastic wild country.

One possibility to day-hiking Ben Aden is to approach by **canoe** up Loch Quoich. Launch the canoes where a track goes down to the waterside (NH 00400 03100) and paddle about 9km to land

NW ridge of Ben Aden

somewhere near the SW tip of the loch at the Allt Coire nan Gall. It is an 8km return walk to Ben Aden along the rough and rocky E ridge over Meall a' Choire Dhuibh before the paddle back along the loch. This could be done in an open canoe or a kayak, but unless you are an expert canoeist you should wait for a windless day as the waves can get quite big and paddling into the wind is tough.

From Sourlies Bothy follow the route to the bridge over the **River Carnach** (35min, 5m, 86570 96460) as described in Route 26. From the bridge follow the track, which soon deteriorates to a path, up the left-hand side of the river. Further up the glen a vehicle track goes off to the left, but you should continue along the faint path along the river bank until you are opposite a sheepfold (1hr 25min, 30m, 88610 97640) just after the Allt Achadh a' Ghlinne joins the River Carnach. Cross the River Carnach, probably getting wet feet, and head roughly NW up the hillside.

See map in Route 26.

You are aiming for the foot of the crags high up on the W ridge of Ben Aden. This is a tough grassy slope, but not difficult. Eventually you pass just below the crags, crossing a gully (at about 625m), and keep going in the same direction until you reach the NW ridge of **Ben Aden** (at about 2hr 45min, 695m, 89580 98920). Head up the grassy ridge, avoiding some quite large crags to reach the summit cairn (3hr 15min, 887m, 89930 98630). The easiest route may not be at all obvious in mist.

Return to the river by the same route (4hr 40min) and back to the bridge (5hr 30min) and the bothy (6hr 5min).

4 NORTH KNOYDART AND KINLOCH HOURN

Loch Quoich from Meall an Spardain (Route 31)

North Knoydart and Kinloch Hourn: Bases and facilities

The 22-mile single-track road with passing places to Kinloch Hourn is unsuitable for caravans.

Base for Routes 28 and 29: Kinloch Hourn

Kinlochhourn Farm has limited accommodation on a full-board or self-catering basis. The tearoom is open all day and the farm provides the parking. In 2012 there was a fee of £1/day for day parking and £2/day for overnight parking. Only open April–October. Tel: 01809 511 253 www.kinlochhourn.com

Camping is available by the bridge 350m E of the farm, but the toilets are at the farm.

Alternative facilities for Routes 28 and 29: Invergarry

See Section 5 for details.

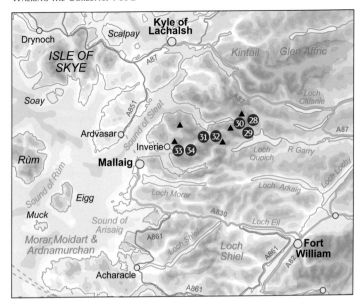

Base for Route 31: Barisdale Bay

Barisdale Bothy is a privately owned and managed bothy comprising a communal room, two bunk rooms and two toilets with cold running water. It cannot be pre-booked and operates on a first come first served basis. Campers in Barisdale Bay are expected to use the designated campsite adjacent to the bothy and may use bothy facilities. The fees in 2012 were £3.00 per person per night for the bothy and £1.00 per person per night for the campsite.

In addition there is a converted stable and stone cottage for those wanting more luxury. These can be pre-booked on an exclusive basis, but if vacant they can be let on site at per person per night prices.
Tel: 01599 522 302 (radio phone) www.barisdale.com

Base for Routes 33 and 34: Inverie

Inverie is a small village on Loch Nevis to the SW of Knoydart. It is not accessible by road so the only access is by ferry from Mallaig or on foot from Loch Arkaig or Loch Hourn. There is a shop, pub and a surprisingly large amount of accommodation.

Knoydart Foundation Bunkhouse
Tel: 01687 462 163 www.knoydart-foundation.com

There is a campsite at Long Beach near the bunkhouse, about 15 minutes' walk from the village.

The Kilchoan Estate offers accommodation in six different properties ranging from the luxurious to a bothy.
Tel: 01687 462 133 www.kilchoan-knoydart.com

The Old Forge is classed by *The Guinness Book of Records* as the remotest pub on mainland Britain. It is open daily and offers showers as well as breakfasts, lunches and dinners, but no accommodation.

Access to Inverie

Access to Inverie is possible on foot from Kinloch Hourn via Barisdale over Mam Barisdale, as described in Routes 30 and 32, or from Loch Arkaig via Sourlies Bothy (Route 25) and over Mam Meadail.

There is a regular ferry service from Mallaig to Inverie.

In 2012 there were sailings from Mallaig Monday–Friday at 10.15 and 14.15, leaving Inverie at 11.00 and 15.00. Sailings on Mondays, Wednesdays and Fridays in winter. Tel: 01687 462 320 www.knoydart-ferry.co.uk

ROUTE 28

Buidhe Bheinn YELLOW MOUNTAIN

Start	Loch Coire Shubh (NG 95860 05530)
Distance	16km (10 mile)
Total ascent	1270m (4200ft)
Difficulty	Although there is no great technical difficulty, this is a rough and tough route which is not recommended for inexperienced walkers in poor weather conditions. There are three burn crossings which can be done dry-shod after dry weather but which could be a problem when they are in spate.
Time	5hr 50min
Summits	Buidhe Bheinn W top (879m), Buidhe Bheinn E top (885m, 2900ft ring contour), Sgurr a' Bhac Chaolais (885m)
Maps	OS Landranger 33
Access	Head W along the A87 from Invergarry and turn left along the minor road to Kinloch Hourn. Continue until Loch Coire Shubh on the right about a mile before the roadhead at Kinloch Hourn. There is limited parking where a path signed to Shiel Bridge goes off right at the NW end of the small loch. There is more parking S of the Coireshubh ruin (95940 05180).
Note	Sgurr a' Bhac Chaolais is often climbed from Glen Shiel to the N and it would be possible to extend this route to include Buidhe Bheinn, returning by the same route or over Sgurr na Sgine.

Buidhe Bheinn is the S peak on the ridge between Kinloch Hourn and Glen Shiel, which also includes Sgurr a' Bhac Chaolais and the Munro Sgurr na Sgine. Until 2012 the OS gave both Buidhe Bheinn and Sgurr a' Bhac Chaolais a height of 885m and they were listed as twin summits in the Corbetts list. They couldn't both be Corbetts as there was only a 400ft descent between them. Recent surveys give Buidhe Bheinn at 885.50 ±0.05m and Sgurr a' Bhac Chaolais at 885.21 ±0.05m and the Corbett is now officially Buidhe Bheinn.

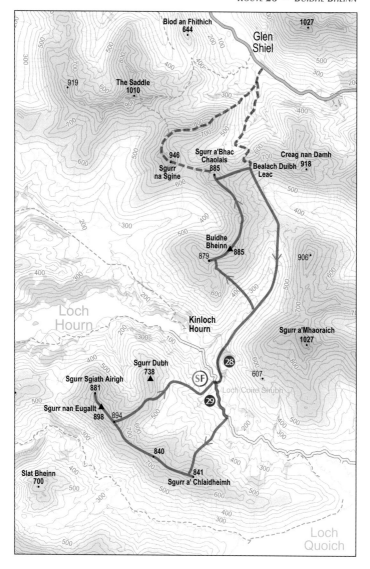

E ridge, Buidhe Bheinn showing W summit

Loch Hourn runs 22km (14 miles) inland from the Sound of Sleat, opposite the island of Skye, to the head of the loch at Kinloch Hourn. Although it is 5km wide at its entrance, it soon narrows to under 2km wide, and after Barisdale Bay it narrows even further, being only 250m at Caolas Mor. This is one of the steepest and most dramatic of the sea lochs, with the Munros Beinn Sgritheall to the N and Ladhar Bheinn to the S.

Follow the rough track signed to Shiel Bridge, crossing the outlet burn from Loch Coire Shubh and then veering left through a gate. Pass through a second gate as you enter the glen of the Allt Coire Sgoireadail, ignoring tracks that go off under the power lines. The track deteriorates to a sometimes boggy path, which you follow until you have passed to the left of a rocky knoll and into an area of flat pasture between two waterfalls (at about 40min, 220m, 96860 07590). Cross the Allt Coire Sgoireadail and head steeply uphill (NW). On reaching the burn which drains Coire Lair, you should follow it up the grass slope until you reach the source of the burn (at about 1hr 35min, 680m, 95950 08550). Head diagonally right (NNE) to the right of the crags to reach the saddle between the two summits of Buidhe Bheinn (1hr 55min, 820m, 96020 08830).

Turn left along the narrow rocky ridge to the **W summit of Buidhe Bheinn** (2hr 5min, 879m, 95720 08750). This ridge is generally easy, but care needs to be taken and occasional use of the hands will be required. Return along the ridge and climb the **E summit** marked by a small cairn (2hr 25min, 885m, 96340 09040). ▸

Any difficulties on the descent down the rocky NE ridge should be bypassed on the left to reach a gully-like saddle (780m, 96500 09400). Continue over a small ridge to a second saddle (780m) and then up the ridge to a minor top (2hr 45min, 835m, 96640 09870) where a wall joins from the right. Continue along the rocky ridge to the left of the wall, down to another saddle (775m, 96610 10010) and over another minor top to a saddle with a pond (3hr, 770m, 96430 10390). Continue up the ridge to a wall junction (855m, 96060 10950) and turn left along the remains of the wall/fence to the cairn on a rock outcrop on the summit of **Sgurr a' Bhac Chaolais** (3hr 25min, 885m, 95840 11030).

Return to the wall junction and follow the wall left down the E ridge of Sgurr a' Bhac Chaolais, over a minor top and down to the **Bealach Duibh Leac** (3hr 50min, 725m, 96820 11230). This saddle is marked by a small cairn. The OS map shows a path crossing this saddle but the path actually only exists to the N of the saddle. Head roughly SE down the grass slope on your right to reach a burn (at about 4hr 10min, 505m, 97180 10720). From here you need to keep heading SE, contouring the grass slope to reach the path descending from the obvious saddle ahead of you (at about 4hr 30min, 505m, 97700 09950). Turn right along the path to a high point (530m) and down as it winds through the crags in Coire Sgoireadail. This path is a little indistinct in places, but is followable, and leads you all the way back the car parking (5hr 50min).

There is confusion because some OS maps label Buidhe Bheinn as the W summit with a spot height of 879m, rather than higher E summit.

ROUTE 29

NW Top, Sgurr nan Eugallt PEAK OF THE PRECIPICES

Start	Loch Coire Shubh (NG 95860 05530)
Distance	11km (7 miles)
Total ascent	1100m (3600ft)
Difficulty	This is a rough, tough walk over mountains covered with crags. It is possible to avoid all difficulties when visibility is good, but it is not recommended for bad weather.
Time	4hr 50min
Summits	Sgurr a' Chlaidheimh (841m), W summit of Sgurr a' Chlaidheimh, Sgurr nan Eugallt (894m, 2933ft), NW top, Sgurr nan Eugallt (898m) , Sgurr Sgiath Airigh (881m)
Maps	OS Landranger 33
Access	Parking as for Route 28
Note	Most walkers ascend and descend by the featured descent route to take advantage of the stalker's path which reaches 600m. The recommended route is longer and tougher but gives a better walk. It would be possible to combine Sgurr nan Eugallt with the Graham Meall nan Eun to the W.

Sgurr nan Eugallt is the rocky peak between Loch Quoich and Loch Hourn. This is another peak where there is confusion as to the highest point. The 'main' summit, with a trig point, has a spot height of 894m but the NW top is actually about 4m higher.

Sgurr nan Eugallt nearly achieved what the Redcoats could not: kill **Charles Edward Stuart**, Bonnie Prince Charlie. After the Battle of Culloden in 1746 he was on the run and heading N through the Rough Bounds. After the hazardous crossing of guarded Glen Cosaidh, his party climbed Sgurr nan Eugallt and had problems descending the wild corries to the N of the long ridge. Somewhere above Coire Shubh, the prince 'fell on a precipice'.

This may be the reason for the name 'peak of the precipices'.

Head S from the parking past Coireshubh ruin and continue until the road crosses a small burn as it climbs after about 1km (10min, 155m, 96120 04680). Head uphill to the left of the burn easily avoiding the multitude of crags and slabs on the N face of Sgurr a' Chlaidheimh. Follow the left-hand tributary (at 245m) and the main branch (left then right) at 520m. Continue until the now trickling burn forks (1hr 30min, 710m, 95340 03220). The right-hand fork avoids the crags and allows you to reach the ridge (830m, 95160 03090) just below the summit. Turn left to the summit cairn on **Sgurr a' Chlaidheimh** (1hr 50min, 841m, 95230 03060).

Head back, following an old fence line along the knobbly ridge down to a saddle (760m) and up to the W summit of Sgurr a' Chlaidheimh (2hr 20min, 840m, 94180 03560). Continue following the fence line past a couple of saddles (730m) and until the fence veers off

See map in Route 28.

W top of Sgurr a' Chlaidheimh

right to head down the NE ridge of Sgurr nan Eugallt. Leave the fence here and climb the steep slope to the trig point on the summit of **Sgurr nan Eugallt** (3hr 5min, 894m, 93090 04480). This isn't the highest point, which is a **top** with a tiny cairn about 450m to the NW (3hr 15min, 898m, 92720 04850).

Continue about 300m NW to the big cairn on the summit of **Sgurr Sgiath Airigh** (3hr 20min, 881m, 92610 05120) to get magnificent views of Knoydart, Loch Hourn and Skye. Return to the trig point on Sgurr nan Eugallt (3hr 40min) and head E veering left down the NE ridge. Care is needed to avoid some small but awkward crags. Regain the old fence line and follow a faint path to the final saddle (4hr 5min, 665m, 94010 05060) before Sgurr Dubh. Head diagonally right (E) down a grassy gully to pick up the top of a stalker's path where it crosses a trickling burn (4hr 10min, 605m, 94170 05060). Turn left and follow this sometimes boggy path easily all the way down to the road at Coireshubh ruin (95890 05400). Turn left and walk 100m back to the parking area (4hr 50min).

ROUTE 30

Access to Barisdale Bothy for Routes 31–34

Start	Kinloch Hourn (NG 94860 06660)
Distance	11km (7 miles)
Total ascent	550m (1800ft)
Difficulty	Easy
Time	2hr 55min
Maps	OS Landranger 33
Access	Head W along the A87 from Invergarry and turn left along minor road to Kinloch Hourn and park at Kinlochhourn Farm, just before the roadhead. There is no parking beyond the car park.
Note	Although easy for walkers, the path is rough and hilly and not really suitable for mountain bikes. If you take the ferry from Mallaig to Inverie you could walk to Barisdale in about 3hr 30min (see Route 32)

From the car park, head W to the roadhead and then along the good, but rough and occasionally boggy, path along the shore of **Loch Hourn**. This path goes up and down quite a bit, including a couple of climbs to over 100m. Eventually reach a junction with the track in **Barisdale Bay** (2hr 30min, 0m, 87280 05880). Turn left past Barisdale House and a cottage to **Barisdale Bothy** and campsite (2hr 55min, 10m, 87180 04210).

Barisdale Bothy

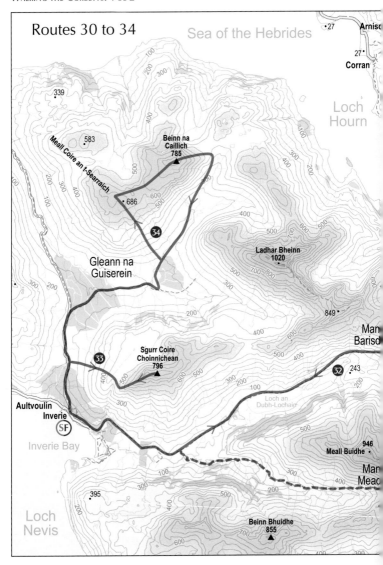

Routes 30 to 34

Sea of the Hebrides

•27

Arniso

27•
Corran

Loch
Hourn

339•

583•

Meall Coire an t-Searraich

Beinn na
Caillich
785

•686

34

Loch
Hourn

Ladhar Bheinn
1020

Gleann na
Guiserein

849•

Man
Bariso

33

Sgurr Coire
Choinnichean
796

32   243

Loch an
Dubh-Lochain

Aultvoulin
Inverie
SF

946
Meall Buidhe

Inverie Bay

Man
Meac

395•

Loch
Nevis

Beinn Bhuidhe
855

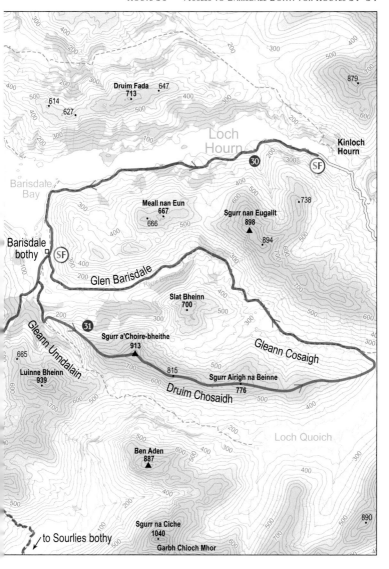

ROUTE 31

Sgurr a' Choire-bheithe PEAK OF THE BIRCH CORRIE

Start	Barisdale Bothy (NG 87180 04210)
Distance	24km (15 miles)
Total ascent	1400m (4600ft)
Difficulty	The featured route, which follows a long rocky ridge with a little easy scrambling and some route-finding difficulties, is not recommended in bad weather.
Time	8hr 30min
Summits	Sgurr a' Choire-bheithe (913m, 2994ft), Sgurr Airigh na Beinne (776m)
Maps	OS Landranger 33
Access	See Route 30
Note	It would just about be feasible for a strong walker to climb Sgurr a' Choire-bheithe in one day from Kinloch Hourn, ascending and descending the suggested ascent route.

Sgurr a' Choire-bheithe is a remote peak to the E of Knoydart peninsular. The best feature of this splendid mountain is Druim Chosaidh, the E ridge, which provides one of the best ridge walks in Scotland. Following surveys of Foinaven and Beinn Dearg on behalf of the Munro Society, Sgurr a 'Choire-bheithe remained the highest Corbett with the possibility of reaching Munro status and was surveyed by John Barnard, Graham Jackson and Myrddyn Phillips in 2009. They recorded a height of 913.32 ±0.07m, confirming the mountain as a Corbett.

In the early 1930s, the Knoydart Estate was bought by **Lord Brocket**, whose family had made their money in the brewing industry. Local lore suggests that the peer was a Nazi sympathiser; what is certain is that he fired most of the estate workers and evicted them from their homes, leaving the land unproductive, keeping it as a recreational area where he and his guests could go hunting and fishing. Fortunately, Knoydart is having new life breathed into it since the estate was purchased by the Knoydart Foundation in 1999.

Cross the bridge by Barisdale Bothy and follow the track, ignoring a left-hand fork, to a cottage and continue to a second fork (10min, 20m, 86910 03550). Fork left to a bridge over the Allt Gleann Unndalain and continue beneath some crags to enter **Gleann Unndalain** (35min, 155m, 87020 02450). Head left and climb the gentle, rough, grassy ridge, easily avoiding any crags, to the W top of Sgurr a' Choire-bheithe (2hr 5min, 810m, 88790 01510). Continue easily E down to a saddle and up to the summit cairn on **Sgurr a' Choire-bheithe** (2hr 30min, 913m, 89560 01560). ▸

See map in Route 30.

The small cairn (89600 01580) on the other side of a small pond was measured during the 2009 survey as being 0.68m higher.

The E ridge, **Druim Chosaidh,** starts by descending to a low point (845m, 89810 01370) and up to a rocky peak (2hr 55min, 875m, 90020 01250). There is then an awkward descent to 840m before climbing to the next top (860m). The 50m steep descent from this top is awkward and is easiest on the left, after which the going is easier, up and down, over or round numerous minor tops, to reach a saddle with a small pond (3hr 35min, 710m, 91490 00720). It's then over the next top (755m), down to a low point (720m) and up to **Sgurr Airigh na Beinne** (4hr 5min, 776m, 92550 00810). It is not at all clear which is the highest point on this knobbly summit plateau.

Now descend fairly easily E, either going over or round many more knolls. There are a few crags on the ridge, which you will need to bypass. Continue down to the old track at the foot of the ridge (possibly at 5hr 25min, 96110 01370). Turn left and follow the track, which soon appears to end in a marsh (220m, 95820 01530). This is a good place to cross the river as the river bed is composed of flat sand or gravel here and it should be a safe ford when water levels are high. You will get your feet wet unless the river is exceptionally low. Continue along the right bank until the track reappears a little further upstream (220m, 95620 01700). The track becomes a little indistinct where it passes through other marshy areas but it should be followable. Pass Loch an Lagain Aintheich as you enter an area where the track winds around many fine examples of *roche moutonnée* caused as the ice ground over the rock in the last ice-age. You reach a high point (6hr 35min, 285m, 93010 03000) and then drop down a better track into **Glen Barisdale**. This track is followed all the way back to Barisdale Bothy (8hr 30min).

ROUTE 32

Access to Inverie from Barisdale
for Routes 33 and 34

Start	Barisdale Bothy (NG 87180 04210)
Distance	14km (9 miles)
Total ascent	600m (2000ft)
Difficulty	Easy
Time	3hr 30min
Maps	OS Landranger 33
Access	See Route 30
Note	Most walkers will want to access Inverie by ferry from Mallaig as detailed in the section introduction.

See map in Route 30.

Cross the bridge at Barisdale Bothy and follow the track, ignoring two left forks, to the pass at **Mam Barisdale** (1hr 20min, 450m, NG 85580 01750). The track deteriorates to a sometimes boggy path on the other side as you descend to the E end of **Loch an Dubh-Lochain** (2hr 5min, 60m, NG 82950 00730). The track improves again as you pass along the N side of the loch and continue to pass below a prominent monument on a knoll to the right of the track. As you approach **Inverie**, fork right at a gate (3hr 20min, 60m, NM 77684 99860) and then keep straight on to the coast road. Turn right to Inverie post office/shop (3hr 30min, 10m, NM 76763 99930).

ROUTE 33

Sgurr Coire Choinnichean PEAK OF THE MOSSY CORRIE

Start	Inverie post office/shop (NM 76763 99930)
Distance	9km (5 miles)
Total ascent	790m (2500ft)
Difficulty	The ascent is easy apart from one small, easy rockstep.
Time	3hr 40min
Summits	Sgurr Coire Choinnichean (796m, 2612ft)
Maps	OS Landranger 33
Access	See Section 4 introduction
Note	This short route shows the best features of this mountain and can be climbed after a lunchtime arrival at Inverie or before an afternoon departure. It would be possible for the experienced mountaineer to devise a dramatic route by connecting Sgurr Coire Choinnichean and Ladhar Bheinn, but this would probably involve some difficult scrambling.

Sgurr Coire Choinnichean is the SW peak in the massif dominated by the magnificent Munro Ladhar Bheinn. The narrow and rocky W ridge, which is climbed, is the finest feature of Sgurr Coire Choinnichean. There are spectacular views towards Rum and Skye as well as over Knoydart.

After World War II, hundreds of returning soldiers from all over the Highlands applied for **crofting land**, but were informed by the Department of Agriculture that no land was available. Yet vast estates all over the Highlands were lying waste in the hands of private and/or absentee landlords. On 9 November 1948, a group of seven young men decided that enough was enough; they occupied a small corner of Lord Brocket's Knoydart Estate and began turning it into crofts. They lost the ensuing legal battle, but are remembered in the song *Men of Knoydart* by Hamish Henderson.

*W ridge of Sgurr
Coire Choinnichean*

See map in Route 30.

Continue W from the post office to the Old Forge pub and turn right up the second track, almost immediately after the pub. Continue to a gate at the top of the forest (20min, 105m, NG 76640 01290). Pass through the gate then turn right up the hint of a path to the left of the forest and continue just S of E to the head of the chasm down which the Allt Slochd a' Mhogha flows (1hr 20min, 470m, NG 77960 00950). Once past the head of the chasm veer right (SSE) along a faint path onto the ridge (535m, NG 78130 00692). The path weaves a way through the crags with only one small rockstep where hands are required. Higher up, the ridge becomes less rocky but narrower before you reach the W top (2hr 5min, 780m, NG 78750 01040). Veer slightly right to a saddle (755m, 78840 01060) and then up to the cairn on the summit of **Sgurr Coire Choinnichean** (2hr 15min, 796m, NG 79080 01070).

Return by the same route (3hr 40min).

ROUTE 34

Beinn na Caillich OLD WOMEN'S HILL

Start	Inverie post office/shop (NM 76763 99930)
Distance	22km (14 miles)
Total ascent	1010m (3300ft)
Difficulty	Beinn na Caillich is one of the easiest peaks in Knoydart, which may account for the name 'old women's hill'. Burn crossings could be a problem when they are in spate and navigation on the summit ridge will be difficult in mist.
Time	6hr 35min
Summits	Beinn na Caillich (785m, 2573ft)
Maps	OS Landranger 33
Access	See Section 4 introduction

Beinn na Caillich is hidden away behind Ladhar Bheinn and is difficult to access – it is therefore rarely climbed. The mountain lacks the attractiveness of most of the Knoydart peaks, but it is placed to give superb views to Rum and Skye.

The **Knoydart Foundation** is a charitable foundation which is a partnership of the local community, the Highland Council, the Chris Brasher Trust, Kilchoan Estate and the John Muir Trust. The Foundation purchased the 17,200 acre Knoydart Estate in 1999 with the objective to preserve, enhance and develop Knoydart for the well-being of the environment and the people. As well as managing some of the wildest land in Britain, the foundation is responsible for several properties, a bunkhouse, deer management and the supply and generation of electricity to the local community. **www.knoydart-foundation.com**

See map in Route 30.

Continue W from the post office to the Old Forge pub and turn right up the second track, almost immediately after the pub. Continue to a gate at the top of the forest (20min, 105m, NG 76640 01290). Pass through the gate and continue to a track junction (40min, 140m, NG 76640 02690). Turn right through the wood and into **Gleann na Guiserein**, through a gate and on until the track ends at a bridge (1hr 10min, 115m, NG 79140 03290). Cross the bridge and turn left along a faint path along the N side of the Allt Coire Torr an Asgaill. ▶ Turn right up a better path along the Abhainn Bheag where waterfalls drop down a small gorge. Pass through a gate in the deer fence (1hr 25min, 145m, NG 79240 04080) and cross the burn. This shouldn't be a problem unless the burn is in spate. Head NW up the slope, veering slightly left as the gradient eases to reach the W top of **Meall Coire an t-Searraich** (3hr 10min, 680m, NG 77790 05670), which has a big cairn and excellent views to Rum and Skye. The grassy ridge to **Beinn na Caillich** is broad and undefined, with many rocky knolls and tops. Head roughly ENE to a saddle (3hr 25min, 630m, NG 78650 05990) before veering a little left to the broad rocky summit (3hr 55min, 785m, NG 79600 06690).

Head down the E ridge, which is fairly steep, rocky and heather covered, but not particularly difficult. At the bottom of the ridge veer right down to the Allt Mam Li burn where you will find a faint path (at about 4hr 35min, 350m, NG 80730 06590). Follow this path down the glen to the Abhainn Bheag. When the path seems to disappear in a grassy area (5hr, 200m, NG 79910 05110), cross the burn. There is a small cairn on the opposite bank. Follow the path, which improves when a path descending from Ladhar Bheinn joins from the left. Continue down to the gate in the deer fence (5hr 15min) and return by the same route to Inverie (6hr 35min).

In dry conditions you could shortcut by crossing this burn where it joins the Abhainn Bheag.

5 GLEN GARRY, GLEN SHIEL, GLEN ELCHAIG AND LOCH HOURN

Ladhar Bheinn from Corran (Route 39)

Glen Garry, Glen Shiel, Glen Elchaig and Loch Hourn: Bases and facilities

Base for Routes 35 and 36: Invergarry

Invergarry has a small shop, post office, restaurant, pub, petrol station, hotel, campsite and two independent hostels.

Invergarry Hotel Tel: 01809 501 206 www.invergarryhotel.co.uk

Invergarry Lodge Independent Hostel Tel: 01809 501 412 www.invergarrylodge.co.uk

Great Glen Hostel at Laggan is 3 miles S of Invergarry. The hostel was formerly Loch Lochy SYHA but has been refurbished and come under private ownership. Tel: 01809 501 430 www.greatglenhostel.com

Faichemard Farm Campsite does not take children (under 18s) Tel: 01809 501 314 www.faichemard-caravancamping.co.uk

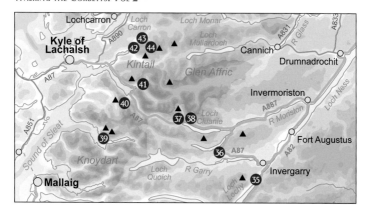

Base for Routes 37–44: Shiel Bridge

Shiel Bridge has a shop, campsite and caravan sites, SYHA hostel and hotel with a bunkhouse.

As well as normal hotel facilities the Kintail Lodge Hotel has a Trekkers Lodge and a bunkhouse. Tel: 01599 511 275 www.kintaillodgehotel.co.uk

Shiel Bridge Caravan Park and Campsite Tel: 01599 511 221 http://shielbridgecaravanpark.co.uk

Morvich Caravan Club Site also takes tents. Tel: 01599 511 354

Ratagan SYHA, Glenshiel, Kyle, IV40 8HP Tel: 01599 511 243

Local facilities for Routes 37 and 38: Cluanie Inn

Cluanie Inn Tel: 01320 340 238 www.cluanieinn.com

Local facilities for Routes 42–44: Dornie

Dornie is a small village with good tourist facilities, including several hotels, B&Bs, caravan and camping site and several shops, including an outdoor equipment store. The main tourist attraction is the Eilean Donan Castle.

Dornie Hotel Tel: 01599 555 205 www.dornie-hotel.co.uk

Whitefalls Retreats at Camas-luinie in Glen Elchaig has self-catering accommodation and a bunkhouse and is ideally placed for climbing Routes 42–44. Tel: 01599 588 205 www.holidayhighlands.co.uk

ROUTE 35

Ben Tee FAIRY HILL

Start	Kilfinnan (NN 27760 95830)
Distance	10km (6 miles)
Total ascent	870m (2900ft)
Difficulty	Relatively easy rough pasture and moorland
Time	3hr 45min
Summits	Ben Tee (901m, 2957ft)
Maps	OS Landranger 34
Access	From Invergarry head S along the A82, turning right along the minor road to Kilfinnan, just before the swing bridge at North Laggan. Park at the roadhead, just before the Kilfinnan Burn.
Note	After climbing Ben Tee it would be possible to complete a tough traverse of the peaks surrounding Coire Glas, including the Munro Sron a' Choire Ghairbh.

Ben Tee is a prominent conical hill when seen from the E, but is hidden away when approached up the A82 along Loch Lochy. There are fine views to Loch Ness to the E and Loch Quoich to the W.

Kilfinnan comes from 'Cill Fhionain' meaning **Finan's Church**, although there is no sign of a church today. Kilfinnan was the burial ground for the chiefs of the MacDonnells of Glengarry. The original burial ground was submerged when the Caledonian Canal was built in the early 19th century and the replacement burial ground, which can be visited today, contains the MacDonnell of Glengarry family mausoleum.

Ignore the path up the Kilfinnan Burn; instead follow the path, which is rather faint in places, up the ridge to the right of the burn. The path traverses right towards the top of the wood to the E. Halfway along the traverse, turn left

151

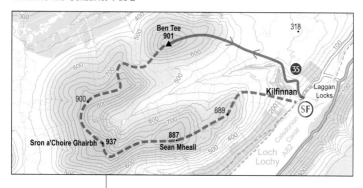

up a small path (205m, 27640 96370) and follow it as it ascends the left side of the ridge to reach a stile in a deer fence (35min, 290m, 27170 96750). Continue along the path to a junction (26730 96740) and turn right. When this path fades away continue WNW over rough pasture and moorland to the E ridge of **Ben Tee** and then follow the ridge easily to the sprawling cairn on the summit (2hr 15min, 901m, 24080 97210).

Summit cairn on Ben Tee

Return by the same route to the stile (3hr 20min) and back to the parking area (3hr 45min).

ROUTE 36

Meall Dubh BLACK HILL

Start	A87 above Loch Loyne (NH 18650 04640)
Distance	15km (9 miles)
Total ascent	600m (2000ft)
Difficulty	There is much rough, pathless moorland to cross and it is only on the higher ground that the going is easy. There are a lot of variations possible as you follow the broad knobbly ridge and navigation would be very challenging in mist. A deer fence must be climbed twice.
Time	5hr
Summits	Clach Criche (674m), Carn Tarsuinn (687m), Meall Dubh (788m, 2581ft)
Maps	OS Landranger 34
Access	Follow the A87 W from Invergarry and park at the high point of the road between Loch Garry and Loch Loyne.
Note	If two cars can be organized it would be possible to traverse the mountain by starting on the A887 to the N. Peakbaggers, or those short of time or energy, might prefer to follow the roads built for the wind farm which would provide an easier ascent of Meall Dubh from the N.

Meall Dubh is the highest point on a sprawling area of moorland N of Loch Garry. The plateau has little structure to it and the higher ridges have a good scattering of rock outcrops. The hill is well protected with forestry on three sides and a wind farm on the E slopes. This isolated peak provides one of the most wide-ranging views in the Highlands and the contrast between the rounded hills S of the Great Glen and the rocky mountains N of the Great Glen is very marked.

The eastern slopes of Meall Dubh are the site of the **Millennium Wind Farm**. Further wind turbines are being added, in line with Scottish Government's policy of producing 100% of its electricity from renewable energy by 2020, and the size of the wind farm is likely to grow in the years to come.

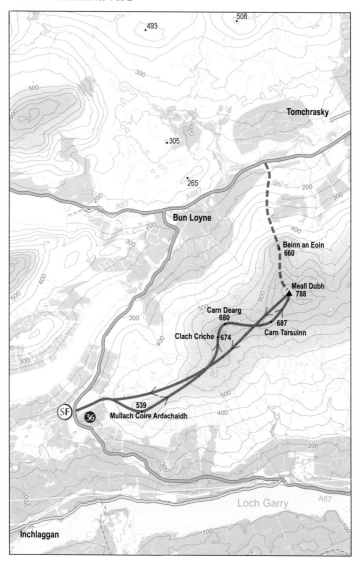

Wind farm on Meall Dubh

Follow a grassy track to the communication masts and then head up the hill aiming for the gap in the forest to a deer fence (25min, 435m, 19760 05240). Climb the deer fence and head ESE to the summit of **Mullach Coire Ardachaidh** (539m, 20510 04680). Head ENE along the ridge to a prominent cairn (1hr 15min, 590m, 21960 05580). It would be possible to take a direct route to Meall Dubh, but it is more interesting to go via **Clach Criche** (674m, 22610 06650), **Carn Dearg** (680) and **Carn Tarsuinn** (687m, 24030 07030) to reach the summit of **Meall Dubh**, which is topped by a very large cairn (2hr 55min, 788m, 24540 07880).

You could return by the same route, but you may prefer a more direct route roughly SW missing the peaks you climbed on the ascent. You should aim to arrive at the prominent cairn you visited on the ascent (3hr 50min). Again you can save time with a direct route (roughly WSW) to the deer fence, which needs climbing again, and back to the parking area (5hr).

ROUTE 37

Beinn Loinne ELEGANT HILL

Start	Cluanie Inn (NH 07900 11690)
Distance	26km (16 miles)
Total ascent	930m (3100ft)
Difficulty	Easy, except for a little boggy moorland to cross.
Time	6hr 40min
Summits	W summit, Beinn Loinne (789m, 2555ft), E summit, Beinn Loinne (775m)
Maps	OS Landranger 33 and 34
Access	Follow the A87 E from Shiel Bridge and park at the start of a tarmac estate road about 200m E of the Cluanie Inn.
Note	The tarmac access road is crumbling in places but easy to cycle using a road bike. The suggested route traverses the ridge from W to E because it is assumed many walkers will just climb the W summit and then return by the same route. If doing the complete walk it would make sense to reverse the route so that you are walking along the ridge towards the magnificent view W down Glen Shiel.

Beinn Loinne is a long ridge sandwiched between Loch Cluanie and Loch Loyne. The mountain consists of heather moorland with many small crags on the ridges. The OS map names the lower E summit on the ridge as Beinn Loinne and the higher W summit is unnamed. Some people have used the name Druim nan Cnamh (bony ridge), which is the name of the W ridge of the mountain, but it seems more sensible to use the name Beinn Loinne (W summit).

Follow the tarmac road, forking right above **Cluanie Lodge**, to the high point of the road (435m, 09950 08140). This crumbling road was the route of the A87 until it was flooded in 1957 when Loch Loyne was created. You can still see where the road drops beneath the loch. It would be possible to head up the W ridge of Beinn Loinne from

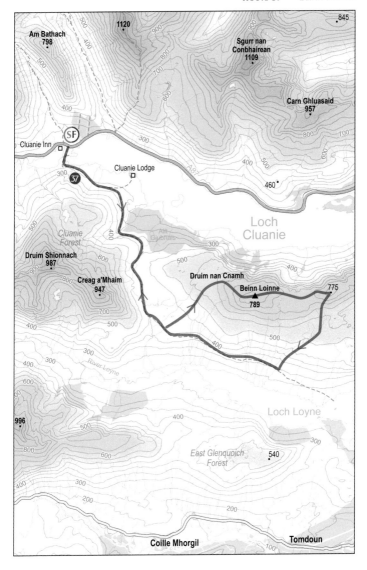

W summit of Beinn Loinne

here, but the moor is particularly rough and boggy so it is better to continue another mile along the road to the third burn flowing from the left (1hr 30min, 395m, 10610 06820). Cyclists will want to leave their bikes here. Turn left up the burn, which provides a pleasant ascent, and follow it until it ends in a bog (560m, 11670 07910). Veer right up the ridge to the trig point on the **W summit of Beinn Loinne** (2hr 55min, 789m, 13100 07680).

Head E down the undefined ridge, dropping about 100m before climbing to the small cairn on the **E summit of Beinn Loinne** (3hr 45min, 775m, 15170 07760). It is easiest to descend SW before heading S down to a burn and follow this, probably on the SE side, down to the tarmac road (4hr 40min, 295m, 13670 05740). Turn right. It's about 3km to where cyclists will have left their bikes, but, assuming you are walking, it's about 10km along the road back to the car park (6hr 40min).

ROUTE 38

Am Bathach THE BYRE

Start	W end of Loch Cluanie (NH 08750 12090)
Distance	8km (5 miles)
Total ascent	620m (2100ft)
Difficulty	Easy
Time	2hr 45min
Summits	Am Bathach (798m, 2605ft)
Maps	OS Landranger 33
Access	Follow the A87 E from Shiel Bridge and park in a layby 1km E of the Cluanie Inn, near the W end of Loch Cluanie, below the forest which was clear-felled in 2011.
Note	Am Bathach is often climbed as a prelude to the ascent of the Munro Ciste Dhubh. It would be possible to descend An Caorann Mor, to the E, instead of An Caorann Beag. It's easiest to descend by the ascent route.

Am Bathach, at the W end of Loch Cluanie, provides a delightful short walk. The narrow, grassy ridge has steep U-shaped glens on either side and has an airy feel to it. As usual, a Corbett surrounded by Munros provides magnificent views.

Walkers on Am Bathach

159

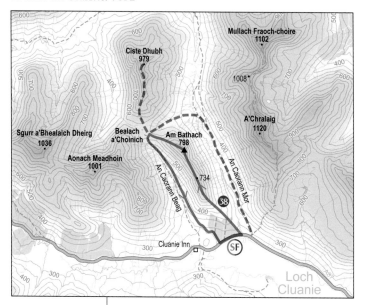

The **Bridge of the Spaniards**, 9km W of the Cluanie Inn, was the site of the last battle fought by foreign troops on mainland Britain, in 1719.

Head E along the road to a gate just beyond the end of the felled forest. Turn left up a good, but small, path alongside the forest then along the well-defined ridge to the S summit of **Am Bathach** (734m, 07750 13630) and along the narrow ridge to the cairn on the N summit (1hr 15min, 798m, 07330 14340).

Follow the faint path along the ridge to the **Bealach a' Choinich** (570m, 06350 14730) where you turn sharp left down an old stalker's path. This path is a little indistinct as the descent starts. If you lose it head down SSE until you relocate the sometimes boggy path, which heads down the E side of **An Caorann Beag** to reach the road at the W end of the forest (220m, 08340 11870). Turn left along the grass verge back to the layby (2hr 45min).

ROUTE 39

Beinn na h-Eaglaise CHURCH HILL *and*
Beinn nan Caorach HILL OF THE MOUNTAIN ASH

Start	Corran car park (NG 84920 09390)
Distance	14km (9 miles)
Total ascent	1080m (3600ft)
Difficulty	Beinn nan Caorach is easy, but the descent from Beinn na h-Eaglaise is steep and would not be comfortable in poor weather.
Time	4hr 50min
Summits	Beinn nan Caorach (774m, 2536ft), Beinn na h-Eaglaise (805m, 2650ft)
Maps	OS Landranger 33
Access	Follow the minor road from Shiel Bridge signed to Elg and Arnisdale. Follow signs to Arnisdale and continue to a car park just before the roadhead at Corran.
Note	For those with plenty of surplus energy it would be possible to continue from Beinn na h-Eaglaise down to Bealach Arnasdail and on to the Munro Beinn Sgritheall. The last house at the E end of Corran has a dilapidated hut attached selling teas, coffees and cakes.

Beinn na h-Eaglaise is a shapely mountain overlooking Arnisdale, with steep slopes on all flanks. By comparison Beinn nan Caorach has gentle E and N ridges.

Arnisdale is best known as the closest settlement to 'Camusfeàrna', where **Gavin Maxwell** wrote *Ring of Bright Water*, the story of his life with his pet otters. This was made into a film starring Bill Travers and Virginia McKenna in 1969. Camusfeàrna is actually Sandaig, about 10km W of Arnisdale. The cottage where Maxwell wrote was burnt down in 1968 and the site is marked by a memorial to Maxwell and the otter, Edal. It is still a good place to see otters.

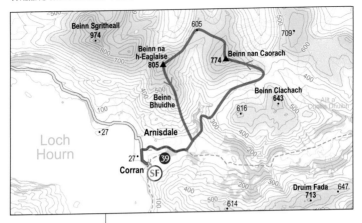

From the car park head back towards Arnisdale and turn right along the track to Glenfield Cottage. Pass behind the cottage and continue until you reach a bridge over the River Arnisdale (20min, 10m, 86110 09720). Don't cross the bridge, but head left across pasture to a footbridge over the Allt Utha. Cross this bridge and follow paths to the track you can see above you. Follow this track above the right bank of the Allt Utha before switchbacking up the lower slopes of Beinn Clachach and past the Eas na Cuingid waterfall, which would be spectacular when in spate. Continue into Coire Chorsalain where the track becomes grassy and no longer follows the line shown on the OS maps. Just before the head of the corrie the track veers off right and you should continue to the obvious saddle just ahead of you (1hr 25min, 410m, 88340 11610). Climb steeply N onto the ridge to the left. The gradient eases as you veer left when clear of the S-facing crags on the ridge. Follow the ridge over a minor top (575m) and continue easily to the summit cairn on **Beinn nan Caorach** (2hr 20min, 774m, 87160 12110).

Head N along the line of old fence posts, which descend a grassy ridge with small rock outcrops. When the fence veers left (it's not obvious as there are a few missing posts) follow it down to a broad saddle (590m,

86750 12840) and up the other side to a **flat-topped hill** (605m). The intermittent fence line now heads SW and takes you down to another saddle (2hr 55min, 550m, 86040 12530). Follow the remains of a deer fence up the ridge ahead, which is not nearly as steep as it looks from below. The formidable looking buttress at 670m is actually easily climbed or bypassed on its left. The deer fence leads all the way to the small cairn marking the summit of **Beinn na h-Eaglaise** (3hr 20min, 805m, 85440 11995). ▸

Follow the deer fence for a short distance then turn left (roughly SE) down the sparse remains of another fence, ignoring the better fence line which heads W towards Bealach Arnasdail. When the fence line veers off right, continue roughly SE down the main ridge and over the tops of **Beinn Bhuidhe** to a small lochan on the summit (3hr 45min, 595m, 85840 11270). It is probably easiest to pass to the left of the lochan, and the crags beyond it, before heading S down the ridge, passing any crags on their left. Continue the steep descent down the grassy slope, veering SSE lower down to come out at the footbridge over the Allt Utha (4hr 25min, 20m, 86300 10050). Return across the pasture, turn right along the track and left along the road back to the car park (4hr 50min).

The author's measurements suggest that Beinn na h-Eaglaise is considerably lower than shown on the maps.

Druim Fada from Corran

ROUTE 40

Sgurr Mhic Bharraich PEAK OF THE SON OF MAURICE

Start	Shiel Bridge (NG93840 18620)
Distance	9km (6 miles)
Total ascent	840m (2800ft)
Difficulty	Fairly easy in good conditions, but care would be needed with navigation in mist.
Time	3hr 30min
Summits	Sgurr Mhic Bharraich (779m, 2553ft)
Maps	OS Landranger 33
Access	Follow the campsite road to the left of the Shiel Bridge shop and park in the large parking area.
Note	To avoid a steep descent return by the ascent route.

Sgurr Mhic Bharraich is actually the end peak on the impressive N ridge of The Saddle, but since the pass between it and the other peaks on the ridge is only 470m it is not normally included in the traverse of this ridge. It provides one of the best viewpoints in the area, with close views to the Five Sisters, South Shiel Ridge, The Saddle and Beinn Sgritheall, as well as more distant views to Knoydart, Skye, Torridon and even the Outer Hebrides.

The old single arch **stone bridge** across the River Shiel was built by Thomas Telford in 1815 as part of the road from Invermoriston on Loch Ness to Kyle of Lochalsh and the crossing to Skye. Before the bridge was built, the old military road would have passed along the S bank of the river, before climbing over the Mam Ratagan to Glenelg Barracks. The bridge is still used for the road to Glenelg. In the summer a small car ferry crosses from Glenelg to Skye.

Continue along the road past the campsite and turn left up the good path between the campsite and the river.

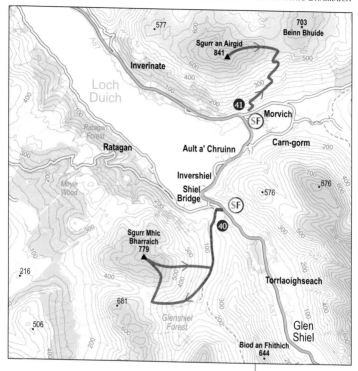

You could take either branch when the path splits but the right-hand one is more pleasant. After about 1km the path crosses a bridge over the Allt Undalain as it flows through a gorge. Continue along the path until you eventually reach a junction (50min, 280m, 92510 16090) where you fork right, and then continue until you can see Loch Coire nan Crogachan on your right. Head for the loch outlet (1hr 15min, 455m, 92040 16340) and then head NE up a small spur which fades into the hillside. Continue NE until you reach the SE ridge of **Sgurr Mhic Bharraich** to the right of the crags (at about 610m 92350 16850) and then turn NW and climb easily to the large cairn on the summit (2hr 10min, 779m, 91770 17350).

The Saddle from Glen Allt Undalain

Head ESE down the ridge, veering E when you are well clear of the dangerous crags on the NE face of Sgurr Mhic Bharraich. The descent is steep in places, but not uncomfortably so, and you should be able to stay on grass with just a little bracken or heather at the bottom of the slope. Reach the access path (at about 3hr 5min, 75m 93620 17060) and turn left back to the car park (3hr 30min).

ROUTE 41

Sgurr an Airgid SILVER PEAK

Start	Clachan Duich Burial Ground car park (NG94610 21200)
Distance	9km (6 miles)
Total ascent	850m (2800ft)
Difficulty	Easy
Time	3hr 10min
Summits	Sgurr an Airgid (841m, 2757ft)
Maps	OS Landranger 33
Access	From Shiel Bridge follow the A87 across the causeway at the head of Loch Duich and turn right up the old road. Park on the right at the Clachan Duich Burial Ground car park.

Sgurr an Airgid is another of those Corbetts which isn't great in its own right, but the magnificent setting makes this a good walk. On the ascent there are views to Sgurr nan Ceathreamhnan, Beinn Fhada, the Five Sisters, The Saddle and Beinn Sgritheall. On reaching the summit Skye fills the view to the W and the peaks of Torridon to the N.

Eilean Donan Castle is one of the most iconic images of Scotland. Situated on an island where Loch Duich, Loch Long and Loch Alsh meet, it is one of the most visited attractions in the Highlands. The first fortified castle was built in the 13th century since when at least four different versions of the castle have been built and re-built. Eilean Donan was partially destroyed in a Jacobite uprising in 1719 and lay in ruins for 200 years before Lieutenant Colonel John MacRae-Gilstrap bought the island and restored the castle to its former glory.

See map in Route 40.

Go through the gate across the road from the car park and follow the path as it goes diagonally right up the hillside to reach the end of a small track (65m, 94750 21420). Turn left up the track, which occasionally becomes a path, soon switchbacking right, and continue until it seems to disappear in some level pasture (180m, 95100 21780). A faint grassy track actually switchbacks left then right again as a small clear track. Continue until you reach a cairn by a small ruin (25min, 225m, 95180 21924). This is where you join the stalker's path marked on the OS maps, but there is little sign of the stalker's path coming up from below. Continue up the track, which becomes a path by the time it passes through a gate in a deer fence. Continue climbing easily until you reach a cairn on the ridge (1hr 5min, 585m, 95680 22940). The stalker's path seems to end here but there is a faint path heading W which is followed to a broad saddle (580m, 95340 22960). The path is clearer as it climbs the ridge to the right of the crags and only fades away when within about 100m of the trig point on the summit of **Sgurr an Airgid** (1hr 55min, 841m, 94030 22700).

Sgurr an Airgid

Return by the same route. In mist care will be needed to locate the path, which is followed easily back to the cairn (2hr 25min) and the car park (3hr 10min).

ROUTE 42

Sguman Coinntich MOSSY PEAK *and Faochaig* THE WHELK

Start	Killilan (NG 94040 30310)
Distance	25km (16 miles)
Total ascent	1410m (4700ft)
Difficulty	The going is easy apart from some rough, steep ground on the descent. Navigation would be very testing in mist.
Time	6hr 55min
Summits	Sguman Coinntich (879m, 2881ft), Faochaig (868m, 2847ft)
Maps	OS Landranger 25
Access	Follow the A87 NW from Shiel Bridge until 1 mile after Dornie when you turn right along the minor road which leads to the N shore of Loch Long. Keep straight on when the road turns right, just after the E end of the loch and immediately park in the parking area on your left. This is the private road to the Inverinate Estate.

These are mountains that could be included in a backpacking trip, possibly involving the Corbetts Aonach Buidhe and Beinn Dronaig, as well as a selection of Munros and Grahams.

Killilan at the head of Loch Long and was the site of the 8th-century St Fillan's Church and its burial ground is said to contain the grave of **St Fillan**, a Columban missionary from Kintail, who died here on the way to Iona. Saint Fillan (Filan, Phillan, Fáelán or Faolan) is the name of at least two Scottish saints, but much of the tradition surrounding Fillan seems to be of a purely legendary character.

Head up the tarmac estate road. Turn left immediately after passing a red telephone box before the bridge over the **Allt a' Choire Mhoir**. Pass to the right of the old schoolhouse (with 1933 plaque) and along a faint path beside the burn. This faint path passes through two gates then continues between some woodland and the burn to reach a track junction

Carnan Cruithneachd from Allt an Daimh

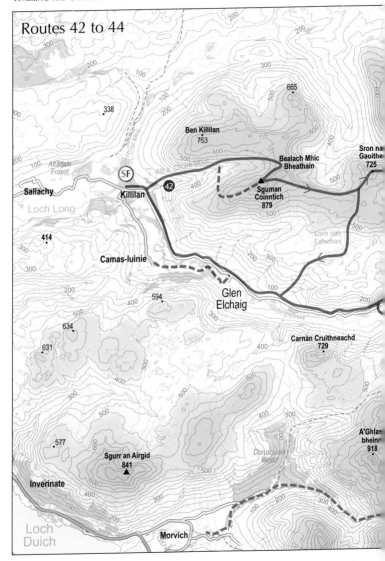

Routes 42 to 44

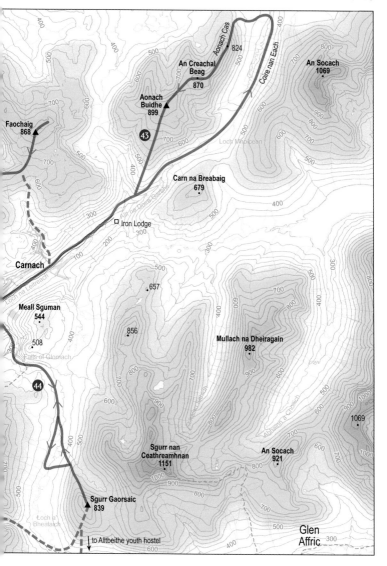

Note the deep
V-shaped valley
rather than the usual
U-shaped valley,
suggesting this valley
was eroded away
by water rather than
ice, probably from
the outflow of a
retreating glacier.

(20min, 155m, NG 95240 30540). Fork left up the rough hill track. ◄ When the gradient eases (at about 55min, 450m, NG 96740 30910) it would be possible to cross the burn and head up the hillside onto the W ridge of Sguman Coinntich and then left to the summit. (If doing the route in reverse, this would be a safer descent, avoiding the crags guarding Bealach Mhic Bheathain.) The featured route continues to the track end (1hr 10min, 590m, NG 97720 31040) before taking a rising traverse ESE towards **Bealach Mhic Bheathain** to reach a big boulder (1hr 30min, NG 98340 30840) just below the pass. Follow a grassy line going diagonally right from the boulder through the lower crags. This easy route could be hard to find in descent, leaving a difficult scramble through the crags. The ascent line leads to a wide grassy ledge which takes you easily below the upper crags to reach the summit ridge (1hr 45min, 830m, NG 98110 30500). Turn right to the disintegrating trig point and summit cairn on **Sguman Coinntich** (1hr 55min, 879m, NG 97700 30350).

Descend the E ridge of Sguman Coinntich to a pond (2hr 10min, 700m, 98910 30350). In good visibility it would be possible to shortcut directly E to the pond, rather than following the ridge ENE then SE. Continue over or round numerous rocky knolls on the broad ridge to a broad saddle with small peat hags (2hr 35min, 640m, NH 00450 30110). Climb NE to the summit of **Sron na Gaoithe** (2hr 50min, 725m, NH 00760 30610). Head roughly E, going round or over rocky knolls on the ridge, to a saddle (3hr 10min, 655m, NH 01860 30830) and climb NNE to the cairn on the summit of **Faochaig** (3hr 40min, 868m, NH 02190 31700).

It is worth heading to the E top (NH 02620 31960), which is about 2m lower, as it is an excellent viewpoint for the mountains and lochs to the E. Return to the main summit (3hr 55min) and to the saddle (4hr 10min). You could descend roughly S to the E end of Loch na Leitreach from here, but it is suggested that you return to Sron na Gaoithe (4hr 35min) and the saddle with the peat hags (4hr 40min). Now head S, just to the right of the knoll with the prominent crags, and down to the head of a small burn (4hr 50min, 605m, NH 00520 29510).

Head down steep grass and heather to the right of this burn. The stalker's path no longer exists where it is shown starting on the OS map, but you can pick it up at the E end of **Loch nan Ealachan** (5hr 10min, 400m, NH 00160 28610). Unfortunately, it disappears again but you can pick it up again along the S shore of the loch from where you can follow it down the right bank of the Allt an Daimh to reach the estate road in **Glen Elchaig** (5hr 55min, 50m, NG 98300 27300). Turn right and follow the road back to Killilan and the car park (6hr 55min).

ROUTE 43
Aonach Buidhe YELLOW RIDGE

Start	Killilan (NG 94040 30310)
Distance	41km (26 miles) from Killilan, 15.8km (10 miles) from Iron Lodge
Total ascent	1470m (4900ft) from Killilan, 1000m (3300ft) from Iron Lodge
Difficulty	Generally easy, although care would be needed with navigation in mist. There is a steep grassy descent from Aonach Buidhe.
Time	10hr from Killilan, 4hr 40min from Iron Lodge
Summits	Aonach Buidhe (899m, 2949ft)
Maps	OS Landranger 25
Access	Parking as for Route 42
Note	In devising this route it has been assumed that walkers will either use bikes to access Iron Lodge or will climb Aonach Buidhe as part of a longer backpacking trip. If you are day-hiking from Killilan you will probably want to make a direct ascent and descent of Aonach Buidhe, saving about 2hr compared with the suggested route. If you are backpacking you may want to stay at the Maol-bhuidhe Bothy (NH 05250 35950) to the N of Aonach Buidhe. Although a mountain bike is recommended for access to Iron Lodge, the track is good enough to use a road bike. If you are walking you could save about a mile in each direction by parking at Camas-luinie (NG 94810 28290).

Aonach Buidhe is remote peak at the head of Glen Elchaig. It is not spectacular when viewed from Glen Elchaig, but the N and E flanks of the mountain have dramatic corries and interesting ridges.

See map in Route 42.

The 63,000-acre **Killilan Estate** is typical of Scottish estates, many of which are owned by absentee landlords, often controlled by offshore holding companies registered in tax havens. Formerly owned by the Wills family, wealthy tobacco industrialists from Bristol, the estate was sold to Sheikh Mohammed al Maktoum, the Crown Prince of Dubai, in the 1990s. These absentee owners rarely manage the estates in the interests of the locals.

Follow the estate road up **Glen Elchaig**. After 4.3km the tarmac road becomes a good dirt road which undulates gently as it heads up the glen. The path to the Falls of Glomach goes off right after 8.7km, after which you pass **Loch na Leitreach** and Carnach Cottage before reaching the turn-off to **Iron Lodge** after 12.8km (2hr 40min, 130m, NH 04200 29420). This is the place to leave road bikes, but those with mountain bikes can cycle a little further. Fork left then right to the bridge across the An Crom-allt, which is where mountain bikes should be left (180m, NH 04660 30010).

Continue up the track to the high point of the pass (3hr 25min, 435m, NH 06630 31250) above **Loch Mhoicean**. Continue past the loch and descend to a track junction (3hr 50min, 405m, NH 07870 32380). Fork right along a grassy track that is not much more than a boggy path in places. Follow the track down **Coire nan Each** and continue until it draws close to the Allt Coire nan Each as you approach An Cruachan. The junction with the stalker's path shown on the OS map is not obvious (4hr 25min, 345m, NH 08730 34880). Cross the burn to the stalker's path, which is clearly visible on the ridge across the burn, and follow it onto the ridge of Aonach Cas. The path is a little indistinct near the top but it can be followed all the way to the ridge (5hr, 595m,

NH 07520 34660), well above where it is shown ending on the OS map. Turn left up the ridge to the NE top of **Aonach Cas** (5hr 35min, 824m, NH 07410 34000) and over a higher top (835m, NH 07210 33530) before veering right to the summit cairn on **An Creachal Beag** (5hr 55min, 870m, NH 06650 33180). Descend roughly SW to a low point (830m, NH 06180 32890) before climbing to the cairn on the summit of **Aonach Buidhe** (6hr 20min, 899m, NH 05770 32450).

Head roughly SSW down the S ridge of Aonach Buidhe. The descent is down fairly steep grass slopes, with some scattered crags to avoid. When you reach the track (at about 7hr 10min, 235m, NH 04970 30000) turn right back to the bridge and Iron Lodge junction (7hr 20min). You now have a 13km walk (or cycle) back to the parking area at Killilan (10hr).

Carn na Breabaig from Loch na Leitreach

ROUTE 44

Sgurr Gaorsaic HORROR PEAK

Start	Killilan (NG 94040 30310)
Distance	32km (20 miles) from Killilan, 15km (9 miles) from Loch na Leitreach
Total ascent	1250m (4100ft) from Killilan, 950m (3100ft) from Loch na Leitreach
Difficulty	There is rough, boggy terrain to cross in Glen Gaorsaic. The path to the Falls of Glomach is exposed with occasional easy rocksteps, and could not be described as a 'tourist' path. This path, which traverses steep slopes, would be extremely dangerous in snow.
Time	8hr 55min from Killilan, 5hr 20min from Loch na Leitreach
Summits	Sgurr Gaorsaic (839m, 2600ft ring contour)
Maps	OS Landranger 33
Access	Parking as for Route 42
Note	You could cycle the first 9km of the route to Loch na Leitreach, which could be done on a road bike. The shortest route to Sgurr Gaorsaic is from Morvich to the W, but this is still a long route and lacks the interest of the recommended route. Sgurr Gaorsaic is surrounded by Munros, which could be combined in a backpacking trip. Sgurr Gaorsaic could easily be climbed from Alltbeithe Youth Hostel in Glen Affric to the E. If you are walking, rather than cycling, you could save about a mile in each direction by parking at Camas-luinie (NG 94810 28290).

Sgurr Gaorsaic is actually just a subsidiary top to the Munro Sgurr nan Ceathreamhnan. This remote peak is at the W end of the long ridge which stretches 30km E to Cannich and includes many Munros. Sgurr Gaorsaic was not recognised as a Corbett based on the OS 1 inch:1 mile map which only showed a 400ft drop to Sgurr nan Ceathreamhnan. However, when the 1:50,000 map was produced, Sgurr Gaorsaic had gained about 50m (170ft) in height and the drop was now about 168m (550ft).

With a drop of 113m (370ft), the remote **Falls of Glomach** (gloomy falls) is one of the highest water-falls in Britain and it is certainly one of the most spectacular. The waterfall is well hidden and it is said to be impossible to capture all of it in one photograph.

Follow the estate road up **Glen Elchaig**. After 4.3km the tarmac road becomes a good dirt road, which undulates gently as it heads up the glen. The path to the Falls of Glomach goes off right after 8.7km (1hr 50min, 95m, NH 00920 27080) just before Loch na Leitreach comes into view. If you are cycling this is where you should leave your bike. Follow the good path down to the bridge over the **River Elchaig** and continue along it until you reach the bridge over the gorge of the Allt a' Ghlomaich (2hr, 110m, NH 01220 26660). Despite the confusing National Trust for Scotland sign, this is not the Falls of Glomach! Cross and follow an exposed path, which has some small rocksteps, high above the steep-sided gorge before drop-ping down to cross the Allt na Laoidhre. The path then climbs steeply before contouring across to the top of the **Falls of Glomach** (2hr 40min, 330m, NH 01840 25590). You still cannot see the falls properly so you will need to turn left down a good path which descends 35m steeply to exposed viewing platforms.

Retrace your steps to the top of the falls then con-tinue along the right-hand side of the Allt a' Ghlomaich. The going is rough and boggy in places. When the burn splits fork right up the Abhainn Gaorsaic and fol-low this burn to Loch Thuill Easaich. ▶ Continue about 300m beyond the loch to find an easy point to cross the Abhainn Gaorsaic (3hr 55min, 385m, NH 02570 22870). Head just N of E to reach the Allt Thuill Easaich and con-tinue up this burn until above the waterfalls (about 4hr 20min, 535m, NH 03300 22950). Head right up the N ridge of **Sgurr Gaorsaic** to the small cairn on a rock out-crop (5hr 5min, 839m, NH 03590 21860). The OS maps show a lochan on the summit, but all that is left is a small peaty marsh.

See map in Route 42.

On the way up Gleann Gaorsaic you will notice extensive tree remains preserved in the peat, showing that this glen, as were most in Scotland, was once forested.

Top of the Falls of Glomach

Return down the ridge and continue down the burn until below the waterfalls where it is possible to cross the burn on boulders (at about 5hr 40min, 385m, NH 02970 23240). Continue N along the Abhainn Gaorsaic until you find a good crossing point (possibly at NH 02980 23990). Cross and follow the left bank back to the Falls of Glomach (6hr 35min) and the track in Glen Elchaig (7hr 10min). Turn left back to the car park (8hr 55min).

6 GLEN AFFRIC, GLEN CANNICH, GLEN STRATHFARRAR AND STRATHCONON

An Tudair across Loch Affric (Route 45)

Glen Affric, Glen Cannich, Glen Strathfarrar and Strathconon: Bases and facilities

Base for Routes 45–50: Beauly or Muir of Ord

Beauly, a very small town, and Muir of Ord, a village just N of Beauly, both have good facilities for tourists. The area is covered by the Inverness Tourist Office.

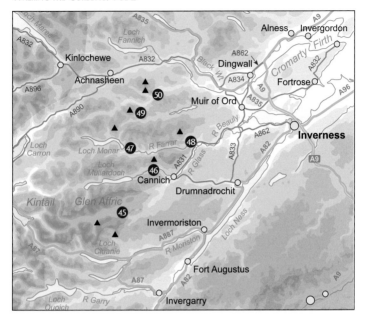

Tourist information: VisitScotland, Castle Wynd, Inverness, IV27 4LX
Tel: 01463 252 401

Lovat Bridge Caravan and Camping Site
Tel: 01463 782 374 www.beaulyholidaypark.co.uk

Alternative bases for Routes 45–50

It would be feasible to base yourself at Strathpeffer, Dingwall, Conon
Bridge, Contin, Drumnadrochit or Inverness for this widespread section.

Local facilities for Routes 45–48: Cannich

Cannich has a small store, two pubs, a camping/caravan site, chalets and
several B&Bs.

Cannich Caravan and Camping Park, which also has static caravans and a
café, has recently been refurbished.
Tel: 01456 415 364 www.highlandcamping.co.uk

ROUTE 45

Aonach Shasuinn RIDGE OF THE SASSENACH *and*
Carn a' Choire Ghairbh CAIRN OF THE ROUGH CORRIE

Start	Glen Affric roadhead (NH 20080 23290)
Distance	26km (16 miles)
Total ascent	1360m (4500ft)
Difficulty	These are pathless mountains with rough heather and grass on the lower slopes, but the going is never particularly tough. The descent path isn't easy to find, even in good visibility, and unless you have GPS it might be more sensible to descend by the alternative route when it is misty.
Time	8hr 15min
Summits	Aonach Shasuinn (888m, 2901ft), An Elric (862m), Carn a' Choire Ghairbh (865m, 2827ft)
Maps	OS Landranger 25 and 34
Access	From Beauly follow the A831 SW to Cannich and follow the minor road SW to a large car park at the roadhead in Glen Affric.
Note	In poor visibility, or for the inexperienced navigator, it might be better to head ENE from Carn a' Choire Ghairbh over Carn Glas Lochdarach and descend the ridge, veering a little right to regain the ascent route at the bridge. If you want to climb these two Corbetts separately you might consider approaching Aonach Shasuinn from the Ceannacroc Bridge on the A887 to the S as there is now a track all the way up to Bealach an Amais. The best way to climb these Corbetts is as part of a backpacking expedition, climbing the Munros surrounding Glen Affric.

Aonach Shasuinn is hidden away behind Carn a' Choire Ghairbh, which is the peak to the S of Loch Affric. These Corbetts are on different branches of the N ridge of the Munro Sgurr nan Conbhairean and you get magnificent views of the Munros surrounding Glen Affric.

Follow the good track from the car park entrance down to the bridge over the **River Affric**. Cross the bridge and

181

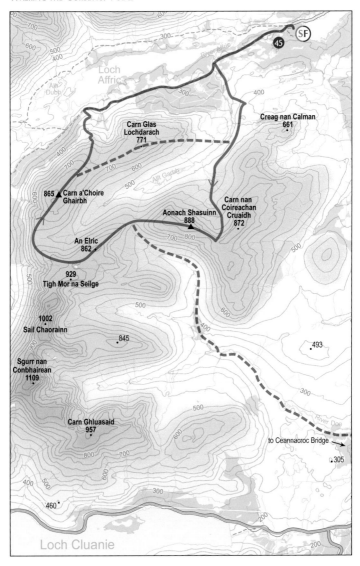

follow the track through natural woodland until a path (18000 22360) signed to Cougie is reached just before the Allt Garbh burn. Turn left up an often boggy path. ▶ Veer left after passing through the gate in a deer fence (330m, 18380 21380) and continue to a junction with an old track (1hr, 410m, 18830 21270). Turn right along the track, descending a little to a bridge over the Allt Garbh (18230 20180). Do not cross, but continue over rough heather and grass along the left bank of the burn, turning left up a tributary into the unnamed corrie NE of Aonach Shasuinn. If in doubt, head S aiming for the pass between Aonach Shasuinn and Carn nan Coireachan Cruaidh. On reaching the head of the corrie veer right up easy grass slopes to the pass (2hr 35 min, 810m, 17930 17730). Turn right to the summit of **Aonach Shasuinn**, which is denoted by a small cairn, not the nearby tall cairn or the wall shelter (2hr 50min, 888m, 17330 18010).

Head W, then WNW to the W top (873m) and then descend steeply W to the Bealach an Amais (650m, 15830 18120), ignoring a track descending left down

The paths are now rather different than shown on the OS map.

Aonach Shasuinn

183

Gleann Fada. Climb the An Elric ridge to **Peak 862** (14750 17410), which is just a minor top on the N ridge of the Munro Sgurr nan Conbhairean. Continue WSW to a little ridge above Lochan a' Choinich (4hr 15min, 860m, 14130 17050) and then head W, gradually veering S down the Carn a' Choire Ghuirm ridge to the pass (665m, 13010 17670) SW of Carn a' Choire Ghairbh. Head roughly NE, picking up the remains of a deer fence that leads to a large well-constructed cairn. Head NNE from here to the summit cairn on **Carn a' Choire Ghairbh**, which is on a small rocky ridge (5hr 30min, 865m, 13680 18870).

Head NE, crossing the old deer fence and keeping left of the upper reaches of the Allt a' Choire Chruim. You are trying to locate a small cairn (6hr 10min, 655m, 14630 20080) marking the beginning of your descent path, which isn't where it is mapped on the OS map! You need to find this path; otherwise it will be a difficult descent down the rough steep corrie. The old Stalker's path, which initially heads WNW, is faint in places but can be followed with care and takes you easily down to the main track up Glen Affric (6hr 55min, 265m, 14310 21050). This junction would be very easy to miss if you were attempting the route in the opposite direction. Turn right and follow the track back to the car park (8hr 15min).

ROUTE 46

Sgorr na Diollaid PEAK OF THE SADDLE

Start	Loch Carrie (NH 26960 33510)
Distance	9km (5 miles)
Total ascent	770m (2500ft)
Difficulty	Although there are no paths, apart from a few animal tracks, the going is generally relatively easy despite some rough heather and grass. There is a short easy scramble to the summit. Navigation on the 'knobbly' ridge could be difficult in mist.
Time	3hr 50min
Summits	Sgorr na Diollaid (818m, 2676ft)
Maps	OS Landranger 25
Access	From Beauly follow the A831 SW to Cannich and follow the minor road up Glen Cannich. One mile after crossing to the N side of the River Cannich you reach Loch Carrie. There is roadside parking where the Allt Charaidh flows into the loch. This is also the best place to swim in Loch Carrie.
Note	A more direct approach can be made up the S ridge from Muchrachd.

Sgorr na Diollaid is a delightful rocky peak between Glen Cannich and Glen Strathfarrar. There are superb views of the Munros which surround these glens.

The 10-mile long **Loch Mullardoch** at the head of Glen Cannich was created in 1951 by the building of the Mullardoch Dam, the largest in Scotland. Before the glen was flooded a drove road stretched from Cannich, up Glen Cannich before dropping down to Loch Alsh via Glen Elchaig. The old Hydro Board had a legal requirement to restore the right of way on completion of the hydro-electric scheme. More than 60 years later we're still waiting!

Head up the left bank of the **Allt Charaidh** and cross over when the burn swings left in a marshy area. Before the burn enters a gully (330m, 27450 34190), head NNE up the ridge to the right of the burn and follow the line of the tributary (which is no more than a trickle) to a plateau. Here you get your first sight of the rocky S ridge of **Sgorr na Diollaid** and you should veer right towards the rocks (1hr 30min, 675m, 28050 35550). Either scramble easily up the rock slabs or climb the short heather and grass slopes to the S summit. Continue roughly N, dodging rock outcrops, to the rocky N summit which has twin tops. The E top is about 1m higher and involves a short,

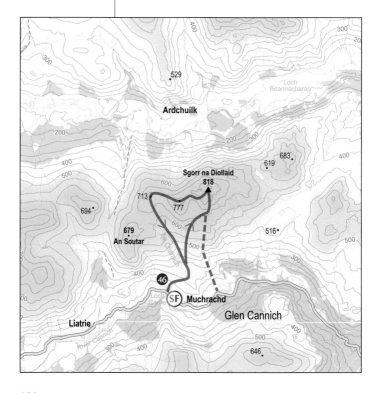

Loch Carrie

very easy scramble to reach the rocky summit (2hr 5min, 818m, 28180 36250).

Head SW, veering W then SW again, along the knobbly summit ridge to **Peak 777** (27340 35850) and then WNW, veering W, to **Peak 713** (2hr 50min, 26490 35980). Head S, veering a little left to the headwaters of Allt Charaidh and continue down above the left bank, crossing to the right bank at the end of the marshy plateau for the final descent to the parking (3hr 50min).

ROUTE 47

An Sidhean THE FAIRY HILL

Start	Monar Dam (NH 20260 39390)
Distance	20km (12 miles)
Total ascent	1020m (3400ft)
Difficulty	Although there are good stalker's tracks on An Sidhean there is rough moor to cross on the ascent and a steep rough descent down to the Allt na Cois. Care would be needed with navigation in mist.
Time	5hr 55min
Summits	An Sidhean (814m, 2661ft)
Maps	OS Landranger 25
Access	Follow the A831 about 10 miles W from Beauly then turn right along the minor road signed to Strathfarrar to reach the gate across the road at Inchmore. There is limited road access to the glen – you can find details on the Mountaineering Council of Scotland's website www.mcofs.org.uk/strathfarrar-access.asp. At the time of writing the road is closed to vehicles on Tuesdays and on Wednesday morning. On other days, access by car is permitted along the estate road from 9.00am–8.00pm in summer, with shorter hours in spring and autumn. Access in winter is only possible by prior arrangement (see website). The gate is likely to be locked but you should ask for access at the cottage beside the gate. Overnight parking is not allowed in Glen Strathfarrar. If you want to camp in the glen you must park before the gate and walk or cycle up the glen. Walkers and cyclists can use the road at any time. It is 13 miles to the roadhead at the Monar Dam where there is limited parking.
Note	Although An Sidhean provides an excellent day-hike, it should really be climbed as part of a backpacking trip over the Munros and Corbetts surrounding Glen Strathfarrar.

An Sidhean is a remote Corbett on the long ridge N of Glen Strathfarrar and Loch Monar. The ridge contains many Munros, including Maoile Lunndaidh and Sgurr a' Choire Ghlais. There are excellent views of Loch Monar as well as the many Munros in this area.

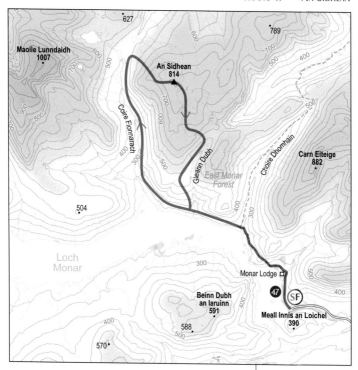

Keep an eye open for **whooper swans** on your drive up Glen Strathfarrar. The 'wild' whooper swan which breeds in Iceland, northern Scandinavia and Siberia winters in Scotland. Unusually, Glen Strathfarrar has a group of whooper swans which breed and remain in the glen throughout the year. Whooper swans are readily distinguished from the mute swan and Bewick's swan because they hold their neck very straight when swimming.

Walk up the private drive to **Monar Lodge** and turn right, uphill, at a green farm building. You soon reach a path junction (20190 40380) where you turn left along

Memorial to Pipe Major WC Ross in Glen Strathfarrar

a good stalker's path, which takes you through a gully behind a knoll and back to **Loch Monar**. Keep straight on at path junctions after the Allt a' Choire Dhomhain and Allt na Cois burns to a path junction close to a bridge over the Allt a' Choire Fhionnaraich (1hr 30min, 235m, 16360 42470). Turn right, then fork right after 300m. The good path becomes a little indistinct further up **Coire Fionnarach**, but it can be followed until it crosses the Allt a' Choire Fhionnaraich (2hr 35min, 445m, 15730 45950). The stalker's paths shown on the OS map on the NW slopes of An Sidhean no longer exist, so head roughly ESE up a rough slope. You soon reach easier going on the summit ridge and continue to the cairn on the summit of **An Sidhean** (3hr 35min, 814m, 17100 45380). The summit plateau has many small rock outcrops.

Head SE to a small marshy lochan (790m, 17330 45180) and then roughly SSE, following the ridge to the left of the outlet burn from this lochan. After a steep descent reach a faint stalker's path where it crosses the burn just above the Allt na Cois (4hr 15min, 530m, 18020 43730). Take care to follow the path as it improves to take you easily down the steep rough slopes to the W of the burn and down to the path along Loch Monar (4hr 50min, 270m, 17650 41960). Turn left back to the Monar Dam (5hr 55min).

ROUTE 48

Beinn a' Bha'ach Ard HILL OF THE HIGH BYRE

Start	Inchmore (NH 39410 40570)
Distance	16km (10 miles)
Total ascent	970m (3200ft)
Difficulty	Beinn a' Bha'ach Ard is surrounded by rough heather and grass moorland. It looks easy on the OS map, but some of the paths shown on the map don't exist so there is much rough terrain to cross on the lower slopes. The summit is shown as surrounded by crags on the OS maps, but these don't exist either!
Time	5hr 5min
Summits	Beinn a' Bha'ach Ard (862m, 2826ft), Sgurr a' Phollain (855m), Carn na Gabhalach (713m)
Maps	OS Landranger 26
Access	Follow the A831 about 10 miles W from Beauly then turn right along the minor road signed to Strathfarrar and park in a small car park at Inchmore just before the gate which is the end of the public road.

Beinn a' Bha'ach Ard is the E peak on the long ridge containing many Munros forming the N wall to Glen Strathfarrar. It feels a little isolated from these peaks, but it does give magnificent views E to Beauly Firth and Cromarty Firth.

In 1757 General Simon Fraser of Lovat raised the 78th Fraser Highlanders. Two hundred men from Strathfarrar volunteered for service in Canada and they became known as the **Lovat Scouts**. The Lovat Scouts distinguished themselves in the Boer war and both World Wars. Many of the Scouts were Gaelic speakers, which gave them a key role as radio operators in World War II when Gaelic became the 'secret language' which the Germans could not understand.

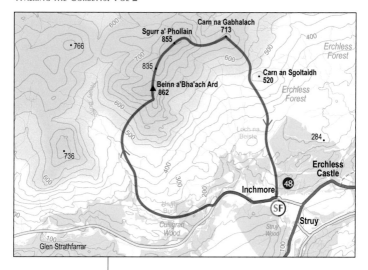

Follow the estate road for 1 mile to the Culligran Power Station. Turn right and almost immediately fork right up the good track which switchbacks, through 'natural' woodland, up the hill before levelling off and following the power lines. The track ends at a water intake dam on the **Neaty Burn** (55min, 200m, 35710 40310). Turn right up an old vehicle track. If you lose this track, which is very indistinct in places, continue up to the right of the Neaty Burn. With a lot of imagination you can follow the 'track' until it crosses the burn draining the SW slopes of Beinn a' Bha'ach Ard (1hr 50min, 505m, 35210 42440). Turn right up the burn and follow it to its source, then continue on the same line to the S ridge of **Beinn a' Bha'ach Ard** (760m, 36150 43160). The going now gets easy as you head N to the stone trig point on the summit (2hr 50min, 862m, 36060 43470).

Head NNE to a saddle (790m) and over **Peak 835** to another saddle (810m, 36360 44340), then veer NE to the small summit cairn on **Sgurr a' Phollain**, which is not a Corbett because it does not meet the 500ft requirement (3hr 20min, 855m, 36800 44720).

The OS map shows an old stalker's path going all the way from here to Inchmore. This path is clear and useful in places, but in other places it has disappeared completely and you will need to descend rough heather and grass. Head E and pick up this stalker's path, which takes you safely SE down the steep lower slopes of the E ridge of Sgurr a' Phollain, avoiding unmapped crags on the E face. You then pick up a line of old fence posts which lead you easily to the summit of **Carn na Gabhalach** (713m, 38090 44850).

Turn right here, following the path when it exists or the line of fence posts. After crossing the shoulder of **Carn an Sgoltaidh** you will probably lose both path and fence posts, but should carry on in the same direction (roughly SSE) until you reach the E end of **Loch na Beiste** (4hr 40min, 235m, 39230 42260) which can easily be located because it is just below a prominent pointed boulder. There should be little difficulty following the path to **Inchmore**. At junctions follow the bigger path/ track, keeping generally S. If in doubt at a couple of forks lower down, fork left, but fork right after passing through a gate in the deer fence just above Inchmore (5hr 5min).

Beinn a' Bha'ach Ard from Loch na Beiste

ROUTE 49

Bac an Eich BANK OF THE HORSE

Start	Inverchoran (NH 26130 50810)
Distance	19km (12 miles)
Total ascent	890m (2900ft)
Difficulty	The ascent route is over rough grassland. The descent is easy but the suggested route along the shore Loch Beannacharain is hard work as the path shown on the OS map does not exist.
Time	5hr 55min
Summits	Bac an Eich (849m, 2791ft)
Maps	OS Landranger 25
Access	From Beauly head N to Muir of Ord and turn left along the A832 to Marybank. Keep straight on here, signed to Strathconon and continue until you see the sign for Inverchoran a mile before reaching Loch Beannacharain where there is limited roadside parking.
Note	If the burns are in flood you might prefer to head to the top of Gleann Chorainn and climb Bac an Eich from the S. You could climb the Sgurr Toll Lochain ridge from Loch Toll Lochain, but this is rather steep. The quickest descent would be to descend S from Bac an Eich and descend down Gleann Chorainn. Although the featured route goes along the S shore of Loch Beannacharain, this section is very rough so you might prefer to walk along the road to the N of the loch. The main alternative would be to park at the roadhead at Scardroy, walk to Corriefeol and follow a path up the S flank of Creag Achadh an Eas before climbing the NW ridge of Bac an Eich.

Bac an Eich is an isolated peak at the head of Strathconon. It is protected by steep slopes and commercial forestry, but spectacular glens surrounding the mountain and wide-ranging views, including Torridon to the NW, make this a very worthwhile walk.

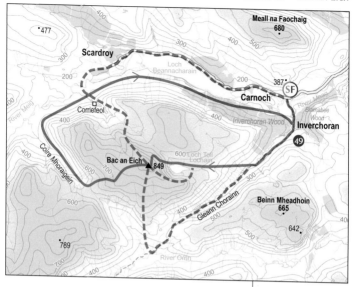

Scardroy Lodge, with its 10,000 acres of hills, lochs, river and forest at the head of Strathconon, exemplifies the diversification that a typical Highland estate has undergone to balance the books. The traditional source of income is from stag and hind stalking, pheasant, partridge and woodcock shooting and fishing. A day's shooting would cost about £500/gun, but you will be pleased to know that lunch is included! The estate lets out three holiday homes and the lodge itself is available for special events.

Cross the bridge and follow the track to Inverchoran House where you turn left across the bridge, right across a ford in front of the kennels and then left up the main track. Veer right up **Gleann Chorainn**. When the track appears to end, just before the end of the forestry, cross the burn (30min, 225m, 25420 49370), possibly getting your feet wet. Turn left along the track which ends at the edge of the wood and then head diagonally uphill, across rough pasture, towards

195

the steep Sgurr Toll Lochain. When you reach the gully of the outlet burn from **Loch Toll Lochain** follow it uphill to the loch (1hr 30min, 520m, 23380 48830). It is easiest to walk along the N shore of the loch and follow the burn which flows into its NW end. When you reach a shallow saddle (620m, 22470 49390) head left up the hill to the stone trig point on the summit of **Bac an Eich** (2hr 35min, 849m, 22220 48940).

Head easily WSW down a broad ridge to a good stalker's path at the head of **Coire Mhoraigein**. Turn right down the corrie, veering right into Gleann Fhiodhaig to reach two ruined cottages at **Corriefeol** (4hr, 175m, 20360 50830). Keep straight on along the S bank of the **River Meig** over improved pasture. The path shown on the OS map is intermittent. Stay on the higher ground to cut across to the S shore of **Loch Beannacharain** and follow the shoreline. About halfway along the loch, the shore is blocked by crags and steep slopes, so it is necessary to climb steeply up to the commercial forestry. Follow the rough grass just below the forest which drops you back to the lakeshore and follow the shore until you reach a fence near the end of the loch (5hr 20min, 155m, 24420 50750). Continue to the left of the forest, eventually picking up a track as it leaves the forest (25360 50390). Follow the track back to Inverchoran House, pass to the right of the house and follow the route back to the parking (5hr 55min).

Corriefeol ruins and Creag Achadh an Eas, Bac an Eich

ROUTE 50

Meallan nan Uan LITTLE ROUNDED HILL OF THE LAMBS
and Sgurr a' Mhuilinn PEAK OF THE MILL

Start	Gleann Meinich (NH 28240 52660)
Distance	17km (11 miles)
Total ascent	1210m (4000ft)
Difficulty	The ascent from Strathconon is steep, but the going is relatively easy if you take the recommended route and the ridges give easy walking. The final descent down to Gleann Meinich is also steep, but is easy underfoot. Care will be needed with navigation in mist.
Time	6hr
Summits	Meallan nan Uan (838m, 2750ft), Sgurr a' Mhuilinn (879m, 2845ft), Sgurr a' Choire-rainich (848m), Sgurr a' Ghlas Leathaid (844m)
Maps	OS Landranger 25
Access	From Beauly head N to Muir of Ord and turn left along the A832 to Marybank. Keep straight on here, signed to Strathconon and continue until you reach Gleann Meinich, about 2.5 miles after the hamlet of Milton. There is plenty of parking just after the burn.
Note	It would be quicker to descend E from Sgurr a' Mhuilinn, but this is a steep descent over rough terrain.

Meallan nan Uan and Sgurr a' Mhuilinn are the attractive peaks that dominate as you drive up Strathconon. In the same group of mountains are the twin summits of Sgurr a' Choire-rainich and Sgurr a' Ghlas Leathaid, which don't quite reach Corbett status as there is only about 460ft of descent to Sgurr a' Mhuilinn. Including these two peaks with the Corbetts makes this a very attractive ridge walk.

The walk down **Gleann Meinich** will give you a reminder of how strong the wind can be in the Scottish Highlands. Winds funnelling down this classic U-shaped valley have caused a lot of

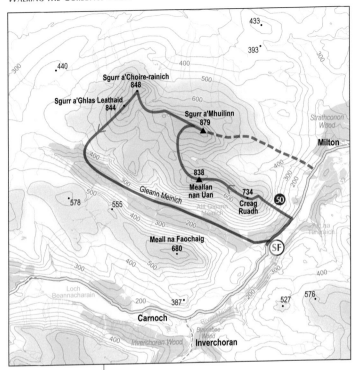

damage to the forestry and you will see not only windblown trees but also many trees which have been snapped by the winds.

Return 1km down the glen and turn left up the hill at the end of the forestry (28940 53360). There are paths (animal tracks?) until you reach the top of the forest, after which you should veer slightly right (NW) for easier going up the steep slope. The slope eases as you reach a cairn on the ridge (660m, 28060 54000). Continue roughly W, following a faint path to the summit of **Creag Ruadh** (1hr 40min, 734m, 27690 53910), then head WNW along the ridge over another top (745m, 27210 54270) and on to the rocky summit of **Meallan nan Uan** (2hr 15min, 838m, 26370 54460).

Keep straight on along the faint path, then veer NW down the steep rocky ridge to a saddle (685m, 25790 54950). Contour right, round a knoll, to a second saddle (700m, 25730 55220) and then head NE to the summit ridge on **Sgurr a' Mhuilinn**. Turn right (E) along the ridge to the trig point (3hr 10min, 879m, 26460 55740).

Return WNW and continue along the summit ridge to a 'lochan', which is not much more than a boggy puddle! Continue roughly W down to a broad saddle (710m, 24860 56420) before veering NW, then N to the summit of **Sgurr a' Choire-rainich** (3hr 55min, 848m, 24800 56900). Head SW down to a saddle and up to the summit of **Sgurr a' Ghlas Leathaid** (844m, 24370 56420). ▸

Don't be tempted to head directly S towards Gleann Meinich as steep slopes and forest would make the descent very difficult. Instead head roughly SW and head for the burn that enters the forest (at 455m, 23160 55510) and follow this burn easily down steep grass to the track in **Gleann Meinich** (4hr 55min, 260m, 23140 54980). Turn left down Gleann Meinich to the road in Strathconon and the parking (6hr).

The author's measurements suggest that Sgurr a' Ghlas Leathaid is the same height as Sgurr a' Choire-rainich.

7 GLEN CARRON, GLEN TORRIDON AND LOCH MAREE

Glen Carron, Glen Torridon and Loch Maree: Bases and facilities

Base for Routes 51–56: Lochcarron or Glen Carron

Loch Carron is a village with several shops, hotel, cafés, campsite and B&Bs.

Lochcarron Hotel Tel: 01520 722 226 www.lochcarronhotel.com

Wee Camp Site Tel: 01520 722 898

Strathcarron Hotel is at the head of Loch Carron.
Tel: 01520 722 227 www.strathcarronhotel.co.uk
Gerry's Hostel at Craig, 2 miles E of Achnashellach Station in Glen Carron, claims to be Scotland's oldest independent hostel.
Tel: 01520 766 232 www.gerryshostel-achnashellach.co.uk

Base for Routes 57–61: Kinlochewe

Kinlochewe is a small village with shop, hotel, café, caravan and a separate campsite and B&Bs.

As well as normal hotel facilities the Kinlochewe Hotel has a bunkhouse.
Tel: 01445 760 253 www.kinlochewehotel.co.uk

Kinlochewe Caravan Club Site does not take tents. Tel: 01445 760 239

Beinn Eighe National Nature Reserve Visitor Centre is well worth visiting. The centre runs a small campsite with basic facilities 1.5 miles N of the village at Taagan Farm. This site, which only takes tents, is aimed at travellers and backpackers who wish to stay for a short period of one or two nights.

Local facilities for Routes 57–59: Torridon

Torridon is a small village with a small store, SYHA hostel, hotel, B&Bs and basic campsite for tents only.

Torridon SYHA, Ross-shire, IV22 2EZ Tel: 01445 791 284

The Torridon Inn is a slightly cheaper base operated by the exclusive Torridon Hotel. Tel: 01445 700 300 www.thetorridon.com

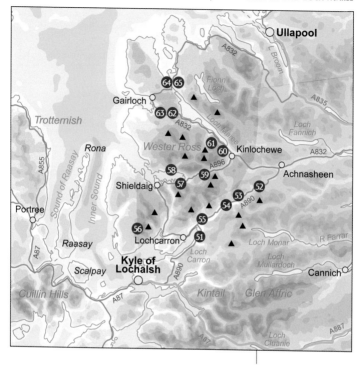

Tigh an Eilean Hotel is at Shieldaig about 11km W of Torridon.
Tel: 01520 755 251 www.tighaneilean.co.uk

Base for Routes 61–65: Gairloch

Gairloch is a fishing village with several shops, SYHA hostel, B&Bs, hotels and campsite.

Carn Dearg SYHA, Gairloch, Ross-shire, IV21 2DJ Tel: 01445 712 219

Gairloch Holiday Park has static caravans and a cottage as well as being a camping and caravan site. Tel: 01445 712 373
www.gairlochcaravanpark.com

The Old Inn, Gairloch, is a traditional Highland coaching inn.
Tel 01445 712 006 www.theoldinn.net

The Millcroft Hotel offers both hotel rooms and self-catering apartments.
Tel: 01445 712 376 www.millcroft-hotel.co.uk

Myrtle Bank Hotel Tel: 01445 712004 www.themyrtlegairloch.co.uk

Local facilities for Route 64 and 65: Poolewe

Poolewe is a small village with a shop, hotel, coffee shop and camping and
caravan site

The Poolewe Hotel was a coaching inn dating back to about 1570.
Tel: 01445 781 769 www.poolewehotel.co.uk

Inverewe Gardens Camping and Caravanning Club Site Tel: 01445 781 249

Gruinard Bay Caravan Park has static caravans as well as being a camping
and caravan site. It is situated in a lovely coastal location between Sections
7 and 8. Tel: 01445 731 225 www.gruinardbay.co.uk

Liathach and Beinn Eighe from lochan on Sgurr Dubh (Route 59)

ROUTE 51

Beinn Dronaig RAGGED HILL

Start	Achintee (NG 94120 41800)
Distance	30km (19 miles)
Total ascent	1480m (4900ft)
Difficulty	An easy, but long walk. Care would be needed with navigation in mist.
Time	8hr 15min
Summits	Beinn Dronaig (797m, 2612ft)
Maps	OS Landranger 25
Access	Head NE from Lochcarron up the A896 and turn right along the A890 to Strathcarron. There is limited parking by a minor tarmac road, signed to Achintee, about 400m S of Strathcarron Hotel and further parking in the vicinity of the hotel.
Note	You could save an hour by descending by the ascent route but you would miss the best section of the route. It would be possible to approach Beinn Dronaig by mountain bike along the estate road from Attadale Gardens. This is really an area for the backpacker and there are many options, including combining with Munros Lurg Mhor and Bidean a' Choire Sheasgaich or Corbetts Sguman Coinntich, Faochaig and Aonach Buidhe as well as a selection of Grahams.

Beinn Dronaig is a remote peak in the Attadale Forest to the E of Loch Carron. The route provides excellent views of the surrounding Munros and Loch Monar to the E.

Begun by Baron Schroder in the late 19th century, **Attadale Gardens** on Loch Carron are worth visiting. There is the original rhododendron walk, in which rowan, maple, cherry and birch have been planted to provide a contrast with the dark green of the rhododendrons, as well as outstanding water gardens and a sunken garden. The gardens are

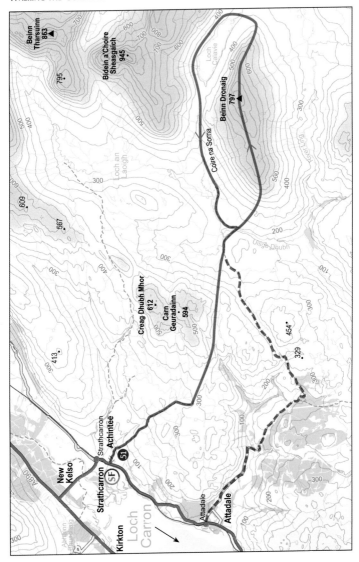

dotted with sculptures and there's a giant 35ft diameter sundial. **www.attadalegardens.com**

Head up the tarmac road signed to Achintee, then left along a tarmac road and right up a track signed 'hillpaths'. Ignore any small tracks off to the right as this track becomes a good stalker's path climbing through rough moorland. Pass to the right of Loch an Fheoir and along the S flank of the Graham Creag Dhubh Mhor. Pass Lochan Fuara and continue until the top of the descent (1hr 40min, 395m, NG 98550 38750) where you get your first proper view of the uninteresting-looking Beinn Dronaig and the shapely Lurg Mhor. Follow the path as it descends to reach pasture where the path fades away. If you lose the path, just continue on the same line to reach the estate road (at about 1hr 55min, 205m, NG 99610 38610). Turn left along the road to a bridge over the gorge of the **Uisge Dhubh** (2hr 10min, 195m, NH 00280 38180). ▸

There are good swimming holes here.

Head roughly ESE up the easy slope to reach the ridge (by 3hr 10min, 625m, NH 01560 37540), then veer left up the ridge and along the broad summit plateau. The plateau has a multitude of small rock outcrops and minor tops which could cause confusion in mist, but continue until you reach the trig point on **Beinn Dronaig** (3hr 55min, 797m, NH 03710 38170).

Although many walkers return by the same route, it is best to descend the E ridge, which gives fantastic views to Loch Monar and the Munros to the E. If your navigation is good you should be able to pick up the top end of a stalker's path on the crest of the ridge (4hr 25min, 540m, NH 05280 37820). This path switchbacks down the remainder of the ridge before veering left towards E end of **Loch Calavie**. You will probably lose the path in the peat hags around the head of the loch, but just keep going and cross the Allt Loch Calavie, on stepping stones when water levels are low. The indistinct stalker's path reaches the track which runs along the N shore of Loch Calavie (4hr 55min, 350m, NH 05760 38660). Turn left along the loch, over the pass (375m) into **Coire na Sorna**

*An Cruachan from
Loch Calavie*

and keep straight on (left) at a junction, immediately crossing the Allt Coire na Sorna (5hr 50min, 215m, NH 01800 39120). Pass Bendronaig Lodge before returning to the bridge over the Uisge Dubh (6hr 15min).

Return by the same route to the top of the climb (6hr 55min) and back to the parking (8hr 15min).

ROUTE 52

Sgurr nan Ceannaichean ROCKY PEAK OF THE PEDLARS

Start	Glen Carron (NH 08040 52030)
Distance	11km (7 miles)
Total ascent	1010m (3300ft)
Difficulty	Easy walking, but navigation could be difficult in mist.
Time	4hr 35min
Summits	Moruisg (928m, Munro), Sgurr nan Ceannaichean (913m, 2986ft)
Maps	OS Landranger 25
Access	Head NE from Lochcarron up the A896 and A890 and park in a layby about 5km E of Craig.
Note	If you don't want to include Moruisg you could ascend by the recommended descent route or climb Sgurr nan Ceannaichean from Craig.

Sgurr nan Ceannaichean is an undistinguished peak to the S of Glen Carron. It was classified as a Corbett until the OS 1:50,000 maps gave it a height of 915m and it was promoted to Munro status. However, a survey carried out by John Barnard, Graham Jackson and Myrddyn Phillips in 2009 gave a height of 913.43 ±0.07m – this has been accepted by the Ordnance Survey and Sgurr nan Ceannaichean has been reclassified as a Corbett.

Founded in 2002, the **Munro Society** is open to mountaineers who have climbed all the Munro summits in Scotland as listed in Munro's Tables – currently there are 283 mountains of Munro status with a height of 3000ft or more above sea level. The official list of members now has more than 4000 names – however, a substantial percentage of 'compleatists' will not have registered their details. **www.themunrosociety.com**

Go through the gate and down to the bridge and follow boggy tracks to a bridge under the **railway** (140m,

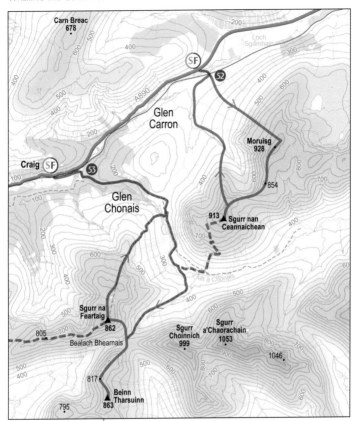

08310 51900), then to a gate in the deer fence which was still being built when the author researched this route in 2012. Follow a faint path through the newly planted woodland to a gate in the deer fence at the top of the plantation (25min, 280m, 08700 51190). Continue straight up the hillside. A path is beginning to develop up the burn to your right, which will ease progress through the rough pasture, but if you lose it just head straight up the hill to reach a large cairn on the N ridge of **Moruisg**

(921m, 10290 50190). Turn right along the ridge to the summit cairn (1hr 55min, 928m, 10120 50190).

Head SSW, gradually veering to W, down the broad mossy ridge to a saddle (2hr 20min, 720m, 09330 48490) and climb easily to the large cairn on **Sgurr nan Ceannaichean** (2hr 50min, 913m, 08680 48130). ▶

Retrace your steps and descend the ridge until it levels off (855m, 08770 48380). Here you should be able to pick up a small path which leads down the N ridge. On the descent of the ridge it's best to head left of any crags before veering right to reach the Alltan na Feola burn (at about 3hr 35min, 345m, 08800 49880) just above a deer fence. You need to cross the burn above a gorge before climbing to the small, sometimes boggy path and turning left along it. Pass through the gate in the deer fence and follow the path through the newly planted woodland to the deer fence at the bottom of the forest (4hr 10min, 170m, 07900 51180). Continue down the path until it fades away as you reach the railway. Continue right, parallel to the railway, to reach the bridge. Turn left under the railway, cross the river and climb back to the parking area (4hr 35min).

The high point (913m, 08730 48050) on the ridge 100m SSE from here was measured in the 2009 survey to be 0.91m higher.

Walker descending Sgurr nan Ceannaichean

ROUTE 53

Beinn Tharsuinn TRANSVERSE MOUNTAIN *and*
Sgurr na Feartaig PEAK OF THE SEA-PINK (THRIFT)

Start	Craig (NH 03980 49240)
Distance	21km (13 miles)
Total ascent	1380m (4600ft)
Difficulty	There is little difficulty in good conditions but navigation could be a problem in mist.
Time	6hr 50min
Summits	Beinn Tharsuinn (863m, 2807ft), Sgurr na Feartaig (862m, 2830ft)
Maps	OS Landranger 25
Access	Head NE from Lochcarron up the A896 and A890 and park in Achnashellach Forest car park on the N side of the A890 at Craig.
Note	If you prefer to climb these Corbetts separately the suggestion would be to climb and descend Beinn Tharsuinn by the recommended ascent route and to climb Sgurr na Feartaig by the suggested descent route and either return by this route or head W along the Sgurr na Feartaig ridge before descending down the stalker's path to the Achnashellach Forest. It would be possible to save some time by cycling the first 4km of the route.

Beinn Tharsuinn is known as 'transverse mountain' because it is the peak between the Munros Sgurr a' Chaorachain and Bidean a' Choire Sheasgaich. The best way to climb Beinn Tharsuinn would be as part of a backpacking trip to climb the many Munros that surround Loch Monar. The Corbetts An Sidhean and Beinn Dronaig and the Grahams An Cruachan and Beinn na Muice could be included in this trip.

The Dingwall and Skye Railway was authorised in 1865 to provide a route to from Inverness to Skye and the Hebrides. The line, which runs down Glen Carron, was opened to Stromeferry in August 1870 with boats providing onward connection to Skye and the Outer Hebrides until the line was extended to Kyle of Lochalsh in 1897. The line never gained much traffic, with the shorter route along the West Highland Railway from Glasgow to Mallaig taking most of the freight traffic. It avoided the Beeching Axe due to 'social necessity', but has often been threatened with closure since.

Return to the A890, cross the road and take the track, signed to Strathconon via Glenuaig. Cross the **railway** and follow the track which veers left. Ignore a track off to the right and fork left after crossing the River Carron. Fork left twice more further up **Glen Chonais** before passing under the steep face of Sgurr nan Ceannaichean. When the track starts climbing again, just after a left-hand bend, a cairn marks a path off to the right (1hr 15min, 275m, 07410 46820).

See map in Route 52.

Sgurr Choinnich from Beinn Tharsuinn

Fork right along the path to the **Allt a' Chonais**. You should be able to cross dry-shod when the water level is low and there is a wire to safeguard the crossing when the river is in spate (285m, 07650 46560). Follow the path up to **Bealach Bhearnais** (2hr 20min, 595m, 06020 44880), the saddle between Beinn Tharsuinn and Sgurr na Feartaig. Do not climb Beinn Tharsuinn directly from here as you need to avoid the big crags on the N face of the ridge, but follow the path which continues diagonally left to reach the saddle (2hr 30min, 640m, 06028 44550) between Beinn Tharsuinn and Sgurr Choinnich. Climb easily up the grass slopes, avoiding a few small crags, and pass over a couple of minor tops before reaching the N top of **Beinn Tharsuinn** (3hr 5min, 817m, 05350 43870). Head SSE to a saddle (785m) and climb the ridge ahead, avoiding some small crags, to reach the small cairn on the summit (3hr 20min, 863m, 05520 43350).

Return to Bealach Bhearnais by the same route, taking care not to drift too far left to the crags on the N face of the ridge. In good visibility you can save a little effort by contouring round the tops on the ridge. The direct route to the summit of **Sgurr na Feartaig** has a lot of boulderfield so instead head roughly N onto the steep SE ridge, gradually veering left to the large cairn on the summit (4hr 35min, 862m, 05510 45380) which is probably just the highest point on the summit plateau.

Head roughly N to pick up the remains of the stalker's path which is marked on the OS maps to the W of Loch Sgurr na Feartaig (4hr 50min, 765m, 05500 45930). This path is no longer visible on the ground but follow its course NNE to the ridge ahead where there is a cairn (5hr, 800m, 05720 46320) marking the point where the stalker's path becomes clear. Follow the path easily all the way down to the Allt a' Chonais just downstream from a bridge (5hr 50min, 240m, 07020 48120). The bridge was in a poor state of repair in 2012 and, unless it is repaired, it may be safer to ford the burn unless it is in flood. Climb up to the track in Glen Chonais and turn left back to **Craig** (6hr 50min).

ROUTE 54

Fuar Tholl COLD HOLE

Start	Achnashellach (NH 00530 48344)
Distance	14km (9 miles)
Total ascent	980m (3200ft)
Difficulty	Fuar Tholl has big crags on the W, N and E-facing slopes and could be dangerous for the inexperienced in bad weather. If you can keep to the suggested route there is little difficulty, except for a short section of steep rocky slope on the ascent of the W ridge.
Time	4hr 5min
Summits	Fuar Tholl (907m, 2975ft)
Maps	OS Landranger 25
Access	Head NE from Lochcarron up the A896 and A890 and park in a layby at Achnashellach, by a red telephone box, opposite the access track to the station.

Fuar Tholl is composed of Torridonian sandstone and is covered in the very steep crags typical of this rock form. The N-facing Creag Mainnrichean is one of the finest rock buttresses in Scotland.

Railway enthusiasts will want to take a trip on the **Royal Scotsman**. Offering tours through the Scottish Highlands of two to seven nights, the train carries just 36 passengers in private cabins with dining car and observation cars. Life on board is relaxed and indulgent, with gastronomic dining. Unfortunately the luxury comes at a price – over £1000 per night. **www.royalscotsman.com**

Follow the track signed to Achnashellach Station, turn sharp right by Garden Cottage, cross the **railway** at Achnashellach Station and turn sharp left at a track junction. Continue along the track until a footpath goes off sharp left (15min, 95m, NG 99750 48660). Turn left

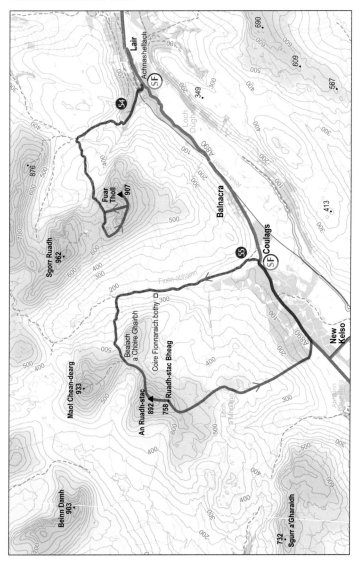

along this good path, which soon turns upstream. Ignore the first turn on the left (at 160m) and continue climbing until a second path on the left, marked by a cairn where the path levels off (40min, 370m, NG 99050 50140). Turn left along the well-maintained stalker's path crossing the River Lair. ▶ Keep going past the dramatic crags on the N face of Fuar Tholl until you reach the high point on the path, marked by a cairn (1hr 40min, 690m, NG 96630 49370). Head roughly SSE past some lochans and up a boulderfield on the W ridge of Fuar Tholl. Skirt right round the crags and pick up a small path that is starting to develop up the steep rocky ridge. The top of the steep section is marked by a cairn (825m, NG 96820 48920). The descent of this ridge would be difficult unless you found this cairn and the easiest route down the steep slope. Continue easily over a minor top (890m), down to a saddle and up to the W summit of **Fuar Tholl** on top of

This could be difficult if the river is in spate, but can be done without getting your feet wet when the water level is low.

Mainnrichean Buttress, Fuar Tholl

the Mainnrichean Buttress (2hr 10min, 895m, NG 97160 48860). Descend to a saddle with a cairn marking the top of the descent route (850m, NG 97350 48730) and climb easily to the summit where you will find the remains of a trig point and a shelter wall (2hr 20min, 907m, NG 97530 48920).

Retrace your steps to the saddle and turn right at the cairn. A path has developed, which makes the descent down the scree slope easy. At the bottom of the scree follow the path down steep grass slopes to regain the stalker's path (at about 2hr 45min, 620m, NG 97140 49370). Turn right and follow the ascent route back to the parking (4hr 5min).

ROUTE 55

An Ruadh-stac STEEP RED HILL

Start	Coulags (NG 95660 45060)
Distance	16km (10 miles)
Total ascent	980m (3200ft)
Difficulty	An Ruadh-stac is not for the inexperienced in poor weather. The ascent is up an intimidating looking ridge, covered with bare quartzite slabs. It is actually much easier than it looks and is barely more than a walk. Higher up broken crags, boulderfields and scree-covered paths aren't difficult, but they are uncomfortable. The suggested descent is initially down boulderfield, after which the going is fairly easy, but navigation would be testing in mist.
Time	5hr 15min
Summits	An Ruadh-stac (892m, 2919ft)
Maps	OS Landranger 25
Access	Head NE from Lochcarron up the A896 and A890 and park in an old quarry just W of the bridge over the Fionn-abhainn at Coulags.
Note	A majority of walkers probably descend by the ascent route. It would be possible to climb the Munro Maol Chean-dearg from the Bealach a' Choire Ghairbh before returning to the pass to climb An Ruadh-stac.

The name An Ruadh-stac is rather misleading. It is certainly a steep mountain but it is incomprehensible how the grey (or white when the sun shines) quartzite of which it is composed could be described as red. Possibly there was a misunderstanding between the surveyor and the local shepherd when the OS surveyor first named the peak. There are certainly many 'red' Torridonian sandstone peaks nearby. All the quartzite mountains in the NW are very rough and An Ruadh-stac is no exception.

When **Strome Castle** was built in about 1400 it was strategically important, guarding the N side of the Strome Narrows near the mouth of Loch Carron. In 1539 the castle was granted by James V to the MacDonalds of Glengarry. For the next 63 years the MacDonalds intermittently fought with their neighbours, the MacKenzies of Kintail, to keep possession of it. In 1602 the castle was besieged by Kenneth Mackenzie, Lord of Kintail. He was on the point of giving up when some MacDonald women who had drawn water from the castle's well accidentally deposited it in the barrel containing the stocks of gunpowder rather than in the water barrel. A Mackenzie prisoner in the castle overheard the argument that followed and in the confusion escaped to inform Kenneth Mackenzie that the castle was now effectively defenceless. The Macdonald garrison negotiated their surrender and safe passage and, after they had departed, the MacKenzies blew up the castle, leaving it very much in the ruined state you see today.

Cross the bridge over the Fionn-abhainn and turn left up the track signed 'Torridon by the Bealach Ban'. At a cattle grid, fork left along a path which detours round the house before joining a good stalker's path. Follow this to a bridge over the Fionn-abhainn (35min, 160m, 95110 47160), past a couple of memorial plaques and the **Coire Fionnaraich Bothy** (50min, 185m, 95000 47960) to a path junction marked by a cairn (1hr 5min, 205m, 94830

See map in Route 54.

217

Don't panic, it may look intimidating but it is much easier than it looks.

49000). Fork left up a good path which takes you easily up to the **Bealach a' Choire Ghairbh** (1hr 50min, 595m, 93120 48780). It is here that you will get your first view of the dramatic E face of An Ruadh-stac. ◀

Contour left to a small saddle (590m, 93180 48590) and turn right along the rocky ridge that separates two lochans and descend to a saddle at the foot of the E ridge of **An Ruadh-stac** (2hr 5min, 575m, 92900 48340). Climb up the centre of the ridge, which is covered with bare slabs of quartzite. This is little more than a walk, with minimal use of your hands. Once you are above the slabs the slopes become much more broken with small outcrops, boulderfields and small paths covered in scree. The ridge takes you to the summit marked by a large cairn (2hr 50min, 892m, 92150 48050).

You could descend by the ascent route, but it is more interesting to descend by the S ridge. Descend boulder-field down the S ridge, veering right to the summit of the rocky knoll **Ruadh-stac Bheag** (3hr 10min, 758m, 92130 47530). You will want to head a little W from here to avoid some small crags, before veering S and getting onto easier terrain (at about 670m). Now head just E of S, aiming for the large lochan, **Loch a' Mhuillin**, which you can see to the S. You will be passing through a curious landscape on the boundary between quartzite rock and Torridonian sandstone, with a confusing jumble of small sandstone and quartzite ridges with many small lochans

An Ruadh-stac from Loch a' Mhuilinn

or ponds. Reach the NE end of the loch (3hr 45min, 490m, 92380 46140).

From here you want to head roughly S, picking the easiest line, until you can see the forest bordering the A890. Aim for the corner of the forest (4hr 30min, 140m, 93100 43950) and follow the deer fence down to a gate. Go through the gate and head diagonally left across the field to the gate at the bottom left corner of the field (4hr 45min, 15m, 93670 43640). Go through the gate and turn left along the road back to the car park (5hr 15min).

ROUTE 56

Sgurr a' Chaorachain PEAK OF THE LITTLE BERRY FIELD
and Beinn Bhan WHITE MOUNTAIN

Start	Bealach na Ba (NG 77430 42580)
Distance	26km (16 miles)
Total ascent	1420m (4700ft)
Difficulty	The suggested ascent route is easy but there is some rough terrain to traverse between Beinn Bhan and Sgurr a' Chaorachain.
Time	7hr 25min (5hr 45min excluding road section)
Summits	Beinn Bhan (896m, 2938ft), Sgurr a' Chaorachain (792m, 2600ft)
Maps	OS Landranger 24
Access	Follow the A896 W from Lochcarron and turn left at Tornapress, up the minor road signed to Applecross. This road climbs steeply to the Bealach na Ba pass. There is a large car park just over the top of the pass.
Note	This route has been planned for two vehicles, one preferably a bicycle, as it starts with a 6-mile descent from the Bealach na Ba. This descent from 2000ft to sea level is Britain's longest road descent and would be an experience for a cyclist. If you want to climb these two Corbetts separately the suggestion is to climb Sgurr a' Chaorachain from the pass (quick, but not very interesting) and to climb Beinn Bhan from the River Kishorn as described below, but to descend easily down the SE ridge.

Beinn Bhan and Sgurr a' Chaorachain have some of the most dramatic corries and rock buttresses in Britain, being composed of the Torridonian sandstone which provides such magnificent scenery throughout NW Scotland. The Applecross hills would be be worth exploring more. The best routes involve scrambling or rock-climbing and the Cicerone guide *Scotland's Mountain Ridges* by Dan Bailey includes the Cioch Nose on Sgurr a' Chaorachain and A' Chioch Ridge on Beinn Bhan.

Bealach na Ba (Pass of the Cattle) is Britain's biggest road climb, rising 626m (2053ft) from sea level in just 10km (6 miles). It was used as a drover's road before a 'Parliamentary' road was built over the pass in 1822. The present twisting single-track road with very tight hairpin bends and gradients that approach 20% was built in the 1950s.

Head back down the Bealach na Ba road, preferably on a bicycle, to the **River Kishorn** at the foot of the pass (on foot 1hr 40min, 10m, NG 83400 42310). Follow a good path to the left of the river to a bridge over a small burn (2hr 15min, 140m, 83230 44480). Fork left up a faint path along the left bank of the burn until this path splits (2hr 30min, 240m, 82700 44420) at a point where there is a small cairn on the other side of the burn. Cross the burn and follow an even fainter path. If you lose it head towards the prominent erratic boulder on the skyline. Turn left when you reach the outlet burn from **Lochan Coire na Poite** (285m, 82490 44750) and follow it to the lochan (2hr 55min, 370m, 81870 45150). ◄ Head round the right-hand side of the lochan and head WNW into the right-hand corrie, Coir' an Fhamair. Continue up the corrie to the foot of the headwall (3hr 35min, 565m, 80360 45770) and head up the steep grassy slope which veers slightly right of the centreline. This slope isn't as steep as it looks and would be feasible for descent; however, other lines of descent into the corrie would be dangerous. On reaching the broad ridge (4hr 5min, 800m, 79960 45940) turn left and follow the edge of the cliffs to the summit of

This lochan has sandy beaches, as have most lochans in these Torridonian sandstone mountains.

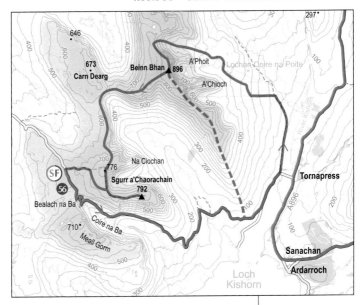

Beinn Bhan, which is marked by a trig point with a surrounding wall (4hr 30min, 896m, 80370 45030).

Head W, veering WSW then W again, down a broad ridge which gradually narrows and becomes rockier as corries bite into it from left and right. Care is needed in the final descent to a saddle (5hr 5min, 595m, 78680 44610). A few cairns mark the start of a path on the left which follows a broad ledge before regaining the ridge (5hr 15min, 580m, 78430 44240). Now head S along a broad ridge with plenty of bare rock heading towards the communications mast. Reach a saddle with a small lochan (5hr 40min, 615m, 78540 43080) and take a rising traverse left, to avoid the crags, before heading easily up to the top with the communications mast (6hr 5min, 776m, 78590 42400). ▸

This is where you get the first magnificent view towards Skye.

Continue S to a top with a cairn marking the start of the Sgurr a' Chaorachain ridge (6hr 15min, 78700 41790). Head W to a rocky top (755m, 79180 41680),

221

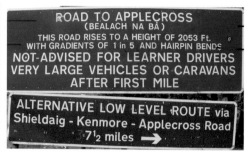

A' Phoit buttress on Beinn Bhan

which can either be climbed or bypassed on its left. The short sharp descent from this top starts on the left, after which it is an easy climb to the sprawling cairn on the summit of **Sgurr a' Chaorachain** (6hr 40min, 792m, 79660 41740). Return by the same route to the start of the ridge (7hr) and head roughly NW to pick up the rough track descending from the communications mast (at about 680m, 78090 42450). Turn left to the road then right to the car park (7hr 25min).

ROUTE 57

Beinn Damh HILL OF THE STAG

Start	Allt Coire Roill (NG 88890 54020)
Distance	11km (7 miles)
Total ascent	1060m (3500ft)
Difficulty	Fairly easy, but there are quartzite boulderfields on the summit plateau. Care will be needed in descent in mist as the big crags would make descent dangerous if you missed the easy route.
Time	4hr 30min
Summits	Spidean Coir an Laoigh, Beinn Damh (903m, 2957ft)
Maps	OS Landranger 24 and 25
Access	The Allt Coire Roill crosses the A896 immediately S of the Loch Torridon Hotel. There are small laybys either side of the bridge over the Allt Coire Roill. If you are starting at Loch Torridon Hotel or Loch Torridon Inn there is a path which brings you out onto the A896 where the path heads S towards Beinn Damh.
Note	It is worth climbing Sgurr na Bana Mhoraire, the peak at the NW end of the Beinn Damh ridge, either before or after climbing Spidean Coir an Laoigh, the main summit. It would be possible to scramble up the NE ridge, Stuc Toll nam Biast, of Beinn Damh, but the author has not climbed that route and cannot confirm the difficulty.

Beinn Daimh is the name of a ridge with many tops to the S of Upper Loch Torridon. The highest top, Spidean Coir an Laoigh, at the SE end of the ridge is often referred to as Beinn Damh, although this name actually refers to the whole ridge rather than the highest summit. This is a fine mountain, but it is the views across to Torridonian giants Liathach, Beinn Eighe and Ben Alligin, NW down Loch Torridon and E to further Torridonian sandstone peaks that make this a magnificent walk.

Shieldaig was established in 1800, with the Admiralty offering grants to support housing and boat-building. Its purported aim was to attract families to take up fishing for a living but the main purpose was to build up a stock of trained seamen who could be called upon by the Royal Navy during the Napoleonic Wars. Fortunately, Napoleon was defeated at Waterloo and the men of Shieldaig were never asked to fight.

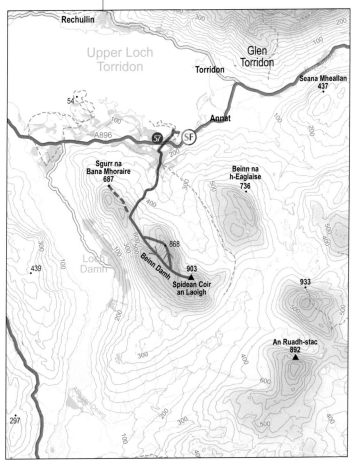

Walkers on Beinn Damh

Head about 100m W along the road from the bridge and then turn left up a good path through rhododendron and conifer forest. At the top of the forest (25min, 185m, 88400 53290), fork right along a good path which eventually deteriorates but is easily followed to a couple of cairns on the Toll Ban saddle (1hr 20min, 585m, 87570 51810). Turn left along a faint cairned path which soon edges to the right of the ridge and bypasses Top 868 of **Beinn Damh** to return to the ridge at the next top (2hr 10min, 835m, 88790 50450). Head SW down a narrowing ridge to a saddle (790m) and then easily up to **Spidean Coir an Laoigh** (2hr 25min, 903m, 89270 50180). ▸

The author's measurements suggest Beinn Damh may not be as high as suggested by the OS maps.

Return down the ridge and, for better views, take the route NNW over **Top 868** (3hr, 868m 88620 51070). Head roughly W, taking care as you descend the quartzite boulderfield, veering NW down the ridge back to the Toll Ban saddle (3hr 35min) and turn right down the path back to the parking (4hr 30min).

ROUTE 58

Beinn Dearg RED HILL

Start	Coire Mhic Nobuil car park (NG 86930 57650)
Distance	17km (11 miles)
Total ascent	1100m (3600ft)
Difficulty	Beinn Dearg is one of the most difficult Corbetts and is not really recommended for inexperienced walkers, or for experienced walkers in bad weather. It is protected by steep slopes with a multitude of crags; there are no safe escape routes once the ridge has been reached and descent routes aren't straightforward. There is some relatively easy but exposed scrambling and you need to be able to select routes up and down steep crag-covered slopes.
Time	5hr 50min
Summits	Stuc Loch na Cabhaig (882m), Beinn Dearg (914m, 2995ft), Carn na Feola (761m)
Maps	OS Landranger 19, 24 and 25
Access	Follow the minor road along the N shore of Upper Loch Torridon and park at the car park where the road crosses the Abhainn Coire Mhic Nobuil.
Note	It would be slightly easier to descend by the ascent route, but that would miss much of the splendour of the route.

Beinn Dearg is one of the finest Corbetts in its own right, with the added advantage of being in one of the most spectacular locations in Scotland with magnificent close views of Munros Beinn Alligin, Liathach and Beinn Eighe, and the Corbetts Baosbheinn, Beinn an Eoin and Meall a' Ghiuthais.

The **National Trust for Scotland** owns 16,000 acres (which includes Beinn Alligin, Liathach, Beinn Eighe and Beinn Dearg) of what is arguably the most magnificent mountain landscape anywhere on the Scottish mainland. The Torridon Countryside Centre, which stands in the shadow of Liathach at the foot of Glen Torridon, is well worth visiting, as is the nearby Deer Museum.

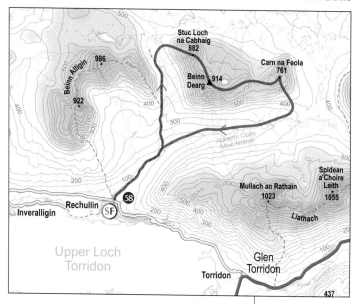

Cross the bridge from the car park and head up the 'tourist' path along the right bank of the **Abhainn Coire Mhic Nobuil**. Cross the bridge (25min, 135m, 88160 58880) and shortly afterwards, at a cairn, fork left up the right bank of the Allt a' Bhealaich. Cross another bridge (40min, 254m, 88220 59660) and continue up the path until a path junction marked by a cairn (45min, 340m, 88250 60130). Fork right, ignoring the left-hand path, which would take you up Beinn Alligin, and follow a path which soon deteriorates but does have a few cairns marking its line. Keep going as the path continues to fade away and at some point, possibly at a large lichen coloured boulder (1hr 10min, 420m. 88010 61380), head diagonally right towards the foot of the W ridge of Stuc Loch na Cabhaig. Study the ridge and pick a route up it. There is a bit of a path going straight up the centre of the ridge, but you may prefer the grassier option to the left of the main crags. Try heading up from a point to the left of

Torridonian sandstone boulders on Beinn Dearg

The latest height measurement of Beinn Dearg of 913.7m ± 0.3m confirms it as a Corbett rather than a Munro.

This is a place where the leader of a party should be carrying a rope and may need to use it to give confidence to a nervous member of the group.

the crags (500m, 88520 61950) to reach a flat shoulder on the ridge (1hr 55min, 800m, 88865 61705). Continue up the ridge, either scrambling up the crags or bypassing them on the right, to reach **Stuc Loch na Cabhaig** (2hr 10min, 882m, 89130 61590).

Descend to a broad saddle (805m, 89180 61200) and climb the ridge to **Beinn Dearg**; again any difficulties can be bypassed on their right, to reach the cairn on the summit (2hr 35min, 914m, 89530 60800). ◄

Drop down SW to a saddle (825m 89790 60660) just before a 'tower' with cliffs dropping near vertically down to Loch a' Choire Mhoir. Follow the small path which contours to the right of the top of the tower. This brings you out above three near vertical rocksteps. These could be intimidating for the inexperienced to down-climb, but climbing down is certainly safer than attempting to skirt round the crags on exposed sloping grass ledges to the right as suggested by at least one other guidebook. There are enough good footholds to make the climb down relatively easy. ◄ Once down the rocksteps it is easy going to the next top (3hr 10min, 795m, 90520 60910). Descend easily to a saddle (665m, 90910 60700) and on to the summit of **Carn na Feola** which is tucked away at the N end of the summit plateau (3hr 50min, 761m, 91560 61230).

Descend SSW. The OS map does not show any crags, but the slope is actually covered on crags and you will need to pick a route carefully down the steep slope avoiding the crags. Eventually you should reach the path in Coire Mhic Nobuil just below Loch Grobaig (at about 4hr 30min, 335m, 91820 59920). Turn right down the rough path which eventually becomes the 'tourist' path. Turn left at the cairned path junction (5hr 25min) and back to the car park (5hr 50min).

ROUTE 59

Sgorr nan Lochan Uaine PEAK OF THE LITTLE GREEN LOCH
and Sgurr Dubh BLACK PEAK

Start	Coire Dubh Mor car park (NG 95790 56800)
Distance	15km (9 miles)
Total ascent	1050m (3500ft)
Difficulty	This route is rough and tough with much pathless rough heather and quartzite boulderfield. The ridge between Sgorr nan Lochan Uaine and Sgurr Dubh is complex, with many small lochans and small ridges covered with unmapped crags. Navigation in mist could make the hard going even harder as it would be impossible to spot the easiest route through the terrain. This route should be only attempted in clear conditions. Walkers need to be competent at route-finding, even in good conditions.
Time	6hr
Summits	Sgorr nan Lochan Uaine (871m, 2840ft), Sgurr Dubh (782m, 2566ft)
Maps	OS Landranger 25
Access	The Coire Dubh Mor car park is in Glen Torridon on the N side of the A896 about 4 miles E of Torridon.
Note	It would be impossible to describe an exact followable line for this route and a few of the grid references and timings are estimations. Walkers will be expected to make their own route choices in many sections.

These two Corbetts are less spectacular than some of the surrounding peaks, but they are fine mountains and the absence of paths means they still maintain a sense of wildness which has been lost on some of the more frequented mountains in Torridon.

Coire a' Cheud-Chnoic (valley of one hundred hills) is a classic drumlin field of hummocky terrain formed by glaciation during the final cold phase of the Ice Age about 12,000 years ago. Some glacial deposits, consisting of stony earth and boulders, were shaped and streamlined as the ice flowed over them and others formed at the edge of the ice as it retreated.

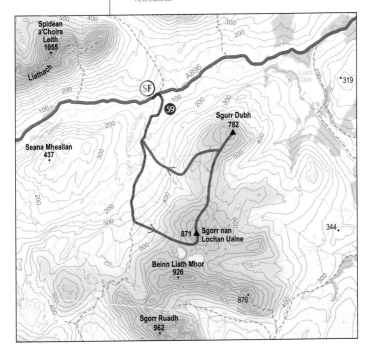

Head E up the **A896**, cross the bridge over the Allt a' Choire Dhuibh Mhoir and, after about 100m, turn right on a good path signed 'Coulags by the Bealach Ban'. Pass the Ling Hut, which belongs to the Scottish Mountaineering Club, and continue up **Coire a' Cheud-Chnoic** through the glacial hummocks until a cairn marks where the path starts to deteriorate (360m, 95190 53490). The latest version of the OS 1:50,000 map shows the path continuing S, then doubling back towards Sgorr nan Lochan Uaine. The author tried to follow this route, but found the path does not exist where it is shown turning E. Therefore head roughly E from the cairn, cross two small burns and follow the third burn all the way up the hill. At the head of the burn follow a dry valley to come out just above Lochan Uaine (2hr, 650m, 96450 52850) and climb roughly E to a ridge (695m 96760 52830). The author headed directly up the hill from here, but you might be better to continue E to the next ridge then head up NE, veering NNW, as the climb will be less steep and on easier terrain. Whichever way you go, you arrive at the inadequate wall shelter on the summit of **Sgorr nan Lochan Uaine** (2hr 45min, 871m, 96920 53140).

Descend roughly NNE down the ridge. In good visibility you can select a route which is mainly on grass, but there are quartzite boulderfields and lots of unmapped crags which will make route-finding difficult in mist. Eventually you reach a small lochan (3hr 25min, 570m, 97360 54410) on the complex saddle between Sgorr nan Lochan Uaine and Sgurr Dubh.

The ascent of Sgurr Dubh is even more complicated, with numerous unmapped crags to confuse navigation. Head roughly N and veer NNE. All routes are likely to reach a large lochan (3hr 50min, 625m, 97590 55390) from where you climb steeply NE to another lochan. Now you can find a route through quartzite crags and boulderfields to the summit of **Sgurr Dubh** with another small wall shelter (4hr 15min, 782m, 97900 55780).

There is no straightforward descent route but the suggestion is you return to the large lochan (4hr 30min) and then head generally WSW. If in doubt go a little left of this

Sgorr nan Lochan Uaine from lochan on Sgurr Dubh

line. This takes you down reasonably gently and keeps you clear of the major crags on the NW face of Sgurr Dubh. Once well clear of these crags (at about 470m, 96450 54750) turn straight down the slope. Take care as there are still plenty of unmapped crags to bypass. Reach the bottom of the slope (at about 5hr 20min, 260m, 96100 54950) and then continue roughly NW through the glacial moraine hummocks to reach the main path (at about 5hr 40min, 130m, 95490 55700). Turn right back to the car park (6hr).

ROUTE 60

Ruadh-stac Beag SMALL RED STACK

Start	Beinn Eighe Visitor Centre (NH 02000 62970)
Distance	15km (9 miles)
Total ascent	930m (3000ft)
Difficulty	Once the pony track is left behind the going is rough and pathless. Ruadh-stac Beag is surrounded by crags and the only weakness in the defences is the S ridge. The final climb up steep boulderfield on this ridge needs care, especially in descent. Climbing this mountain in bad weather conditions is not recommended.
Time	4hr 45min
Summits	Ruadh-stac Beag (896m, 2850ft)
Maps	OS Landranger 19
Access	The Beinn Eighe Visitor Centre is on the A832 1km NW of Kinlochewe.
Note	It would be possible to combine Ruadh-stac Beag with Meall a' Ghiuthais by climbing the SE ridge of Meall a' Ghiuthais after climbing Ruadh-stac Beag.

Ruadh-stac Beag is an outlier on the N ridge of Spidean Coire nan Clach, on the main Beinn Eighe ridge, and it is the best viewpoint for the crags on the N face of Beinn Eighe. It is well protected by big crags and long scree slopes consisting mainly of white quartzite rocks, so it is unclear how it gets the name Ruadh-stac Beag.

From the early 1600s English ironmasters set up **furnaces** at Letterewe on the NE shore of Loch Maree and at the E end of the loch. Iron ore was imported by sea from England because it was far easier to transport the ore than the vast amounts of charcoal needed to process it. The industry flourished for over 50 years, but it ceased after it had consumed all the readily available woodland in a wide area of Wester Ross. During World War II much of the

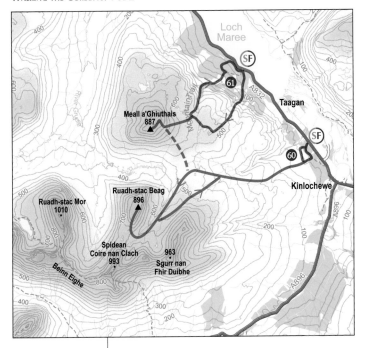

woodland that had recovered since the 1600s was cut down to make ammunition boxes to support the war effort.

Follow the 'pink square' waymarks to the right of the Visitor Centre along the Rhymy Trail, which leads to the Ridge Trail. Turn left along the Ridge Trail to reach a junction with the Pony Track (35m, NH 02020 62650), an old stalker's path. Turn right across the bridge up the Pony Track, sharing the path with the Ridge Trail, and continue straight on when the Ridge Trail goes off to the right. Fork right at two further junctions, where paths head left towards Beinn Eighe, and continue until you reach a small pond (1hr 20min, 490m, NG 98490 62820) as you approach the high point of the track. Leave the path here and head S, veering SW, down moraine ridges to reach the Allt Toll a' Ghiubhais burn (at about 1hr 35min, 450m NG 98180 61780). Continue up the left bank of the burn, taking advantage of a faint path which is starting to develop up this 'Alpine' valley. Keep to the right-hand tributary as the burn branches and continue until you are well clear of the screes on the E slopes of Ruadh-stac Beag. Cross the burn (at about 650m, NG 97290 60610) and climb onto the ridge on your right. Then turn right (N) to the foot of the boulderfields on the S ridge of **Ruadh-stac Beag** (at about 720m, NG 97170 60730). Climb the boulderfield and pass the crags higher up the ridge on their left to arrive at a fairly flat summit plateau with quartzite outcrops and boulderfields. The summit cairn is at the far end of the plateau (2hr 40min, 896m, NG 97280 61330).

In mist you would need to be very careful to find the top of the descent as it would be dangerous to attempt a descent except on the S ridge. Return to the Allt Toll a' Ghiubhais by the ascent route. The easiest option is to

Ruadh-stac Beag

descend this burn and just follow the ascent route, but many walkers will be tempted to take a shortcut. You could take advantage of an intermittent path which contours above the burn, then head roughly NE over boulderfield to cross the N ridge of Sgurr nan Fhir Duibhe and then to descend roughly NW down short heather and stony ground to reach the Pony Track (at roughly 3hr 55min, 395m, NG 99450 62310). Turn right and follow the Pony Track down to the Ridge Trail (4hr 35min, 70m NH 01820 62490). For variety, turn left and follow the Ridge Trail back to the Visitor Centre (4hr 45min).

ROUTE 61

Meall a' Ghiuthais HILL OF THE PINE TREE

Start	Beinn Eighe National Nature Reserve (Glas Leitire) car park (NH 00170 65000)
Distance	9km (6 miles)
Total ascent	930m (3000ft)
Difficulty	Fairly easy, although there is some boulderfield to cross on the summit and care would be needed in descent in mist.
Time	3hr 45min
Summits	Meall a' Ghiuthais (887m, 2882ft)
Maps	OS Landranger 19
Access	Beinn Eighe NNR (Glas Leitire) car park is the first car park along the S shore of Loch Maree on the A832 NW of Kinlochewe.
Note	After climbing Ruadh-stac Beag it would be possible to climb the SE ridge of Meall a' Ghiuthais.

Meall a' Ghiuthais is a Torridonian Sandstone peak sitting on a base of Cambrian quartzite rock. The recommended ascent through the Beinn Eighe National Nature Reserve is of great interest to the geologist and there are well-written free leaflets available in the car park giving notes on the geology as well as the plants and animals that you will see as you climb the Mountain Trail.

Set up in 1951 **Beinn Eighe National Nature Reserve** was Britain's first National Nature Reserve. This beautiful reserve stretches from the shores of Loch Maree, up through ancient pinewoods with some birch, juniper and holly, to the grey quartzite screes of Beinn Eighe. The reserve is a stronghold of the pine marten, and golden eagle breed here as do Scottish crossbill, redpoll, siskin and golden crest. There is a visitor centre, picnic sites and a basic campsite on the reserve.

Meall a' Ghiuthais

From the car park follow the signs for the **Mountain Trail** under the road bridge and up the left bank of the Allt na h-Airighe burn. This well-engineered path climbs easily through the woodland before climbing steeply through a landscape dominated by quartzite crags and outcrops. ▶ Just after the '460m' cairn (actually at about 475m) there are very good examples of pipe rock (called 'trumpet rock' in the Nature Reserve leaflet). Continue to the Conservation Cairn on the summit of the quartzite ridge (1hr 15min, 560m, NG 99320 63310). Continue

See map in Route 60.

Don't set your altimeter by the cairn at '305m' – according to the author's GPS this is actually at 268m. The '305m' cairn on the descent was measured at 336m!

237

NW along the Mountain Trail past Lochan Allt an Daraich to a cairn marking the small Lunar Loch (1hr 30min, 540m, NG 98870 63730).

Continue to the next cairn then head WSW up the quartzite ridge above the loch. You soon reach a good wall shelter where you will notice you are right on the fault line, with quartzite on your left and Torridonian sandstone on your right. Continue WSW gradually veering W and NW once you are clear of the big crags on the NE face of Meall a' Ghiuthais. The climb is mainly up grass, short heather and moss, but there are boulderfields near the top. ◀ You reach the NE summit of Meall a' Ghiuthais (865m, NG 97840 63730) and head roughly 400m SW to the main summit on **Meall a' Ghiuthais** (2hr 15min, 887m, NG 97610 63430). Return to Lunar Loch (2hr 50min) taking care not to get mixed up in the big crags on the E and NE face of Meall a' Ghiuthais. Turn left and follow the Mountain Trail until you eventually meet the Woodland Trail. Turn left along the Woodland Trail, which soon swings E and takes you back to the car park (3hr 45min).

The boulderfields are composed of both sandstone and quartzite – the peak was covered in ice during the last ice-age and the quartzite boulders were deposited when the ice melted.

ROUTE 62

Beinn an Eoin HILL OF THE BIRD

Start	Am Feur-Loch (NG 85650 72060)
Distance	21km (13 miles)
Total ascent	1060m (3500ft)
Difficulty	The ascent is relatively easy. The suggested descent down the steep craggy S ridge of Beinn an Eoin requires route-finding skills and occasional use of the hands. This descent is only recommended for experienced mountaineers – the less experienced should descend by the ascent route.
Time	6hr 10min
Summits	Beinn an Eoin (855m, 2805ft)
Maps	OS Landranger 19
Access	There is parking behind a green shed (previously known as the 'Red Shed') by the small Am Feur-Loch just before Loch Bad an Sgalaig on the A832 between Loch Maree and Loch Gairloch.
Note	Inexperienced walkers should descend by the ascent route. See Route 63 for combining Baosbheinn and Beinn an Eoin.

Beinn an Eoin is another fine Torridonian sandstone mountain, on the opposite side of Loch na h-Oidhche to Baosbheinn. Views towards Beinn Eighe, Beinn Dearg, Beinn Alligin and Baosbheinn are particularly spectacular.

On the approach to Beinn an Eoin you pass the **Grouse Stone**. This Torridonian sandstone boulder is an erratic deposited in the glen when the ice retreated after the last ice age. In the 19th century shooting parties would stay up on the hill for a few days and each day the ghillie would leave the 'bag' of grouse on top of the Grouse Stone to be collected by another ghillie who would travel up from Gairloch and take them back to the game larder for use in the estate kitchens.

Enter the newly planted Bad na Sgalaig Native Pinewood by the bridge opposite the car park at the W end of Am Feur-Loch and follow the rough track until the deer fence at the top of the pinewood (1hr, 280m, 88160 68830). Continue up the track, passing to the right of a rocky knoll and crossing the **Abhainn Loch na h-Oidhche** burn. As you climb away from the burn there is a cairn beside the track and this is as good a place as any to leave the track (1hr 30min, 370m, 88590 67410). Head roughly

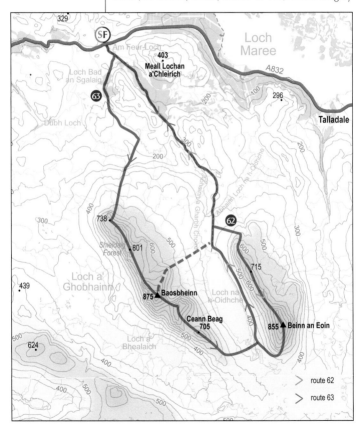

Natural 'modern art' on the N ridge of Beinn an Eoin

ESE towards a gully to the left of the main band of crags on the N ridge of **Beinn an Eoin**. On reaching the gully just below the crags (495m, 89210 67040) skirt round to the left and then climb easily up the grassy N ridge to the first top (2hr 20min, 680m, 89350 66530). Continue along the broad, fairly flat, ridge, passing over a number of minor tops, until the ridge narrows a little at the foot of the final climb. Climb steeply then continue along a narrow ridge to a wall sheltering the base of a trig point. The summit is marked by a tiny cairn a few metres further along the ridge (3hr 5min, 855m, 90520 64620).

The suggested descent is S down a gradually steepening ridge with horizontal bands of Torridonian sandstone crags that make route-finding difficult. Some downclimbing of the crags is required. If in doubt it is probably safer to veer left than right when avoiding obstacles. You should eventually reach Gorm-Loch na Beinne at the foot of the slope (at about 3hr 45min, 410m, 90350 63600). Contour right round the foot of the slope, hopefully picking up the path that leads to the Poca Buidhe Bothy (4hr, 425m, 89890 64290) at the SE end of Loch na h-Oidhche. ▶

Note that this bothy is no longer available for public use.

Continue 10km down the track back to the car park (6hr 10min).

ROUTE 63

Baosbheinn WIZARD'S HILL

Start	Am Feur-Loch (NG 85650 72060)
Distance	22km (14 miles)
Total ascent	1290m (4300ft)
Difficulty	There are no great difficulties, but there is much rough, possibly boggy, heather moorland to cross on the approach to Baosbheinn and some steep but easy slopes to ascend and descend. This would be a demanding route in poor weather.
Time	7hr
Summits	Baosbheinn (875m, 2869ft)
Maps	OS Landranger 19
Access	Parking as for Route 62
Note	A strong walker could combine Baosbheinn with Beinn an Eoin by continuing on to Beinn an Eoin after climbing Baosbheinn, but this would make a long day. The shortest way to climb Baosbheinn would be to use the An Reidh-choire (NE) ridge, but that would miss the essence of the mountain.

The traverse of Baosbheinn makes a magnificent expedition on one of the finest ridges in Scotland. Apart from the merits of the Torridonian sandstone mountain, the close views of the N faces of Beinn Alligin, Beinn Dearg, Liathach and Beinn Eighe are awe-inspiring. There are also good views out to Outer Hebrides with its only Corbett, Am Cliseam clearly visible on the horizon.

On this route you will pass some information boards about the history of the area, but you should really visit the **Gairloch Heritage Museum** for a full picture of how local people have lived from the Stone Age to the present day. History is all around you, from the Bronze Age hut circles by the River Sand, the remains of the vitrified fort of An Dùn by Gairloch beach to the Destitution Roads and the magnificent family seat of the Clan Mackenzie in the wooded Flowerdale Glen. Place names speak both of Viking invaders and of the traditional Gaelic culture. **www.gairlochheritagemuseum.org**

Enter the newly planted Bad na Sgalaig Native Pinewood by the bridge opposite the car park at the W end of Am Feur Loch and follow the rough track for about 8min before a small burn crosses the track (115m, 85990 71710). Turn right along a faint, possibly boggy, path, marked ahead, but not at the junction, by posts with yellow markers which lead to **Loch Bad na Sgalaig**. The path continues beside a deer fence along the shore of the loch to the cascading waterfall of **Abhainn a' Gharbh Choire**. Follow the path up the left-hand side of this burn to a bridge, cross and continue up the right-hand side. You may pass the remains of a bridge which has seen better days, but continue until you reach a good bridge in a

See map in Route 62.

NW ridge of Baosbheinn

large flat valley (1hr, 190m, 86650 69480). Don't cross the bridge, but head roughly S across possibly boggy moorland until you reach a deer fence. Turn right along the deer fence until you reach a fence post with some rungs (230m, 86340 68970). Climb the fence and continue along it to the Allt na Cosaig burn. Follow this up steep heather-covered slopes, probably climbing the left bank of the right-hand tributary. When the burn fades away continue up the same line, roughly S, to the foot of the left-hand edge of the Creag an Fhithich buttress (2hr, 525m, 86020 67630). Climb the steep but easy grass slopes to the left of the buttress to reach a narrow ridge at the top (2hr 25min, 695m, 85760 67540). Climb to a minor top (738m, 85740 67410) where the ridge broadens and follow this ridge over another minor top to the NW summit of Baosbheinn (2hr 50min, 801m, 86230 66860).

Continue to the foot of the big buttresses on the NW ridge of Baosbheinn (725m, 86680 65910). There is a small path up the ridge which bypasses the difficulties on the left and leads easily to a saddle. Continue up the ridge and again bypass the crags on their left to reach another saddle and climb easily to the small grassy summit plateau of **Baosbheinn** (3hr 20min, 875m, 87050 65410).

Descend steeply, but with little difficulty, ESE to a saddle (705m, 87400 65190) and up the other side (800m, 87680 65170). Turn S down a ridge which gradually veers ESE to another saddle (625m, 87090 64540) and climb to the final top, **Ceann Beag**, on the ridge (4hr 10min, 705m, 88210 64440). Descend roughly SE down grass slopes, easily avoiding the many crags on the ridge, until you reach a small lochan (505m, 88880 63880). From here head ENE down rough heather to the S end of **Loch na h-Oidhche** (395m, 89600 64100) and climb to the bothy at the SE end of the loch (4hr 50min, 420m, 89890 64290). ◄

Turn left down the rough track which takes you about 10km back to the car park (7hr).

Note that this bothy is no longer open to the public but is solely for the use of the Gairloch Estate.

ROUTE 64

Beinn Airigh Charr ROUGH SHIELING HILL

Start	Poolewe (NG 85820 80800)
Distance	25km (15 miles)
Total ascent	1160m (3800ft)
Difficulty	This is one of the easiest Corbetts in Section 7, but care would be needed with navigation in mist.
Time	6hr 20min
Summits	Beinn Airigh Charr (791m, 2593ft)
Maps	OS Landranger 19
Access	From Gairloch head NE along the A832 to Poolewe and turn right (SE) along the minor road down the N bank of the River Ewe and immediately park in the car park on the left. It is no longer permitted to drive down the private road to Inveran.
Note	It is possible to cycle the first 8km of this route.

Beinn Airigh Charr is the prominent mountain seen from Poolewe to the N of Loch Maree. Although it is a rocky mountain, the Lewisian Gneiss does not provide such spectacular crags as the many Torridian sandstone peaks in this area.

The National Trust for Scotland owns the world-famous **Inverewe Garden and Estate** in Poolewe. This 50-acre garden, created in 1862, is an oasis of exotic plants, bursting with vibrant colour, thanks to the warm currents of the Gulf Stream that flows along the W Scottish coastline. The Trust also manages over 2,000 acres for conservation, including the Pinewood Trail, Inverewe Trail and Kernsary Path. At the edge of Loch Ewe is a hide where seals, otters, divers and a rich variety of wildlife can be seen. **www.nts.org.uk/Property/Inverewe-Garden-Estate**

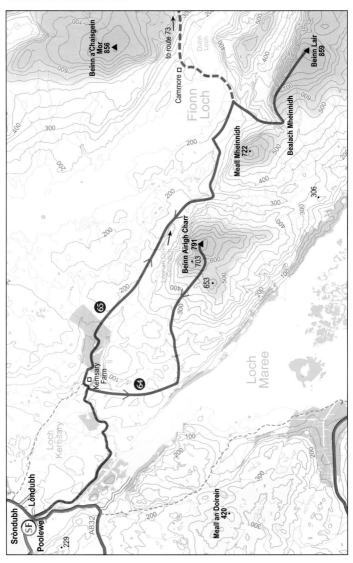

Head down the tarmac road past the church and down the tarmac estate road. After 2.5km fork left along a good track signed to Kernsary Estate. At Kernsary Farm (24m, 89250 79260) turn right along the right-hand side of the burn. This track is less good but is still just about good enough to ride on a road bike. The track climbs to about 100m and, about 600m after the high point, a small cairn (1hr 40min, 100m, 89380 76880) marks a faint path just below an old shieling.

Burn on Beinn Airigh Charr

Turn left along this path, which becomes a good stalker's path after the shieling. Follow this path to a fork marked by a small cairn (2hr 10min, 200m, 91090 77070). Fork right and follow the path until it ends (or fades away) in a corrie (at about 3hr, 575m, 92100 76380). Keep going, picking up a path to the left of the burn which leads to a small cairn on the saddle between Spidean nan Clach (703m) and Meall Chnaimhean (653m). Keep straight on until clear of the crags on your left then turn roughly ENE up easy slopes to the saddle between Spidean nan Clach and Beinn Airigh Charr (685m, 92730 76230). Climb roughly E up the steep ridge on your right to the summit cairn on **Beinn Airigh Charr** (3hr 30min, 791m, 93030 76170).

Return by the same route to the track (4hr 40min) and the car park (6hr 20min).

ROUTE 65

Beinn Lair HILL OF THE MARE

Start	Poolewe (NG 85820 80800)
Distance	38km (24 miles)
Total ascent	1560m (5100ft)
Difficulty	This would be one of the easiest mountains in this guide if it weren't for the fact the summit is 19km from the road access. Care would be needed with navigation in mist on the big summit plateau.
Time	9hr 35min
Summits	Beinn Lair (859m, 2817ft)
Maps	OS Landranger 19
Access	Parking as for Route 64
Note	The first 6km could be cycled on a road bike. Experienced cyclists on a mountain bike could cycle a lot further than this but the occasional cyclist might prefer to walk once the track gets rough and muddy. It would make sense to include Beinn Lair on a backpacking trip which could also include Beinn Airigh Charr, Meall Mheinnidh, Slioch and possibly the mountains to the N of Lochan Fada and Fionn Loch.

Beinn Lair looks uninteresting when viewed across Loch Maree, but when viewed from the N you will see one of the biggest rock walls in Scotland. The glen occupied by Fionn Loch is one of the most spectacular in Scotland and would be a massive tourist attraction if it weren't so remote. The suggested route is much more interesting than the equally long alternative from Kinlochewe, which features the 'boring' S slopes rather than the dramatic N slopes.

Following the sinking of HMS Royal Oak at Scapa Flow in 1939, **Loch Ewe** became an important safe haven for naval warships supporting the Arctic convoys. Access to Wester Ross was restricted by road barriers, one of which was located close to the present site of the Gairloch Heritage Museum.

When the barrier disappeared under mysterious circumstances, an incomer to the area was suspected of being a Nazi sympathizer, but the police were unable to implicate him in the crime. A sawn-off section of the barrier was found in his house when he died in 1958 and can now be seen in the Gairloch Heritage Museum

Head down the tarmac road past the church and down the tarmac estate road. After 2.5km fork left along a good track signed to Kernsary Estate. At **Kernsary Farm** (24m, 89250 79260) fork left past the farmhouse and continue to a track junction halfway up the hill (1hr 15min, 50m, 89730 79260). This is where most cyclists will want to leave their bikes. Turn right through the gate and into the wood and continue along a muddy track. You should note that the next section has been realigned and is different than shown on many maps. Fork R along a path, marked by a cairn (1hr 35min, 130m, 90900 78970). You soon reach a stile over a deer fence at the edge of the wood

See map in Route 64.

Crags on the N face, Beinn Lair

and continue along a good stalker's path through heather moorland. The path takes you over a high point (240m) before dropping down to **Loch an Doire Crionaich** (2hr 15min, 205m, 93240 77190). Beyond this lochan you will see massive rockfalls on Beinn Airigh Charr to your right before passing another lochan and reaching a path junction at the foot of the pass between Beinn Airigh Charr and Meall Mheinnidh (2hr 35min, 216m, 94350 76080). Fork left, cross the burn and climb the other side to another path junction. Turn left and continue to another path junction, marked by a small cairn, at the base of **Beinn Lair** (3hr 15min, 185m, 96860 75320). Turn right up a less well maintained stalker's path, ignoring a track off to the left (240m) and a path to the left (440m), and keep going to the pass of **Bealach Mheinnidh** (3hr 50min, 485m, 96300 73910). Turn left, roughly ENE, up the easy ridge on your left. ◀ In mist, don't get confused by a cairn on a knoll (835m, 97590 73890) but continue SE onto the large summit plateau. The summit is marked by one of the biggest cairns on a Corbett (4hr 55min). There are other options in descent but on such a remote mountain most walkers will want the quickest option which is to return by the ascent route.

Care will be needed in mist to find the stalking path (5hr 45min) to the foot of Beinn Lair (6hr 20min). You are now back on the excellent stalker's path and it will be another 2hr back to the point where most cyclists will have left their bikes and further 1hr 15min back to the car park if you are walking (9hr 35min).

Stay close to the edge to get spectacular views of the cliffs on the N face of Beinn Lair.

8 STRATH GARVE, FISHERFIELD AND INVERPOLLY

Strath Garve, Fisherfield and Inverpolly: Bases and facilities

Base for Routes 66–76: Ullapool

Ullapool, the biggest town on the NW coast of Scotland, is a major tourist resort with plenty of accommodation and excellent facilities for walkers.

Ullapool Tourist Office Tel: 01854 613 031

Ullapool SYHA Tel: 01854 612 254

Broomfield Holiday Park in Ullapool is a large camping and caravan site. Tel: 01854 612 020

Ardmair Holiday Park, 4km N of Ullapool on the A835, is in a beautiful setting. It is a camping and caravan site with self-catering chalets and a small store. Tel: 01854 612 054 www.ardmair.com

Alternative base for Routes 66–69: Aultguish Inn

Aultguish Inn, an ancient drover's inn at the E end of Loch Glascarnoch on the A835, has a bunkhouse and snack bar as well as normal hotel facilities. Tel: 01997 455 254 www.aultguish.co.uk

Alternative base for Routes 66–74: Forest Way Bunkhouse

Forest Way Bunkhouse is on the A835, 2 miles N of the junction with the A832 (NH 19500 81100). Tel: 01854 655 330 www.forestway.co.uk

Alternative base for Routes 71–73: Shenavall Bothy

Shenavall Bothy is a small bothy maintained by the Mountain Bothies Association. It is not available during stag stalking season from 15 September to 20 October.

Alternative bases for Routes 70–74: Dundonnell and Gruinard Bay

Dundonnell Hotel Tel: 01854 633204 www.dundonnellhotel.com

Sail Mhor Croft Hostel is situated at the foot of An Teallach on the shore of Little Loch Broom. Tel: 01854 633 224 www.sailmhor.co.uk

Gruinard Bay Caravan Park: See Section 7 introduction.

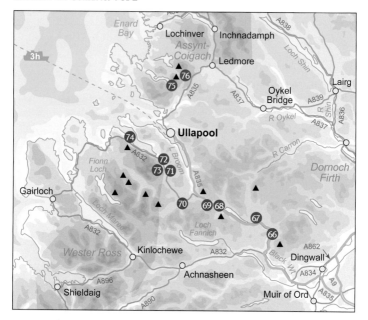

Beinn a' Chlaidheimh from Gleann na Muice Beag (Route 72)

ROUTE 66

Little Wyvis LITTLE AWESOME HILL

Start	Ben Wyvis car park (NH 41010 67100)
Distance	12km (7 miles)l
Total ascent	670m (2200ft)
Difficulty	The suggested ascent route does involve climbing a steep heather-covered slope. The summit ridge and descent are easy.
Time	3hr 50min
Summits	Little Wyvis (764m, 2497ft)
Maps	OS Landranger 20
Access	Follow the A835 S from Ullapool and park at the Ben Wyvis car park 2 miles S of the Inchbae Lodge Hotel.
Note	There's much to be said in favour of climbing and descending the suggested descent route. This route would not have much interest, but it would save a lot of effort.

Little Wyvis is an outlier on the SW ridge of Ben Wyvis. Unfortunately this is a rare occasion when the Munro is a much better mountain than the Corbett. Little Wyvis has little to recommend it apart from wide views from the summit ridge. The mountain was under 2500ft on the OS 1 inch:1 mile map but was promoted to Corbett status when the metric maps were produced. This is a peak to climb to stretch the legs on the drive N to better mountains.

The rare **dotterel** is the symbol of the Ben Wyvis National Nature Reserve. This wader breeds in Scotland, Scandinavia and Siberia, wintering in North Africa. By 1986 Scottish numbers had increased to about 600 breeding pairs, possibly due to a reduction in disturbance by sheep on the high ridges where the dotterel nests. The distinctive marks are the white eye-stripe and white line separating the grey upper breast from the rufous lower breast and black belly.

Follow the well-maintained tourist path NE from the car park, soon crossing the Allt a' Bhealaich Mhoir and then turning right up the left bank of the burn. Continue to the top of the forest (45min, 350m, 43130 66510). If you want an easy ascent, cross the burn, follow the edge of the forest and then head up an old fence line to the summit ridge. The suggested route continues up the path until it veers left up An Cabar. Leave the path here (43400 66450) and follow the burn on a faint vehicle track or the now indistinct stalker's path until the burn starts veering left up Ben Wyvis (1hr 20min, 460m, 44670 65440). Head right (WSW), over heather moorland, until you reach a line of old fence posts then follow these posts up the steep heather slopes to the summit of **Tom na Caillich** (705m, 43900 65360). Head W to a broad saddle (43510 65390) where you should turn left along another line of

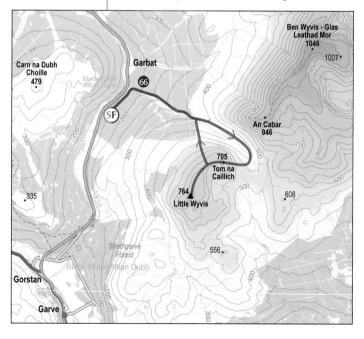

fence posts which is followed over the N summit of **Little Wyvis** (750m, 43240 64950) and on to the cairn on the S summit (2hr 35min, 764m, 42960 64470). The summit ridge is scarred by a number of vehicle tracks.

Retrace your steps to the saddle then turn left when you reach a line of old fence posts (665m, 43480 65370) heading NNW. Follow this easily down to the forest corner and down the edge of the forest to the Allt a' Bhealaich Mhoir. Cross the burn and turn left along the path back to the car park (3hr 50min).

An Cabar Ridge on Ben Wyvis from the Allt a' Bhealaich Mhor

ROUTE 67

Beinn a' Chaisteil HILL OF THE CASTLE

Start	Black Bridge, Glascarnoch River (NH 37390 70810)
Distance	26km (16 miles)
Total ascent	920m (3000ft)
Difficulty	The ascent is up easy rough pasture and the going along the stony moss-covered ridge is easy; however, the descent to Strath Vaich is rather steep.
Time	6hr 20min
Summits	Meall a' Ghrianain (772m), Beinn a' Chaisteil (787m, 2580ft)
Maps	OS Landranger 20
Access	Follow the A835 S from Ullapool and park beside the Black Bridge over the Glascarnoch River 2 miles S of the Loch Glascarnoch dam.
Note	The descent will be slightly quicker if you return to the saddle between Beinn a' Chaisteil and Meall a' Ghrianain and descend to the right of the burn to Lubachlaggan. It would be possible cycle up Strath Vaich.

Beinn a' Chaisteil is a remote peak on the ridge to the E of Loch Vaich. The southern summit on the ridge, Meall a' Ghrianain, doesn't quite reach Corbett status because of an insufficient drop to Beinn a' Chaisteil.

Low-flying is an essential skill for military aircrew. In the UK, fixed wing aircraft are considered to be low-flying when operating below 2000ft and they are required to maintain a minimum separation of 250ft from the terrain. However, there are three designated low-flying areas where this limit is reduced to 100ft and the largest of these includes the NW of Scotland. On mountain ridges you will frequently see jet aircraft well below your feet as they shoot through the glens. Strath Vaich is often used on these training flights.

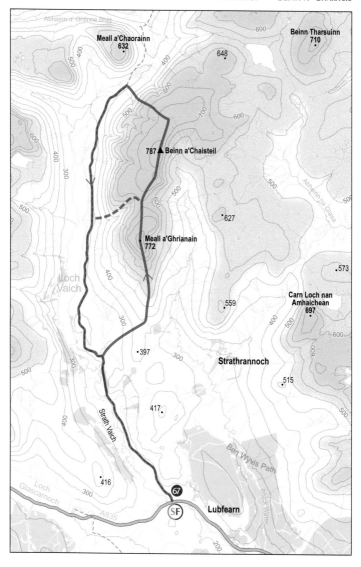

*Strath Vaich from
Black Bridge*

Head along the tarmac estate road up **Strath Vaich** and after 3.5km fork right up a good track, just before the estate road crosses the Abhainn Srath a' Bhathaich. Turn right at a track junction (265m, 35420 74640) and head alongside a small canal until about 150m before the canal emerges from a tunnel (1hr, 285m, 35890 75070). Head roughly ENE across rough pasture, taking advantage of some animal tracks to reach the ridge (at about 395m, 36550 75560) and then turn N up the ridge. You will find it easier to follow the ridge rather than the old fence line which joins the ridge higher up. Ignore the fence when it goes off left. When the ridge steepens you can pick up the remains of an old stalker's path to climb easily to the summit cairn on **Meall a' Ghrianain** (2hr 20min, 772m, 36550 77580).

Head N down the broad ridge to a saddle (650m, 36530 78710) and NNE up to the stone trig point on the summit of **Beinn a' Chaisteil** (3hr 5min, 787m, 37000 80100).

Head NNE to a small tarn on the summit plateau (725m, 37330 81000) then head NW. Don't head too far left as the slope will be uncomfortably steep and rougher. Eventually veer left to reach the good track at the head of Strath Vaich (3hr 55min, 340m, 36040 81780). Turn left and follow the track down Strath Vaich to the tarmac estate road (5hr 40min) and turn left back to the parking (6hr 20min).

ROUTE 68

Beinn Liath Mhor a' Ghiubhais Li

BIG GREY HILL WITH COLOURED PINE TREES

Start	Abhainn an Torrain Duibh (NH 27750 74240)
Distance	9km (6 miles)
Total ascent	570m (1900ft)
Difficulty	There is some rough heather, tough in places, but most of the boulderfields higher up the hill can be bypassed.
Time	2hr 50min
Summits	Beinn Liath Mhor a' Ghiubhais Li (766m, 2464ft), Meall Daimh (532m)
Maps	OS Landranger 20
Access	Follow the A835 S from Ullapool. There is a small car park just W of the Abhainn an Torrain Duibh at the W end of Loch Glascarnoch.
Note	It would save a little energy to descend by the ascent route. Not the most interesting of the Corbetts, Beinn Liath Mhor a' Ghiubhais Li could be classed as a mountain to be saved for a wet weather day.

Beinn Liath Mhor a' Ghiubhais Li is squeezed between Sgurr Mhor and Loch Glascarnoch. It is a featureless dome with rough pasture and heather moorland and boulderfields on the summit producing the grey cap to the hill. This is another peak that was below 2500ft on the 1 inch:1 mile OS maps but was promoted to Corbett status when the 1:50,000 maps were produced.

Cross the bridge and head E along the **A835** to a track signed to Beinn Liath Mhor Fannich. Follow this track through the deer fence and immediately turn left along the main track and follow this track to the fence at the SW end of the forest (40min, 385m, 26680 72250). Head uphill over rough heather, dodging boulderfields higher up, to the summit of **Beinn Liath Mhor a' Ghiubhais Li.** It isn't clear which is the highest point, but it is probably the

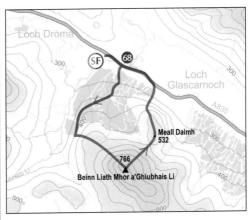

low shelter rather than the sprawling cairn (1hr 35min, 766m, 28090 71300).

Head NE down to a broad saddle (505m, 28760 71990) and up to the summit of **Meall Daimh** (532m, 28870 72130). Head NNW down the ridge, veering N to the edge of the forest. Continue down and climb a fixed gate in the deer fence to reach the A835. Turn left back to the parking area (2hr 50min).

Beinn Liath Mhor a' Ghiubhais Li

ROUTE 69

Beinn Enaiglair HILL OF THE TIMID BIRDS

Start	Loch Droma (NH 25360 75500)
Distance	15km (9 miles)
Total ascent	700m (2300ft)
Difficulty	Beinn Enaiglair is well provided with stalker's paths and the suggested route is easy. The mountain has rough, steep N and S slopes which make some of the possible alternative routes difficult.
Time	4hr
Summits	Beinn Enaiglair (889m 2915ft)
Maps	OS Landranger 20
Access	Follow the A835 S from Ullapool and park at the dam at the W end of Loch Droma.
Note	If you can arrange transport it makes sense to climb the mountain from Braemore Junction to the SW and descend by the recommended route.

Beinn Enaiglair is a summit on the W ridge of the Beinn Dearg and could easily be combined with an ascent of this Munro.

The 60m deep, mile-long **Corrieshalloch Gorge** at Braemore Junction is a fine example of a box canyon. The river plunges 45m over the Falls of Measach which can be seen from a new viewing platform or from the suspension bridge built in 1874 by John Fowler, joint designer of the Forth Railway Bridge.

Cross the road and go through the gate (or climb the fence) to the right of Lochdrum Cottage. Follow the faint path up the left bank of the burn. This stalker's path becomes clear by the time it crosses the burn (380m, 25570 76270) and is easily followed to the ridge. The

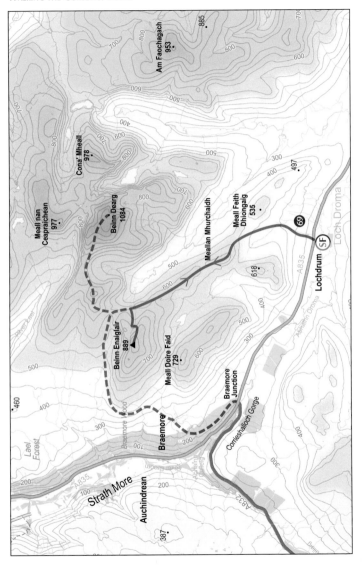

path skirts the summit of **Meallan Mhurchaidh** and follows the pleasant ridge to a path junction, marked by a small cairn (1hr 25min, 620m, 23790 79590). Turn right, continue to a burn (660m, 23420 80440) and head up it to pick up an old stalker's path (745m, 22970 80530) just below the saddle. Turn left up the path which switchbacks easily to the summit ridge. Turn right to the summit cairn on **Beinn Enaiglair**, which is at the far end of the summit plateau (2hr 20min, 889m, 22510 80510).

Return by the same route (4hr).

Beinn Dearg from the W ridge of Beinn Enaiglair

ROUTE 70

Creag Rainich BRACKEN COVERED CRAG

Start	A832 'Destitution Road' (NH 16150 76130)
Distance	20km (12 miles)
Total ascent	790m (2600ft)
Difficulty	The ascent is over easy rough pasture, with some rocky patches as the summit is approached. The ridge along to Meall an t-sithe is easy going, but care would be needed with navigation in mist. The final descent is rough and boggy in places.
Time	5hr 55min
Summits	Creag Rainich (807m, 2646ft), Meall an t-sithe (601m)
Maps	OS Landranger 19 and 20
Access	Follow the A835 S from Ullapool then turn right along the A832 at Braemore Junction. There is limited parking on the long right-hand bend just after the track off to Loch a' Bhraoin.
Note	It will save a little energy to descend to Loch a' Bhraoin from the low point on the ridge.

Creag Rainich is a remote mountain to the W of Loch a' Bhraoin. The mountain is splendidly placed, giving a unique view of the fantastic slabs on the E face of Mullach Coire Mhic Fhearchair as well as a good view of majestic An Teallach. Keep an eye open for a herd of wild goats on Creag Rainich.

The **Highland potato famine** caused by potato blight resulted in over 1.7 million people leaving Scotland between 1846 and 1852. Famine relief programmes were better organised in the Highlands than in Ireland and relatively few people died of starvation, with the Navy distributing oatmeal and other supplies. However, the crofters were expected to work for their rations, eight hours a day, six days a week. Much of this work was the building

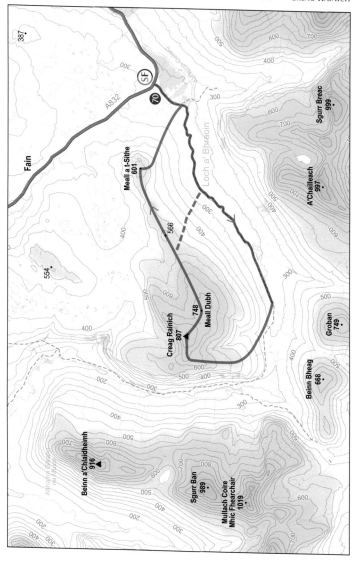

of what became known as 'Destitution Roads' and the stretch of road from Dundonnell to Braemore Junction is still known as the Destitution Road.

Head back down the road and turn right down the track towards **Loch a' Bhraoin**. Turn right along a new footpath (250m, 15700 75320) which takes you down to Loch a' Bhraoin and turn right along the good track to Lochivraon Cottage at the W end of the loch (1hr 15min, 255m, 11790 73350). Continue along the track, which gradually deteriorates to a path and becomes unclear in places. Stay on the right-hand side of the burn, ignoring a cairned crossing place, until the path ends just before the burn enters a gully (1hr 55min, 315m, 09820 73060). Cross the burn and head uphill, veering to the left edge of the ridge to get a good view of the bare slabs on the E face of Mullach Coire Mhic Fhearchair. The remains of an old fence guide you up the ridge which eventually turns E to the summit of **Creag Rainich**. The fence veers off left just before the summit, which has twin tops about 50m apart. It is the W top (3hr 30min, 807m, 09610 75140) which is higher, not the E top with the stone trig point.

Beinn Dearg from Meall an t-Sithe

Head SE to a saddle with a small lochan (715m, 10000 74750), then ESE over Meall Dubh (748m) to

another shallow lochan (10570 74670) and ENE to a broad saddle (4hr 15min, 540m, 12050 75500). It is easier to descend to Loch a' Bhraoin from here, but it is more scenic to continue ENE along the knobbly ridge to the large cairn on the summit of **Meall an t-Sithe** (5hr, 601m, 14100 76490).

Head SSE, veering SE when you have passed the crags on the upper slopes, and descend across rough, sometimes boggy pasture towards the E end of Loch a' Bhraoin. Reach the track/path junction and turn left, back to the A832 and the parking area (5hr 55min).

ROUTE 71

Beinn a' Chlaidheimh HILL OF THE SWORD

Start	Corrie Hallie (NH 11410 85100)
Distance	23km (14 miles)
Total ascent	1470m (4900ft)
Difficulty	There is pathless heather moorland and boulderfields to cross. Route-finding skills are needed and fording the Abhainn Loch an Nid could be difficult if it is in flood.
Time	7hr 40min
Summits	Beinn a' Chlaidheimh (914m, 2800ft ring contour)
Maps	OS Landranger 19
Access	Head S down the A835 from Ullapool and turn right along the A832. After about 10 miles, park in the layby about 200m S of the arts and craft shop at Corrie Hallie. Please don't park outside the shop.
Note	It is recommended that you climb Beinn a' Chlaidheimh as part of a backpacking trip, including the peaks in Routes 72 and 73 and the Munros in the Fisherfield Forest. The main alternative to backpacking these three routes would be to base yourself at the Shenavall Bothy. If you are staying at Shenavall Bothy (see Route 72) then you start by heading SW on a combination of track and path up the N bank of the Abhainn Loch an Nid burn, passing Achneigie Cottage, reaching the track from Corrie Hallie after about 50min.

Beinn a' Chlaidheimh is the N summit of the N ridge of the spectacular Munro, Mullach Coire Mhic Fhearchair. The best option would be to climb it on a backpacking trip involving this and other Munros in the Fisherfield Forest.

The 1929 OS 6 inch:1 mile map showed **Beinn a' Chlaidheimh** as a 3000ft ring contour, whereas the 1955 1 inch:1 mile map showed a 2800ft ring contour. It was promoted to a Munro in 1974 when it appeared on the new metric maps at 914m and later 916m. In 2011 a survey on behalf of the Munro Society measured it at 913.96 ±0.1m (2998ft). This has been accepted by the OS and Beinn a' Chlaidheimh has been demoted from a Munro to a Corbett.

Head up the track signed to Kinlochewe and continue until the top of the hill. Just after the top a path, marked by two cairns, forks right to Shenavall (1hr, 390m, 10080 82310). Ignore this path and fork left down the track which reaches the **Abhainn Loch an Nid** burn at the S end of some woodland (2hr, 130m, 08990 78830). There are good campsites here.

Cross the burn, which will only be possible dry-shod when the water level is low. Climb, roughly WSW veering W, easily up the broad **Creag Ghlas** ridge with Torridonian sandstone outcrops. ◀ As you approach the big crags on the NE ridge above (at about 3hr 15min, 605m, 06830 78560) you should start climbing the small rocky ridge on your left. Contour into the grassy gully between the small ridge and the big crags and climb the gully. Once level with the top of the small ridge on your left (675m, 06720 78420), a small path is beginning to develop. This path, which you follow diagonally right uphill, takes you left of the crags (to about 730m, 06630 78300) and then climbs straight up the hill to reach the ridge (825m, 06450 78200). ◀ Turn left to the N top (900m, 06350 78010), now on quartzite rather than

Notice the mixture of Torridonian sandstone and quartzite boulders dumped by glaciers.

The top of this route is insufficiently cairned to contemplate as a descent route in mist.

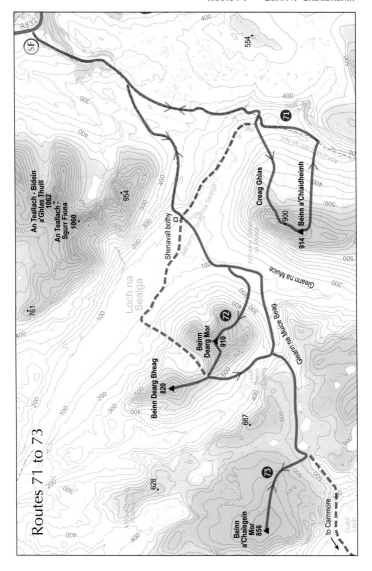

Routes 71 to 73

An Teallach - Bidein a'Ghlas Thuill 1062
An Teallach - Sgurr Fiona 1060
954
761
Shenavall bothy
Loch na Sealga
Creag Ghlas
Beinn a'Chlaidheimh 914
900
Abhainn Srath na Sealga
Abhainn Gleann na Muice
Gleann na Muice
Beinn Dearg Mor 910
Beinn Dearg Bheag 820
687
Gleann na Muice Beag
Loch Beinn Dearg
628
to Carnmore
Dubh Loch
Beinn a'Chaisgein Mor 856

Camping beside Abhainn Loch an Nid

Torridonian sandstone, and follow the narrow ridge over a minor top to the summit cairn on **Beinn a' Chlaidheimh** near the far end of the ridge (4hr 10min, 914m, 06140 77570)

Keep straight on but gradually veer SE then E, keeping right of the crags on the left flank of the E ridge. Reach the Abhainn Loch an Nid burn (at about 5hr 10min, 155m, 08420 77180) and follow the burn downstream. When convenient, cross the burn and follow the track down the right bank and back to the track from Corrie Hallie (5hr 40min). Follow this track back to the parking (7hr 40min).

ROUTE 72

Beinn Dearg Bheag SMALL RED MOUNTAIN
and Beinn Dearg Mor BIG RED MOUNTAIN

Start	Corrie Hallie (NH 11410 85100)
Distance	30km (19 miles) from Corrie Hallie, 16km (10 miles) from Shenavall
Total ascent	1820m (6000ft) from Corrie Hallie, 1120m (3700ft) from Shenavall
Difficulty	Accurate route-finding is needed in these steep rocky mountains, which means that they are not suitable for inexperienced walkers in poor weather conditions. There are two burn crossings and quite a lot of boggy ground on the approach, which could cause difficulties in wet weather.
Time	10hr 40min from Corrie Hallie, 6hr 20min from Shenavall
Summits	Beinn Dearg Mor (910m, 2974ft), Beinn Dearg Bheag (820m, 2550ft)
Maps	OS Landranger 19
Access	Parking as for Route 71
Note	See note to Route 71

These magnificent Torridonian sandstone peaks are hidden away to the S of the equally magnificent Munro An Teallach in the Fisherfield Forest. The view of the Beinn Dearg ridge from Shenavall is stunning and the bothy would be a good base for climbing the mountain.

The An Teallach Ale Company is a **small brewery** operating out of a croft at Camasnagaul, near Dundonnell, on the shore of Little Loch Broom. Its beers include Beinn Dearg Ale and An Teallach Ale.

Head up the track, signed to Kinlochewe, and continue to the top of the hill. Just after the top a fork in the path is marked by two cairns (1hr, 390m, 10080 82310). Fork right and follow a rough, occasionally boggy path down to **Shenavall Bothy** (2hr 10min, 120m, NH 06590 80980).

See map in Route 71.

Head SW down to the **Abhainn Srath na Sealga** (95m, NH 06360 80720). You should be able to cross safely here, but will only be able to keep dry feet in unusually dry conditions. Head WSW across very boggy moor directly towards Larachantivore Cottage and cross the **Abhainn Gleann na Muice** (2hr 40min, 95m, NH 05350 80150). This is another safe river crossing, but again you are likely to get wet feet.

Turn left after crossing the Abhainn Gleann na Muice and, after about 400m, cross a small burn (05290 79730). ◄ Turn right along the small burn, which follows the foot of Beinn Dearg Mor before heading up the hill. Follow the burn until it eventually goes underground (by 3hr 30min, 325m, 04150 79080). Head straight uphill, weaving through crags, then veering left as you approach the rim of the corrie where you will see big chasms in the Torridonian sandstone (4hr 10min, 580m, 03690 79160).

The craggy ridge on your left looks like an intimidating scramble. You could climb the ridge on your right to the E top of Beinn Dearg Mor, but the easiest thing is to head NNW up the right-hand side of the corrie to reach the ridge at the saddle between the E top and the main summit and continue easily up the ridge, noting the spectacular crags on your right, to the large summit cairn on **Beinn Dearg Mor** (4hr 55min, 910m, 03220 79930).

Head SW to the end of the summit ridge before veering right (WNW) down a steep slope to the low point (5hr 30min, 590m, 02200 80340). Continue NNW veering N up **Beinn Dearg Bheag**. This ridge becomes a little craggy with some boulderfields but doesn't present any real difficulties. The summit is marked by a small cairn (6hr 5min, 820m, 02000 81120).

Return to the low point (6hr 25min). The 'normal' descent is left, steeply down to Loch Toll an Lochain and Loch na Sealga, but the descent to the right is easier and gentler. Head roughly S down easy slopes reaching **Loch Beinn Dearg** (at about 6hr 50min, 340m, 02390 79100). Turn left along the loch and continue to the SE tip, then head S to pick up a good stalker's path (7hr 10min, 335m, 02820 78370). Turn left down **Gleann na Muice**

If you are backpacking this would be a good place to camp.

Beinn Dearg Mor over Larachantivore

Beag to a path junction in **Gleann na Muice** (7hr 40min, 125m, 04910 78590) and turn left back to Larachantivore Cottage (8hr). Return by the same route to Shenavall (8hr 30min) and Corrie Hallie (10hr 40min).

ROUTE 73

Beinn a' Chaisgein Mor LARGE FORBIDDING HILL

Start	Corrie Hallie (NH 11410 85100)
Distance	37km (23 miles) from Corrie Hallie, 22km (14 miles) from Shenavall
Total ascent	1570m (5200ft) from Corrie Hallie, 870m (2900ft) from Shenavall
Difficulty	The only significant problem will be the burn crossings and the boggy terrain in wet conditions. Care would be needed with navigation in mist.
Time	10hr 40min from Corrie Hallie, 6hr 25min from Shenavall
Summits	Beinn a' Chaisgein Mor (856m, 2802ft)
Maps	OS Landranger 19
Access	Parking as for Route 71
Note	See note to Route 71. Beinn a' Chaisgein Mor could also climbed from Poolewe by following the approach to Beinn Lair (Section 7) and turning left past Carnmore to join the featured route.

Beinn a' Chaisgein Mor is a remote peak in the wild Fisherfield Forest where the Torridonian sandstone peaks provide some of the most magnificent mountain scenery in Scotland.

You might fancy a day's **fishing** on the remote Fionn Loch immediately W of Beinn a' Chaisgein Mor, but you could be disappointed. The Letterewe Estate does allow the Gairloch Angling Club to use a boat on the loch, but you must have a local address to take advantage of this concession. You could of course fish when staying as a guest of the Letterewe Estate, but this is only possible for those with a very full wallet.

See map in Route 71.

Follow Route 72 to **Shenavall Bothy** (2hr 10min, 120m, 06590 80980) and the **Abhainn Gleann na Muice** (2hr 40min, 95m, 05350 80150).

Continue up the Abhainn Gleann na Muice to a path junction at the mouth of the **Gleann na Muice Beag** (3hr 5min, 125m, NH 04910 78580) and fork right. The stalker's path takes you almost to the SE tip of **Loch Beinn Dearg** (3hr 40min, 345m, NH 02820 78360) before switchbacking up the slope to the left (S). The path levels at the top of the hill, then leads you easily through rough moorland past three lochans with the impressive Munros Ruadh Stac Mhor and A' Mhaighdean on your left. Continue to a path junction (4hr 35min, 535m, NH 00240 77500) just after the third lochan. If you are backpacking there are campsites here beside a lovely sandy beach. ◀

This is where the alternative route from Poolewe via Carnmore joins our route.

Head roughly NW across the pathless moorland, veering left when you reach the broad mossy summit ridge. Continue to the summit of Beinn a' Chaisgein Mor, which is a flat plateau with many small rock outcrops. The summit cairn is set on the top of a bigger cairn which appears to be an old burial mound. This isn't actually the highest point which is a rock outcrop about 20m away (5hr 30min, 856m, NG 98250 78540).

Backpacking tents at Loch Feith Mhic'-illean

Return by the same route to the stalker's path (6hr 10min), Lochan Beinn Dearg (6hr 50min), Larachantivore Cottage (8hr), Shenavall (8hr 35min) and Corrie Hallie (10hr 40min).

ROUTE 74

Sail Mhor BIG HEEL

Start	Ardessie (NH 05430 89570)
Distance	11km (7 miles)
Total ascent	840m (2800ft)
Difficulty	There is some rough, possibly boggy, moorland to cross. The Allt Airdeasaidh burn will be difficult to cross when in spate.
Time	4hr
Summits	Sail Mhor (767m, 2508ft), Ruigh Mheallain (594m)
Maps	OS Landranger 19
Access	Head S down the A835 from Ullapool and turn right along the A832. There is limited roadside parking on the A832 where it crosses the Allt Airdeasaidh at Ardessie about 4km W of Dundonnell.
Note	You could shorten the route by not climbing Ruigh Mheallain.

Sail Mhor is an outlier on the NW ridge of the impressive Munro An Teallach. Although it is one of the gentler Torridonian sandstone peaks, it is a worthy mountain in its own right as well as giving spectacular views of An Teallach, Beinn Dearg Mor and Beinn Dearg Bheag. The walk would be worthwhile just for the waterfalls on the Allt Airdeasaidh burn.

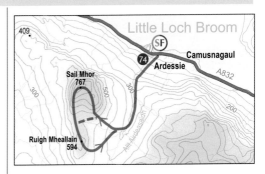

Gruinard Island, visible to the NW, was the site of one of the most disreputable experiments committed in the name of scientific research. In 1942, the killing power of anthrax was demonstrated by releasing this most feared agent of biological warfare on Gruinard Island to wipe out a flock of sheep. The plan was that linseed cakes contaminated with anthrax would be air dropped over Germany. Fortunately this plan was shelved but Gruinard Island was quarantined for almost 50 years. The Government paid £500,000 for the island to be decontaminated in 1986 and it was declared safe in 1990 but many scientists are not convinced by this assurance.

You should be able to keep your feet dry if the water is low, but the crossing could be difficult when the burn is in spate.

Head up a rough boggy track along the left bank of the **Allt Airdeasaidh burn**. This path has many strands and is sometimes unclear. Continue until you reach an island in the burn once the burn has levelled off (1hr, 340m, 04630 87600). This is as easy a place as any to cross. ◄ Head roughly W above the right bank of a small burn and continue up it until it fades away (at about 1hr 30min, 490m, 03540 87770). Head roughly NNE up the ridge on your right passing over a small top before reaching the SE summit of **Sail Mhor** (715m, 03710 88480). Continue NNW, gradually veering to the W to reach a shelter wall (765m, 03400 88780). The highest point is a small cairn (2hr 15min, 767m, 03300 88690) a little to the WSW.

Head easily down the S ridge to a broad saddle (520m, 03190 87770). You could descend E from here to regain the ascent route, but it is worth continuing SSE to **Ruigh Mheallain** (2hr 50min, 594m, 03350 87240) to get better views of Beinn Dearg Mor and Beinn Dearg Bheag.

Start down the S ridge and when the gradient eases veer E and then NE to reach the Allt Airdeasaidh roughly where you left it. Cross the burn and return down the right bank back to the parking (4hr).

Waterfall, Allt Airdeasaidh and Sail Mhor

ROUTE 75

Cul Beag SMALL BACK

Start	Loch Lurgainn (NC 12690 08830)
Distance	7km (5 miles)
Total ascent	760m (2500ft)
Difficulty	This route isn't recommended for inexperienced walkers in bad weather. You will be climbing and descending through rough heather on steep slopes and will need to navigate through the many small crags on the N and S ridges. You need to stay clear of the big crags on the W face of Cul Beag. In mist it is probably safer to descend by the ascent route.
Time	3hr 30min
Summits	Cul Beag (769m, 2523ft)
Maps	OS Landranger 15
Access	Follow the A835 N from Ullapool and turn left along the minor road signed to Achiltibuie. Continue until you see a small stalker's path on your right just before the left-hand bend above Loch Lurgainn. There is very limited parking in a passing place.
Note	The approach from the E is less steep, but it is still over very rough terrain.

Cul Beag is a spectacular little peak with horizontal bands of Torridonian sandstone cliffs, surrounded by numerous sparkling lochs and lochans in wild heather moorland. Those walkers who only think in terms of Munros should visit Cul Beag. It has views of Beinn Mhor na Coigach, Stac Pollaidh and Suilven, three of the most impressive mountains in Scotland and none of them a Corbett, let alone a Munro!

Stac Pollaidh to the WNW is a fine advert for the Grahams. Despite its modest height of 612m it is one of the finest mountains in Scotland with a rocky crest of Torridonian sandstone, with many pinnacles and steep gullies. The crest is extremely weathered suggesting that it was not covered in ice during

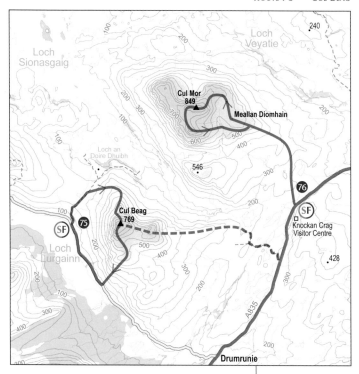

the last ice age. Some scrambling and a good head
for heights are required to reach the summit.

Follow the stalker's path N past Lochan Fhionnlaidh
to some large fallen boulders (20min, 170m, 13150
09670). Head roughly E across heather moorland to the
ridge and turn right up the ridge. At the foot of a steep
buttress (430m, 13950 09480) it is easier to contour to
the right, below the fallen rocks, before climbing up
a very faint path to a cairn on a small saddle (545m,
14060 09170). There is then a path up the steep slopes
leading directly to the summit cairn on **Cul Beag** (2hr,
769m, 14040 08820).

Cul Mor from Knockan Crag National Nature Reserve

Take care on the descent to stay clear of the big crags on the W face of Cul Beag as you weave your way through the smaller crags on the S ridge. You need to veer SE to avoid big crags to a gully (500m, 14200 08090) from where you climb briefly before descending S then SW to the road (at about 13700 07000). Turn right back to the parking (3hr 30min).

ROUTE 76

Cul Mor BIG BACK

Start	Knockan Crag Visitor Centre (NC 18890 09380)
Distance	11km (7 miles)
Total ascent	720m (2400ft)
Difficulty	The route is relatively easy going in good weather, but in mist the crags on most faces and ridges of the mountain would make accurate navigation essential. The mountain is not recommended for the inexperienced in bad weather. There is a short distance of quartzite boulderfield to cross as well as some easy but boggy moorland.
Time	3hr 55min
Summits	Cul Mor (849m, 2786ft)
Maps	OS Landranger 15
Access	Follow the A835 N from Ullapool. There is parking area about 200m N of the entrance to the Knockan Crag National Nature Reserve and Visitor Centre, on the A835 about 2 miles SW of Elphin.
Note	In bad weather it would be wise to descend by the ascent route.

Cul Mor is an impressive mountain in its own right, but its position makes it a spectacular mountain, being surrounded by sparkling lochs and with close views of Suilven, Stac Pollaidh and Cul Beag. The crags on the mountain are composed of Torridonian sandstone with the approach ridge and summit being capped by quartzite.

Knockan Crag is one of the most important geological sites in the world; this was where the evidence for continental drift was first recognised. At the visitor centre the story of the geology and landscape of the area is told with displays, poetry and sculptures. Knockan Crag is part of the North West Highlands Geopark with many visitor centres and roadside displays explaining the evolution of the fantastic

landscape of NW Scotland. **www.knockan-crag.
co.uk**

See map in Route 75.

Head N, veering WNW, up the maintained footpath from
the parking area. The path deteriorates (at about 345m,
18510 11150), becoming boggy in places. When the
path fades away continue WNW up the ridge, marked
with occasional cairns, reaching a cairn (590m, 17280
11650) from where you can see the NE ridge of Cul Mor.
Veer round the right-hand side of **Meallan Diomhain**
and contour to a broad saddle (1hr 15min, 585m, 16970
11850) where Torridonian sandstone replaces quartzite.
**Do not attempt to climb (or descend) the crag-bound E
ridge of Cul Mor.** Head roughly NNW to a small lochan
(610m, 16840 12260) where a path is developing which
can be followed up the NE ridge of Cul Mor. The ascent
is easy until the final quartzite boulderfield, which is
climbed to the trig point on the summit of **Cul Mor** (2hr,
849m, 16200 11900).

Head W, skirting left of a sandstone crag before veering S to the saddle (750m, 15880 11600) between the
two summits of Cul Mor and continue to the S summit
(2hr 20min, 830m, 15940 11340). In windy conditions
stay well clear of the near vertical cliffs on the W face of
Cul Mor. Descend SE, veering E then ENE, to cross the
burn draining Cul Mor (535m, 16900 11420). Contour
E, veering left, to reach the access path (at about 500m,
17770 11490) and follow this back to the parking area
(3hr 55min).

9 STRATHCARRON AND NW SCOTLAND

Family on Spidean Coinich (Route 82)

Strathcarron and NW Scotland: Bases and facilities

Base for Routes 77 and 78: Bonar Bridge

Bonar Bridge is a village with limited facilities for tourists. Carbisdale Castle SYHA is 5km N of the town.

The Bridge Hotel Tel: 01863 760 003

Carbisdale Castle SYHA, Culrain, Sutherland, IV24 3DP.
Tel: 01549 421 232

Base for Routes 79–82: Inchnadamph

There is nothing at Inchnadamph apart from a hotel, hostel and car park. The location at the SW end of Loch Assynt is magnificent and is a good base for the Corbetts as well as the Munro Ben More Assynt.

Inchnadamph Hotel was originally a coaching inn, over 200 years old.
Tel: 01571 822 202 www.inchnadamphhotel.com

Inchnadamph Lodge has hostel accommodation as well as offering B&B.
Tel: 01571 822 218 www.inch-lodge.co.uk

Alternative base for Routes 79–82: Lochinver

Lochinver is a small fishing village with a several shops, plenty of accommodation and excellent facilities for tourists. www.assynt.info

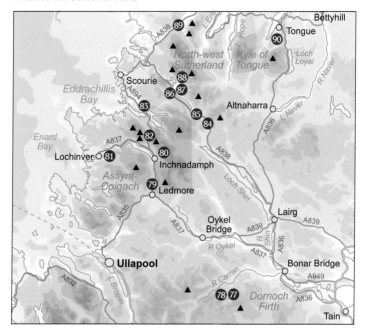

The Assynt Visitor Centre in Lochinver is well worth a visit.

When the Royal National Mission to Deep Sea Fishermen closed its hostel in Lochinver it was taken over by the local community and turned into a bunkhouse for walkers and tourists.
Tel: 01571 844 324 www.lochinvermission.org.uk

Culag Hotel Tel: 01571 844 270 http://culaghotel.co.uk

Achmelvich Beach SYHA, Recharn, Lochinver Sutherland, IV27 4JB. This hostel, which is about 6km NW of Lochinver, overlooks a white sandy beach.

Clachtol Beach campsite is also at Achmelvich.
Tel: 01571 855 377 www.clachtollbeachcampsite.co.uk

Drumbeg Hotel is on the coast road between Lochinver and Kylesku Bridge. Tel: 01571 833 236 www.drumbeghotel.co.uk

Base for Routes 82–88: Scourie

Scourie is a small fishing village with a shop, hotel, B&Bs and campsite.

Scourie Hotel Tel: 01971 502 396 www.scourie-hotel.co.uk

Scourie Caravan & Camp Site Tel: 01971 502 060

Local facilities for Route 83: Kylesku

Kylesku is a small fishing hamlet with a hotel and a jetty from which boat trips are organised.

Kylesku Hotel Tel: 01971 502 231 www.kyleskuhotel.co.uk

Alternative base for Routes 77, 78 and 84–88: Lairg

Lairg is a village with several shops and plenty of accommodation for tourists.

Lairg Highland Hotel Tel: 01549 402 243 www.highland-hotel.co.uk

Dunroanin Caravan and Camping Park
Tel: 01549 402 447 www.lairgcaravanpark.co.uk

Woodend Camping and Caravan Park at Achnairn is 6km N of Lairg.
Tel: 01549 402248

Local facilities for Routes 84–88: Overscaig House Hotel

The Overscaig House Hotel is near the N end of Loch Shin.
Tel: 01549 431 203 www.overscaig.com

Base for Routes 89 and 90: Durness

Durness has a bunkhouse, SYHA hostel, several B&Bs, hotels, shop, visitor centre, cafés and campsite.

Tourist information: VisitScotland, Durness, IV27 4PZ Tel: 01971 511 368

Mackays Rooms and Restaurant has both a self-catering cottage and bunkhouse accommodation. Tel: 01971 511 202 www.visitdurness.com

Durness SYHA Tel: 01971 511 264

Smoo Cave Hotel Tel: 01971 511 227 www.smoocavehotel.co.uk

Sango Sands Oasis campsite has static caravans as well as being a camping and caravan site. Tel: 01971 511 726 www.sangosands.com

Local facilities for Route 90: Tongue

Tongue has two hotels, SYHA hostel and a store.

Ben Loyal Hotel Tel: 01847 611 216 www.benloyal.co.uk

The Tongue Hotel Tel: 01847 611 206 www.tonguehotel.co.uk

Tongue SYHA, Sutherland, IV27 4XH Tel: 01847 611 789

ROUTE 77
Carn Chuinneag HILL OF THE CHURN

Start	Glencalvie Lodge (NH 46440 89130)
Distance	18km (12 miles)
Total ascent	890m (2900ft)
Difficulty	The described route involves crossing awkward boulderfields and rough boggy moorland. If you want an easy time follow the alternative route.
Time	4hr 50min
Summits	W summit, Carn Chuinneag (830m), E summit, Carn Chuinneag (838m, 2749ft), Carn Maire (736m)
Maps	OS Landranger 20
Access	From Bonar Bridge follow the A836 S to Ardgay and turn right up the minor road signed to Croick. Follow this road until a road junction with signs for the Glencalvie Estate. Turn left to Glencalvie Lodge where there is a car park on the right at the roadhead by the drive to Glencalvie Lodge.
Note	It is possible to follow the stalker's path until you are just below the saddle between the two summits of Carn Chuinneag and climb easily up to the E summit, returning by the same route.

Carn Chuinneag is the highest point in an area of heather moorland in Easter Ross. Its geology is similar to the Cairngorm Mountains and, as in the Cairngorms, there is a good selection of access tracks and stalker's paths to ease movement through the rough terrain.

Held annually in May, the **Glencalvie Challenge** is a charity fundraising event organised by the Rotary Club of Inverness Culloden, for walkers, runners or cyclists. The route follows 18 miles (29 km) of estate roads over the watershed from Black Bridge on the A835 up Strath Vaich and down Gleann Mor to Glencalvie Lodge.

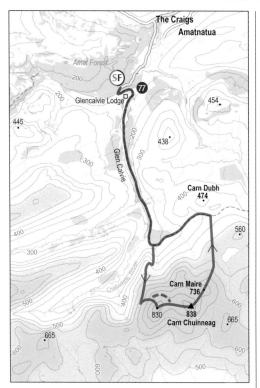

Follow the tarmac drive towards **Glencalvie Lodge**, cross the bridge, veer left through the lodge gates and keep straight on past the lodge. The road veers right by the Water of Glencalvie and continues as a good track up **Glen Calvie**. Follow the track up the picturesque glen to a junction as you reach open hillside and continue a few metres to the junction with a stalker's path (1hr, 285m, 47320 84940). Turn right and continue up to a cairned path junction (660m, 47070 83410). Turn sharp left and climb until the path levels off after some switchbacks (2hr 5min, 725m, 47320 83600). You should continue along the path if you are following the easier alternative route,

Water of Glencalvie on approach to Carn Chuinneag

The author's measurements suggest that this summit is only a couple of metres lower than the E summit.

but otherwise turn SE up the hillside, much of which is boulderfield, to the **W summit of Carn Chuinneag** (830m, 47510 83370). ◄ Head roughly E, on easier going, to the broad saddle between the two summits and up to the stone trig point on the **E summit of Carn Chuinneag** (2hr 35min, 838m, 48360 83320).

Head NNE, veering NE to the summit of **Carn Maire** (736m, 48810 83820) and descend NNE down an awkward boulderfield until you reach the stalker's path W of Loch Chuinneag. Follow the path until it veers right above the loch (3hr 15min, 525m, 49050 84680), then head N across boggy moorland until you reach the good track (405m, 48840 85740) below **Carn Dubh**. Turn left, ignoring a turn-off right by a plantation, and follow the track down Glen Calvie, back to Glencalvie Lodge and the parking (4hr 50min).

ROUTE 78

Carn Ban WHITE CAIRN

Start	Glencalvie Lodge (NH 46440 89130)
Distance	36km (22 miles)
Total ascent	1270m (4200ft)
Difficulty	Although there are few paths once you leave the access tracks, the going is relatively easy. Care will be needed with navigation in mist.
Time	8hr 45min
Summits	Bodach Mor (822m), Bodach Beag (837m), Carn Ban (845m, 2762ft)
Maps	OS Landranger 20
Access	Parking as for Route 77
Note	Possibly the best solution to Carn Ban would be to include it on a backpacking trip including Beinn a' Chaisteil and Carn Chuinneag and possibly also the Munros Seana Braigh and Ben Dearg. It would be possible to cycle up Gleann Mor, or from the S up Strath Vaich, to Gleann Beag and then to climb the S ridge of Carn Ban.

Carn Ban is a very remote peak in the Freevater Forest in Easter Ross. The closest access is from Strathcarron to the E and the suggested route gives a very good walk through majestic glens and along the NE ridge of Carn Ban. Bodach Beag almost makes Corbett status, but there is only about 470ft descent between it and Carn Ban.

The Highlands are considered one of Europe's last great areas of wilderness, yet many of the plants and animals that once thrived here has been driven to extinction by the activities of humans. Alladale Estate has created a **Wilderness Reserve** to restore a remote area of the Highlands to its former natural glory. There have been plans to reintroduce certain native species, including wild boar, lynx, brown bears and, most controversially, wolves. You may be

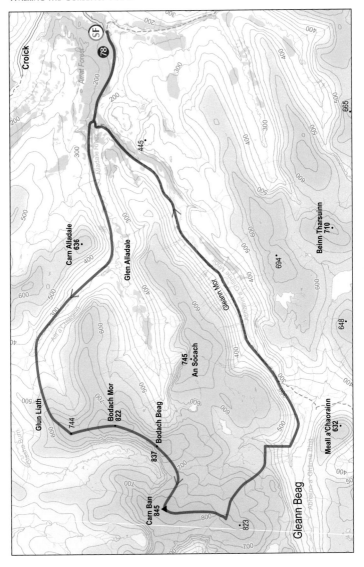

Alladale River

lucky enough to see wild boar and European elk inside an electrified fenced enclosure on the E ridge of An Socach. **www.alladale.com**

Follow the good track to Alladale Lodge. Keep straight on, then fork left at a junction signed 'Ghillie's Rest' and 'Eagles Crag'. Follow the good track up **Glen Alladale** and then fork right up the glen down which the Allt a' Chlaiginn flows and continue until the track ends (1hr 50min, 325m, 38540 90990). Drop down to the Allt a' Chlaiginn burn and follow it upstream until there is an easy crossing place where a burn comes down from the left (38120 91100). Climb WSW up the ridge to the right of the burn. An old vehicle track gives an easy route through the rough heather moorland. The Glun Liath ridge takes you easily up to **Peak 744** (3hr 10min, 35880 90100).

The ridge is easy going on a mixture of stones and moss. Head just left of S to **Bodach Mor** (822m, 36080 89210), S to Craig Riabhach and SSW down to a saddle and up to **Bodach Beag** (4hr 5min, 837m, 35500 87770). ◄ Head WSW to a broad saddle (700m, 34811 87310) and continue in the same direction, veering NW when you reach the ridge up to the cairn on the flat summit plateau of **Carn Ban** (4hr 35min, 845m, 33860 87580).

Head S over the S top of Carn Ban and SSW down to a broad saddle. As you start climbing towards Peak 823 you should see a cairn (805m, 33650 85890) on your left. This marks the top of a cairned route that takes you down the ridge to the E. Follow these cairns, which are too far apart to confidently followed in mist, down the ridge, veering S to reach the top of an old stalker's path (5hr 20min, 645m, 34650 85100). Follow this old, sometimes boggy path as it switchbacks down to a track (350m, 35540 84330) just above **Gleann Beag**. Follow the track down to its final switchback then follow the burn down to the footbridge on the Allt Bheargais (35570 84130). Cross the bridge and follow the path, sometimes boggy, to a bridge over the **Abhainn a' Ghlinne Mhoir** and the track down **Gleann Mor** (6hr 25min, 280m, 37180 84430). Turn left down the track and follow it down to the bridge over the **Alladale River** (44060 89460). Cross the bridge and turn right at a junction back to the parking area (8hr 45min).

The author's measurements suggest that Bodach Beag may be much higher than this and only a couple of metres lower than Carn Ban; too close to be sure it isn't actually higher!

ROUTE 79

Breabag LITTLE BACK

Start	Bone Caves car park (NC 25350 17890)
Distance	21km (13 miles)
Total ascent	950m (3100ft)
Difficulty	Navigation will be very difficult in mist and the route isn't recommended for the inexperienced in bad weather. There is rough, possibly boggy, moorland to cross and the summit ridge has quartzite boulderfields. There are many crags, which could cause problems in poor visibility.
Time	6hr 30min
Summits	Breabag (815m, 2670ft), N summit, Breabag (718m)
Maps	OS Landranger 15
Access	Follow the A837 4km S from Inchnadamph where there is a large car park, signed to Bone Caves. If you are staying at Inchnadamph it would make sense to start from there, doing the road walk first.
Note	It would be easier and quicker to descend by the ascent route, but this would miss much of the interest on the walk.

A glance at the map might suggest that Breabag is just a point on the S ridge of the Munro Ben More Assynt, but it actually provides one of the most interesting walks in the Scottish Highlands. There are magnificent views on this walk.

The Durness limestone rock of the **Inchnadamph National Nature Reserve** makes this an area of great geological and landform interest. At ground level cave entrances, disappearing rivers and limestone pavements can be seen, while underground there is the biggest cave system in Scotland. The featured route visits Bone Caves where archaeologists have found human remains dating back 4500 years along with the bones of animals long extinct in Scotland, including Eurasian lynx, brown bear,

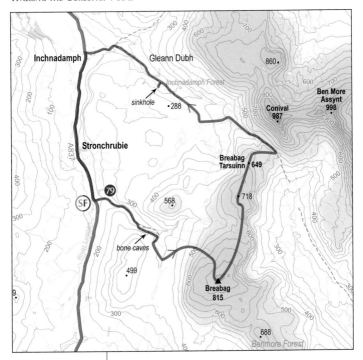

Arctic fox, reindeer and even polar bear. Breabag itself is a rocky quartzite plateau. The descent is made down the Traligill River, which disappears intermittently into sinkholes on its way down the glen.

This is a very unusual spring where water wells up through the gravel. The flow is actually larger than in the Allt nan Fuaran burn which flows down the glen.

Head W up the track from the car park, soon joining a maintained path. After 850m you pass the Fuaran Allt nan Uamh. ◀ As you continue up the glen the burn disappears underground and you come to a path junction (25min, 225m, 26440 17280). Paths are not as shown on the OS map. Fork right across the dry stream bed and follow the path up to the **Bone Caves** (310m, 26830 17020). Fork right at the end of the crags and follow the path up to a pothole entrance (375m, 26900 16760). Keep out! Head SE across moorland to a dry valley (27160 16400) and then head just N of E. You should head for the left-hand end of the slabs and crags guarding the W face of Breabag. After passing the slabs veer right up grassy slopes, avoiding boulderfields, to the summit of **Breabag** (2hr 10min, 815m, 28680 15720). The summit is a small cairn with a nearby shelter round the base of an old trig point. On the approach the lower E top (810m, 28950 15830) would have appeared more prominent.

The route follows the N ridge of Breabag. It is easier to head ENE for about 100m before turning NNE so that the descent of the ridge can be made on grass rather than boulderfield. Continue down to a saddle (635m, 29300 16940) and head N over a complex landscape of quartz-ite boulders, slabs and crags to the **N summit of Breabag** (3hr 10min, 718m, 29230 17970). Continue NNE over another two tops and down to a third (630m, 29600 19010) before veering E down a grassy ridge, avoiding

Sinkhole on River Traligill

the dangerous crags on the N face of **Breabag Tarsuinn**. Near the bottom of this ridge (30320 18970), after passing the crags, head N to the deep gully below **Conival** (3hr 55min, 510m, 30280 19100).

Turn left along the gully and, when a burn appears, avoid the crags down which the burn drops by following a path (sheep track?) which rises slightly on your right. Don't be tempted to drop down left too soon, but contour until you pass a deep gully on your left (495m, 29730 19540). It is now safe to descend down the boggy moorland to the Allt a' Bhealach burn and follow it down until it disappears underground. Continue down the dry valley, which disappears briefly, until a path crosses the valley (4hr 55min, 245m, 27650 20350). Follow the path right down to a bridge over the River Traligill. Cross the bridge and turn left along the burn to see the **sinkhole** down which the River Traligill disappears. Retrace your steps; turn left just before the bridge and then turn left along the path down **Gleann Dubh**. This path becomes a track which passes Glenbain Cottage before crossing the Allt Poll an Droighinn and passing Inchnadamph Lodge to reach the A837 (5hr 40min, 75m, 25070 21800).

Unless you have arranged transport, turn left for the 4km road walk back to the car park (6hr 30min).

ROUTE 80

Glas Bheinn GREY HILL

Start	Inchnadamph (NC25100 21590)
Distance	15km (10 miles)
Total ascent	790m (2600ft)
Difficulty	Most of the route is on an old stalker's path, but there is some boulderfield to traverse and some rough terrain on the suggested descent route. Care would be needed with navigation on the summit plateau in mist.
Time	5hr
Summits	Glas Bheinn (776m, 2541ft)
Maps	OS Landranger 15
Access	Park at a large car park beside the A837 at Inchnadamph.
Note	In bad visibility it would be sensible to descend by the ascent route. A very tough possibility is to head SE from Glas Bheinn to Ben More Assynt and possibly on to Breabag. An alternative is the short but steep and rough climb of Glas Bheinn from the NW.

Glas Bheinn is the end peak on the NW ridge of the Munro Ben More Assynt to the E of Loch Assynt. This is a wild rocky wilderness but a stalker's path allows easy access to the mountain. There are good views from Glas Bheinn, particularly to the nearby Quinag.

Ardvreck Castle, the seat of the McLeods of Assynt, was built in the 15th century and is now a ruin on a promontory on the N shore of Loch Assynt just N of Inchnadamph. The castle came under frequent attacks as the McLeods fought among themselves and against the MacKenzie clan from Wester Ross. The MacKenzies attacked and captured the castle in 1672 and it was never reoccupied. In 1726 it was replaced by Calda House, a modern manor house, but this was burnt down in 1727 and the ruins can be seen beside the road.

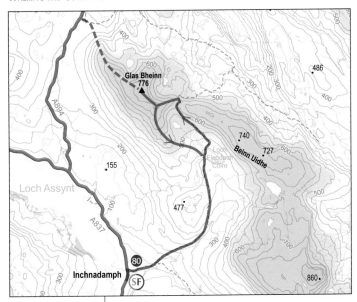

Head N along the main road, cross the Allt Poll an Droighinn and turn right up a good track past Inchnadamph Lodge. After about 900m there is a stalker's path on the left, opposite a footbridge across the river (15min, 105m, 25850 21980). Turn left up the path and follow it easily to a path junction with a small turf-covered shelter (425m, 27360 23930). Fork left, passing two small lochans to reach the outlet at the W end of **Loch Fleodach Coire** (1hr 30min, 400m, 27230 24740). Cross this burn on stepping stones and two more burns at the NW corner of the loch. Follow the path as it continues N and veer NW when the path seems to disappear at a cairn (450m, 27320 25170). The path reappears, but you may lose it again, in which case you should head NW to the pass between Glas Bheinn and Beinn Uidhe (2hr 15min, 625m, 26470 26170). Turn left up a path which is beginning to develop through the boulderfield. The ridge narrows before opening out at the summit plateau.

Veer right to the large summit cairn on **Glas Bheinn** (2hr 50min, 776m, 25480 26480).

Return to the SE end of the summit plateau and head S across boulderfields. Easier terrain is soon reached as you descend to a small lochan (615m, 26030 25350) on the ridge. Veer ESE back to Loch Fleodach Coire (3hr 45min) and follow the path back to the car park at Inchnadamph (5hr).

ROUTE 81

Canisp ROOF

Start	Glencanisp Lodge (NC 10730 21980)
Distance	23km (14 miles)
Total ascent	1200m (4000ft)
Difficulty	The access is on a good stalker's track. There is a short section of boggy ground to cross and the summit is a quartzite boulderfield.
Time	6hr 5min
Summits	Canisp (846m, 2779ft)
Maps	OS Landranger 15
Access	From Inchnadamph follow the A837 to Lochinver then follow the narrow minor road, signed to Glencanisp Lodge. After 1 mile, park at the head of the public road where there is parking for about five cars. On sunny summer days these parking places will quickly fill up and it would be sensible to park in the car park behind the visitor centre (09400 22400) in Lochinver.
Note	The shortest approach is from the A837 to the SE, but that route is rougher and doesn't give the fine views of Suilven that you get on the recommended route. If transport could be organised a traverse from Lochinver to the A837 would be a good idea.

Canisp is a distinctive mountain with a steep-sided NW ridge. It is climbed as much for the magnificent views of the adjacent peaks, including Suilven, than it is for its own merit.

A view of Suilven from the route

As you climb Canisp, the dominant mountain on your right, with its steep sandstone crags guarding its serrated ridge, is **Suilven** (Sula Bheinn). From the coast Suilven looks like a large grey pillar, hence the name which it was given by sea-borne Vikings. The peak is only 731m high and therefore not even a Corbett, but it is one of the most distinctive mountains in Scotland.

Continue up the tarmac road and fork left behind Canisp Lodge and fork right along a track at the far end of the house. Follow this track for a further 5.5km, ignoring a track off left, to a bridge across the Abhainn na Clach Airigh (1hr 25min, 140m, 16560 20240). Follow the track across the bridge and soon pass the path to Suilven before crossing the Abhainn na Clach Airigh again. Continue to a fork in the track just N of **Loch na Gainimh** (1hr 45min, 185m, 17310 19260). Fork left and follow the track until it deteriorates then ends (455m, 18820 19430) on a boggy plateau. Continue ENE to the NW ridge of Canisp. Turn right up the easy grass ridge, dodging a few sandstone crags. The final section of the ridge is up a quartzite boulderfield which soon leads to the small summit plateau on **Canisp**. The highest point on the flat plateau is not obvious and there is a shelter wall at either end of the short plateau. The better shelter at the SE end of the plateau contains the base of an old trig point (3hr 25min, 846m, 20310 18750).

Return by the same route to Loch na Gainimh (4hr 25min) and the parking area (6hr 5min).

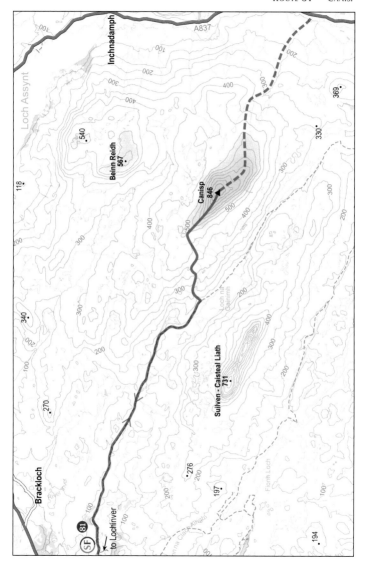

ROUTE 82

Spidean Coinich MOSSY PEAK, *Sail Ghorm* BLUE HEEL
and Sail Gharbh ROUGH HEEL *on Quinag* MILK BUCKET

Start	A894, N of Skiag Bridge (NC 23290 27370)
Distance	13km (8 miles)
Total ascent	1150m (3800ft)
Difficulty	The recommended route is relatively easy considering the formidable look of the mountain. There are a few small rocksteps with very easy scrambling and some narrow ridges as well as some relatively easy boulderfields to cross, but paths have developed along all the ridges.
Time	5hr 55min
Summits	Spidean Coinich (764m, 2508ft), Sail Ghorm (776m, 2551ft), Sail Gharbh (808m, 2653ft)
Maps	OS Landranger 15
Access	From Inchnadamph follow the A837 N to Skiag Bridge then fork right along the A894. After 2 miles there is a large parking area on the right.
Note	There are alternative routes on the mountain, but many of these will involve rock-climbing skills. If you want to split the route into two walks then the obvious thing is to climb Spidean Coinich separately.

Quinag, N of Loch Assynt, is one of the most majestic mountains in Scotland. There are at least seven tops, three of which are Corbetts. The Torridonian sandstone crags are particularly spectacular when the buttresses of Sail Ghorm and Sail Gharbh are viewed from Kylesku to the NW. The sandstone is capped by quartzite, which forms the slabs and boulderfields on the SE ridge of Spidean Coinich and the boulderfield on the summit of Sail Gharbh. From Sail Ghorm there is a good view W to the Isle of Lewis and on a clear day it is even possible to see the small island of Rona 100km to the NNW.

The **John Muir Trust** (www.jmt.org) is the leading wild land conservation charity in the UK, inspired by the work and spirit of the pioneering Scots-born American conservationist. The Trust owns

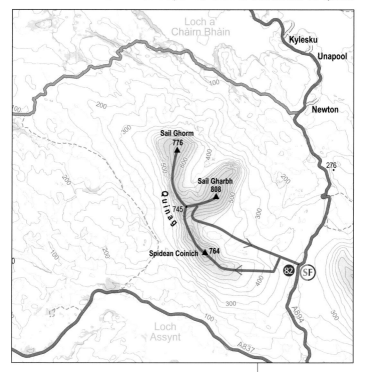

land throughout the Highlands, including Quinag. Quinag encompasses a wide range of habitats, from the coast where seabirds, seals and dolphins may be seen to the tops where you may encounter ptarmigan, Arctic hare and ring ouzel. The estate is also home to otters, pine martens, water voles and Britain's largest mammal, the red deer.

Head a few metres S along the road then turn right along a path and across a footbridge. Ignore the old path which used to be the route up Spidean Coinich and in 2011 was a boggy scar. Turn left up a new path and reach quartzite slabs about 500m from the road. Turn left up

Crags on the S ridge of Sail Ghorm

a combination of path and quartzite slab to reach the ridge and continue up slabs joined by paths through easy grass and boulderfields to a minor rocky summit (615m, 21120 27340). Descend 25m then follow the paths which are developing through boulderfields to the summit of **Spidean Coinich** where there is a large cairn close to the small cairn marking the summit (1hr 30min, 764m, 20610 27720).

Head a few metres left before turning right down the path along a narrow ridge and then steeply down to a small lochan (655m, 20370 27990). Continue over a minor top (713m, 20210 28200) and down another narrow ridge to the Bealach a' Chornaidh (2hr 10min, 575m, 20110 28460). It would be easy to escape E from here to descend down the main path back to the parking area. Continue N along the path which finds its way easily through rock outcrops to the summit of **Peak 745** (20090 28910) and continue to a low point (655m, 19930 29110) with spectacular views of the crags on the W face of the mountain. Continue over another minor top and then to the summit cairn on **Sail Ghorm** (3hr 25min, 776m, 19840 30410).

Return down the ridge. Peak 745 can be contoured on its left to reach the cairns marking the top of the descent path on the broad saddle (710m, 20400 28930) between Peak 745 and Sail Gharbh. Climb easily NNE to the trig point on the summit of **Sail Gharbh** (4hr 25min, 808m, 20930 29180).

Return to the saddle (20400 28930) and follow the path down to Lochan Bealach Chornaidh and back to the parking area (5hr 55min).

ROUTE 83

Beinn Leoid SLOPING HILL

Start	Kylestrome (NC 21800 34510)
Distance	29km (18 miles)
Total ascent	1470m (4900ft)
Difficulty	There is a good track to the foot of the mountain, after which there is a short section of peat bog to cross. There are short sections of awkward boulderfield on the final ascent up the NW ridge. Care would be needed with navigation in mist.
Time	7hr 55min
Summits	Sail na Slataich (652m), Beinn Leoid (792m, 2597ft)
Maps	OS Landranger 15
Access	From Inchnadamph follow the A837 N to Skiag Bridge then fork right along the A894. One mile N of the Kylesku Bridge, turn right down an unsigned private road where there is a car park on the right after a few metres.
Note	The quickest and shortest ascent is by using the stalker's path between Loch More and Loch Merkland on the A838 to the NE, but this route lacks interest. An interesting way to approach Beinn Leoid would be by canoe or boat from Kylesku to Glencoul or Glendhu. The area is great for backpacking and Beinn Leoid could be climbed as part of a trip involving Glas Bheinn, Beinn More Assynt and Breabag.

Beinn Leoid is a remote mountain between Kylesku and Loch Shin. The terrain to the W and NW of Beinn Leoid is particularly spectacular with much bare rock, deep glens and an approach along impressive sea lochs. It would be possible to use a mountain bike as far as Glendhu Bothy.

A stone cairn on the N side of the Kylesku Bridge was erected in 1993 to honour the men of the **XIIth Submarine Flotilla** who manned the X-craft and human torpedo midget submarines that trained in these waters in 1943 and 1944. These craft were designed to be carried to the enemy coastline by submarine and then used to attack enemy warships

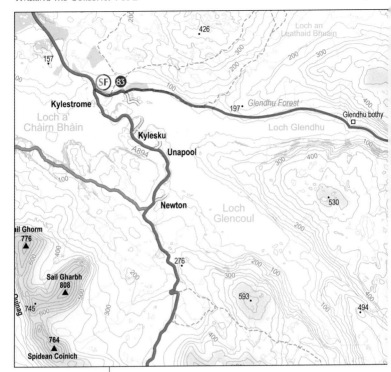

in harbour with limpet mines. The best known operation was the attack, in September 1943, on the German battleship *Tirpitz*, which was based in the Altenfjord in Norway. The *Tirpitz* was badly damaged and put out of action for eight months.

Follow the tarmac estate road past the estate buildings and down to **Loch Glendhu**. Leave the tarmac road when it heads across a bridge onto Eilean na Rainich, turning left along a good track (22550 34500). Follow this track along the N shore of the sea loch, forking right after 3km and continuing to the **Glendhu Bothy** (1hr 30min, 5m, 28320 33700). ◄ The track continues up the spectacular

This bothy at the head of Loch Glendhu is maintained by the Mountain Bothies Association.

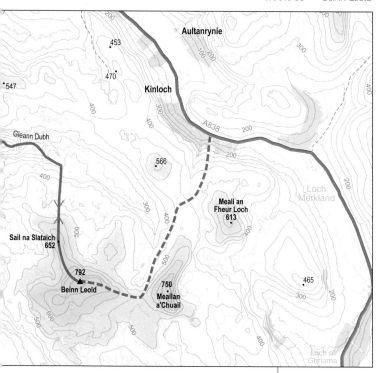

Gleann Dubh to reach a 'hidden valley' with rough boggy pasture. The track crosses a bridge (180m, 30990 32910) at the head of grassy flat before climbing to the SE. Continue until the good track splits into two grassy stalker's paths (355m, 31690 32160). Fork right and continue until a cairn marks the end of the path (2hr 50min, 405m, 31770 32060).

Head roughly S across boggy moor and peat hags, soon reaching a broad grassy ridge and veering right to the summit of **Sail na Slataich** (3hr 45min, 652m, 31450 30400). Head SSE, gently downhill, to a broad saddle (610m) and climb SE up the steep final slopes of **Beinn Leoid**. The final ascent to the trig point on the summit is

Abhainn a' Ghlinne Dhuibh, Beinn Leoid

over a mixture of grass and slightly awkward boulderfield (4hr 20min, 792m, 32030 29480).

Return by the same route to the path end (5hr 20min), bothy (6hr 20min) and car park (7hr 55min).

ROUTE 84

Ben Hee FAIRY HILL

Start	West Merkland (NC 38380 32950)
Distance	15km (10 miles)
Total ascent	920m (3000ft)
Difficulty	Stalker's paths take the walker through the roughest of the heather moorland. There are boulderfields on the upper parts of the mountain, but they are not particularly difficult as long as the visibility is good enough to see the easier routes through them.
Time	5hr
Summits	NE summit, Ben Hee (851m), Ben Hee (873m, 2864ft)
Maps	OS Landranger 16
Access	Follow the A838 S from Durness, turning left at Laxford Bridge to Loch Merkland. There is a track to the left beside the cottage at West Merkland where there is limited parking.
Note	It is possible to shortcut from the corrie lochan up the N ridge of Ben Hee. The quickest route is to ascend and descend by the recommended descent route, but this misses all the best points of the mountain.

When viewed from Loch Merkland, Ben Hee appears as a rounded hill covered in heather moorland, but the lochs and corries on the approach from the N provide plenty of interest. There are magnificent views over Ben Hope, the most northerly Munro, and Ben Loyal to the N coast of Scotland as well as to all the Corbetts in Assynt.

The track over the **Bealach nam Meirleach** (robber's pass) joining West Merkland on Loch Merkland to Allnabad on the Strath More road was built between 1866 and 1869. A 1940s guidebook stated that this was an old drove road but there doesn't seem to be any evidence for this. However, the name suggests that the route may have been used by cattle rustlers.

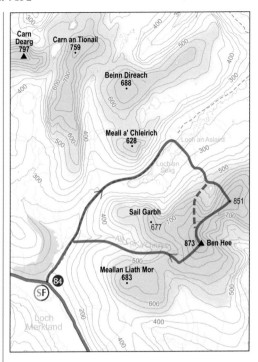

Head up the good track to the right of the burn, keeping straight on at a couple of junctions. The track veers right over Bealach nam Meirleach and follows the shores of Loch an Tuim Bhuidhe and **Loch an t-Seilg**. At the end of Loch an t-Seilg an old, faint stalker's path goes off to the right (1hr 10min, 255m, 41900 36650).

These may be under water in wet weather.

Turn right and cross the burn flowing from Loch an t-Seilg to Loch an Aslaird on stepping stones. ◄ Continue until the stalker's path ends (325m, 42460 36110) and then up rough heather beside the Allt a' Gharbh-choire Bhig. Follow the stalker's path when it reappears and then veers left to easier terrain (410m, 42750 35950). Head easily uphill to the corrie lochan and then climb the ridge to the left of the lochan. There is a relatively easy route up the boulderfield, but it may be difficult to see in mist. The ridge takes you to the **NE summit of Ben Hee** (2hr 55min, 851m, 43480 35040).

Head SW along the ridge towards Ben Hee. There are crags on your left as well as old landslips. Continue SW from the low-point (755m, 42980 34640) before veering left to the summit of **Ben Hee**. The summit is marked by a small cairn, not the trig point about 30m further SE (3hr 25min, 873m, 42630 33960).

Head roughly SW down the broad ridge, veering right to the source of the **Allt Coir' a' Chruiteir**. Continue down the left-hand side of the burn, picking up a path at about 530m. This leads to the end of a stalker's path beside a shooting butt (490m, 41230 33730). In places this path is boggy and, in several places, washed away by the burn, but it does lead you relatively easily through some very rough moorland. Eventually you reach the track, the junction being marked by a cairn (4hr 40min, 190m, 39200 34160). Turn left back to West Merkland (5hr).

Allt Coir' a' Chruiteir on Ben Hee

311

ROUTE 85

Meallan Liath Coire Mhic Dhughaill SMALL GREY
ROUNDED HILL OF MACDOUGAL'S CORRIE *or*
Carn Dearg RED CAIRN

Start	Kinloch, Loch More (NC 34820 34290)
Distance	18km (11 miles)
Total ascent	1040m (3400ft)
Difficulty	The going is relatively easy for such a wild area. There are boulderfields and small crags on the ridges, but they don't pose big problems. Navigation would be difficult in misty conditions.
Time	5hr 35min
Summits	Meallan Liath Coire Mhic Dhughaill (801m, 2627ft), Carn Dearg (797m, 2613ft)
Maps	OS Landranger 15 and 16
Access	Follow the A838 S from Durness, turning left at Laxford Bridge to park at Kinloch just after the S end of Loch More where a track goes sharp left.
Note	It would be interesting to approach the mountain from the N with its deep crag-lined corries, but the distance would make this a better idea when backpacking rather than day-hiking. At the time of writing the approach track was being upgraded prior to clear-felling the forest at the SE end of Loch More.

Meallan Liath Coire Mhic Dhughaill is a complex hill to the NE of Loch More, with many ridges and subsidiary peaks. The recommended route gives superb views of Ben Stack, Foinaven and Arkle. Measurements of altitude with a hand-held GPS suggest that it may actually be Carn Dearg that is the highest summit – and therefore the Corbett – rather than Meallan Liath Coire Mhic Dhughaill.

Ben Stack is the prominent mountain at the head of Loch More, looking like a miniature version of the Matterhorn. Only 721m, it doesn't reach Corbett status, but it is a popular mountain with an easy

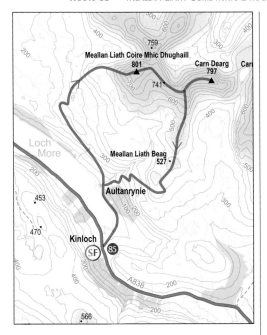

route up the SE ridge. On 6 August 2005 former
Foreign Secretary Robin Cook died after collapsing
with a heart attack while walking down from the
summit of Ben Stack.

Follow the good track until a track goes off to the right just
before Aultanrynie Cottage (25min, 50m, 34690 36010).
Turn right then, after 150m, turn left and cross the bridge
over the Allt an Reinidh. Follow the track diagonally up
the hillside to emerge, with splendid views of Ben Stack,
Arkle and Foinaven as the track veers right to cross a burn
with plenty of stepping stones (1hr 5 min, 275m, 33730
38330). Ignore the 'wooden roadway' and follow a faint
track up the ridge on your left where it ends at a cairn
(305m, 33790 38550). Head roughly NE up the broad
ridge, veering E after reaching a plateau with a large

Crags on the W ridge of Meallan Liath Coire Mhic Dhughaill

lochan. There are easy boulderfields and small crags of the ridge which leads to the trig point on the summit of **Meallan Liath Coire Mhic Dhughaill** (2hr 30min, 801m, 35720 39140).

Head ENE, veering SE over **Top 741**, to the low point on the ridge (700m, 36660 38750). Continue roughly E veering ENE then E to the summit cairn on **Carn Dearg** (3hr 15min, 797m, 37700 38920).

Return along the ridge until it splits at a small cairn and head S down the ridge to a marshy lochan. Continue roughly SSW over the many tops of **Meallan Liath Beag** to the knoll at the end of the ridge (4hr 35min, 513m, 36160 35990). Head SE down to a track, turn right and follow the track easily down to Loch More (5hr 10min). Turn left back to the parking area (5hr 35min).

ROUTE 86

Meall Horn HILL OF THE EAGLE

Start	N of Achfary (NC 29780 40200)
Distance	21km (13 miles)
Total ascent	980m (3200ft)
Difficulty	The going is easy on the broad grassy ridges, with occasional stony areas and a few small crags. The ascent and descent is over rough moorland. Careful navigation would be needed in mist.
Time	6hr 5min
Summits	Meall Horn (777m, 2548ft)
Maps	OS Landranger 9
Access	Follow the A838 S from Durness, turning left at Laxford Bridge and after passing Loch Stack there is a track on the left about 700m before reaching Achfary. There is limited parking at this junction, but it is permitted to drive 100m down this private road to a parking area beside the bridge.
Note	The quickest ascent would be to follow the track up the Allt Horn and climb steeply up to Creagan Meall Horn, but this route lacks interest.

Meall Horn looks a rather uninteresting mountain when viewed from Arkle, but it has big crags and corrie lakes on its N slopes. The suggested route gives a good walk following the ridges that surround Coire Granda.

Traditionally, **peat** has been an important natural fuel source in the Scottish Highlands and you will be able to see peat cuttings on the approach to Meall Horn. Peat would normally be cut in the spring and left to dry over two or three weeks of good weather. The peats would then be stacked into small (five peat) piles called *rudhan* for a further two weeks, before being put into bigger piles called *rudhan mor* for further drying. When fully dry the peat would be carted home.

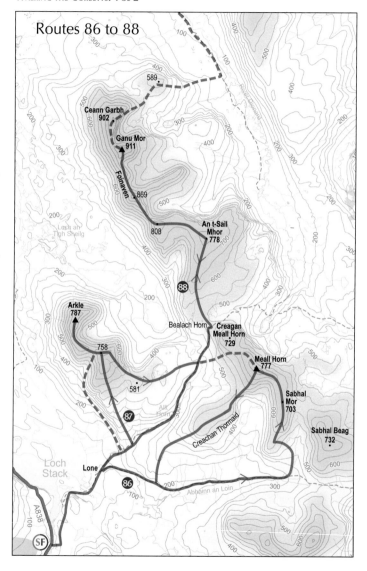

Routes 86 to 88

Ceann Garbh
902

Ganu Mor
911

Foinaven

869

808

An t-Sail
Mhor
778

88

Arkle
787

758

Bealach Horn

Creagan
Meall Horn
729

Meall Horn
777

581

87

Sabhal
Mor
703

Sabhal Beag
732

Creachan Thormaid

Loch
Stack

Lone

86

Abhainn an Loin

A838

SF

Cross the bridge and follow the estate road past Airdachuilinn Cottage to the bridge by the farm buildings at **Lone** (35min, 45m, 30920 42130). Cross the bridge and, after 100m, fork right and follow the track diagonally up the hillside and then down to the **Abhainn an Loin**. Continue along the burn to the second stone bridge (2hr, 315m, 36260 42080), after passing the buttress of the Sail Eilid a' Mhoraire ridge.

Turn left up the burn and then veer left once you are past the crags on Sail Eilid a' Mhoraire. Climb the slope to an inadequate shelter wall on Sail Eilid a' Mhoraire (575m, 35690 42960). Turn right (NNE veering N) up the broad ridge, over **Sabhal Mor** (703m, 36000 44040) and continue veering left to the large summit cairn on **Meall Horn** (3hr 45min, 777m, 35270 44910).

Descend SSW, veering SW to a saddle with shallow ponds trapped by the rock outcrops. Continue roughly SW up Creachan Thormaid to a small cairn at the SW end of this broad level ridge (4hr 25min, 600m, 33820 43240). Care is needed in descent to avoid crags on either flank of the ridge. Initially head W, gradually veering WSW (to about 330m, 32680 42900) then head roughly S to reach the track to the left of the crags (5hr 15min, 185m, 32420 41910). Turn right, following the track back to Lone and then back to the parking area (6hr 5min).

Meall Horn from Lochan na Faoileige on Arkle

ROUTE 87

Arkle PEAK OF THE CHEST

Start	Achfary (NC 29810 40090)
Distance	20km (12 miles)
Total ascent	1100m (3600ft)
Difficulty	Although much of the going is fairly straightforward, there are areas of boulderfield to cross and an exposed ridge with some very easy scrambling, which would be daunting for the inexperienced in strong winds.
Time	5hr 55min
Summits	SE summit, Arkle (758m), Arkle (787m, 2580ft)
Maps	OS Landranger 9
Access	Parking as for Route 86
Note	Those with excess energy could climb Meall Horn when they reach the track on the suggested descent. In bad weather descend by the ascent route, but this route is much less interesting than the recommended route. Another possibility, which isn't obvious from the map but is reasonably easy, is to descend SSW on scree from the low point between the two main summits on Arkle. When below the crags, turn left just below the scree to return to Lone.

Arkle is the prominent mountain seen across Loch Stack with a line of quartzite crags and screes facing the loch. There is a narrow, almost knife-edge, ridge separating the two highest summits on the mountain. There are fine views in all direction and Arkle is the best viewpoint to appreciate the grandeur of Foinaven.

You can expect to see **ravens** around the rocky mountains of NW Scotland. These massive all-black birds were once widespread throughout Britain but persecution from farmers and gamekeepers in the 19th century caused the bird to retreat to the mountains and sea-cliffs to the N and W of Britain. The raven is larger than a crow or a rook, and can be readily identified by its diamond-shaped tail and its habit of doing spectacular aerobatics in air uplifting off the cliffs.

Cross the bridge and follow the estate road past Airdachuilinn Cottage to a bridge by the farm buildings at **Lone** (35min, 45m, 30920 43130). Cross the bridge and fork left after 100m and follow the track up the **Allt Horn**. There is a small cairn on the left at the top of the switch-backs marking the start of a faint path (160m, 31730 42820) to the left. Follow this path, NNW, up the hillside until it fades away among bare rock slabs (at about 385m, 31540 43680). Continue easily up the broad ridge to the summit cairn on the **SE summit of Arkle** (2hr 25min, 758m, 31030 45330).

See map in Route 86.

There is a small cairn just to the W of the sum-mit cairn which marks the beginning of the rough path descending down to a saddle (685m, 30780 45400). The path continues over a minor top onto a narrowing ridge. There is some easy scrambling along this ridge which

Arkle seen from its SE summit

leads to the cairn on the summit plateau on the main summit of **Arkle** (3hr, 787m, 30270 46170).

Return to the SE summit of Arkle then head E to the end of the summit plateau before descending the SE ridge, down easy stony terrain to the saddle (3hr 55min, 560m, 31850 44670) before Meall Aonghais. Head E over boulderfield, skirting Meall Aonghais, down to the E shore of Lochan na Faoileige. Continue roughly ENE down grassy slopes to the left of a line of low crags and, just above an unnamed lochan, veer right below the crags and head E to the track (4hr 30min, 395m, 33690 45160).

Turn right down the track to Lone and back to the parking area (5hr 55min).

ROUTE 88

Ganu Mor, Foinaven BIG WEDGE, WHITE MOUNTAIN

Start	Achfary (NC 29810 40090)
Distance	29km (18 miles)
Total ascent	1700m (5600ft)
Difficulty	Once the approach track is left behind much of the route is over quartzite boulders which provide slow and tough walking. There is a little easy scrambling on the descent to Cadha na Beucaich from Peak 808. The ridge approaches 'knife-edge' status in places and would not be a good place to be in strong winds. Once you are embarked on the ridge there is no safe escape route if you are caught out in bad weather.
Time	9hr 20min
Summits	Ganu Mor, Foinaven (911m, 2980ft)
Maps	OS Landranger 9
Access	Parking as for Route 86
Note	It is possible to approach Foinaven up Srath Dionard to the N and then climb Cnoc a' Mhadaidh, Ceann Garbh and on to Ganu Mor. This would enable a traverse of the mountain by descending the recommended route if transport could be arranged at either end. The author has not checked this route, which involves a steep climb up Ceann Garbh.

Foinaven is one of the most impressive mountains in Scotland with a long ridge, narrow and rocky in places, with many summits. The flanks of the mountain are protected by vast quartzite screes which appear white on a sunny day. The high point is the W top which is about 2m higher than the E top.

Main ridge on Foinaven

An **Irish racehorse** was named after this mountain. Virtually unknown until the 1967 Grand National, Foinaven was lagging near the back when a loose horse veered across the field at the 23rd fence, bringing down all the leaders. Foinaven was so far behind that its jockey had time to steer his mount clear of the chaos and jump on the wide outside gaining a 100-length lead before the others got back into the chase. Even this lead was reduced 20 lengths by the winning post.

See map in Route 86.

Cross the bridge and follow the estate road past Airdachuilinn Cottage to a bridge by the farm buildings at **Lone** (35min, 45m, 30920 43130). Cross the bridge and fork left after 100m and follow the track up the **Allt Horn** and to the high point of the track at **Bealach Horn** (2hr 5min, 530m, 33950 45990). Head NNW, veering N, to **An t-Sail Mhor**. It is easier going if you stay on grass to the right of the crest of the ridge, rather than on boulderfields on the ridge. The summit is marked by the remains of a trig point surrounded by a good sheltering wall (778m, 33860, 48360).

Recent measurements have confirmed Fionhaven as a Corbett rather than a Munro at 911.05 ±0.3m. The highest point is the W top.

Head WNW, veering W, from here along a broad ridge to **Peak 808** (3hr 45min, 32510 48720). This is where the committing part of the route begins. Descend steeply NW to the Cadha na Beucaich (690m, 32330 48870). There is some very easy scrambling down a crag towards the bottom of this descent. Climb steeply to **Peak 869** (31880 49430) and down to a low point (785m, 31670 49650). You have to pass over a minor top on the narrow ridge before the final climb to **Ganu Mor**, the highest summit on Foinaven (5hr 15min, 911m, 31520 50690). ◀

Return back along the ridge to Peak 808 (6hr 40min), the track (7hr 45min) and back to the parking area (9hr 20min).

ROUTE 89

Cranstackie RUGGED HILL *and Beinn Spionnaidh*

STRONG HILL

Start	Carbreck (NC 33000 59030)
Distance	12km (8 miles)
Total ascent	1100m (3600ft)
Difficulty	The NW-facing slopes of these mountains is steep pasture, but the ridges are covered with quartzite boulderfields edged by crags. Care is needed on the steep boulderfields on Cranstackie and this route wouldn't be recommended to inexperienced walkers in bad weather.
Time	5hr 30min
Summits	Cranstackie (801m, 2630ft), Beinn Spionnaidh (773m, 2535ft)
Maps	OS Landranger 9
Access	Follow the A838 12km SW from Durness to a track on the left, signed to Rhigolter, by the cottage at Carbreck. There is a large parking area about 300m past the cottage. Please don't drive down the private track.
Note	It is possible to climb the steep slopes of Calbhach Coire to the saddle between Cranstackie and Beinn Spionnaidh. It would also be possible to climb these Corbetts from Polla at the SW end of Loch Eriboll, but this ascent is not recommended as it is rough and featureless.

Cranstackie appears as a rocky wilderness when viewed from Foinaven but when approached from the NW these Corbetts are surprisingly grassy. Beinn Spionnaidh is the most northerly Corbett.

Cape Wrath, the NW tip of mainland Scotland, can be seen from these Corbetts. Named *hvarf* (turning point) in Norse, Cape Wrath was where the Viking longboats turned S to their settlements in the Hebrides and Ireland. The Cape Wrath Long-Distance Trail is a 200-mile trek from Fort William to Cape Wrath through the wildest terrain in Britain, including Morar, Knoydart, Applecross, Torridon and Assynt.

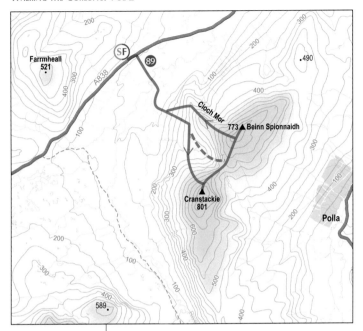

Head back to the track, turn right and follow it across the **River Dionard** to Rhigolter Cottage (25min, 45m, 33940 57680). Head straight up the hillside, then veer right when the gradient eases, at about 350m, and contour into Calbhach Coire to cross the burn at the corrie entrance (1hr 15min, 315m, 34750 56690). Head S to the broad NW ridge of **Cranstackie**, veering left straight up the steep grass slopes. At 700m you reach a steep boulderfield consisting of blocks fallen down from the crags which edge the summit of Cranstackie. Climb this boulderfield, breaching the crags on the left. On reaching the summit plateau turn right to the large summit cairn (2hr 35min, 801m, 35070 55590).

Head down the boulderfields on the NE ridge, taking care to stay left of the crags on the E side of the ridge. Once down to 720m the going becomes easy and you soon reach the saddle between Cranstackie and Beinn Spionnaidh (565m, 35710 56180). Climb easily NNE over grass, then boulderfield, to a cairn at the W end of the summit plateau and NE to the walled-in trig point on **Beinn Spionnaidh** (3hr 50min, 773m, 36200 57280). The highest point on the plateau is not clear, but it may be a slight rise (36140 57200) about 100m SW of the trig point.

Head back to the cairn (35940 56980) at the SW end of the plateau and turn right (WNW) down the ridge. Care is needed descending the boulderfield, but you soon reach easy, but steep, grass slopes. Continue over a saddle to the summit of **Cioch Mor** (555m, 35120 57500) and steeply down to a second saddle (4hr 45min, 350m, 34830 57900). Head roughly WSW down steep grass slopes to Rhigolter Cottage and follow the track back to the parking area (5hr 30min).

Crags on the NE face of Cranstackie

ROUTE 90

An Caisteal, Ben Loyal THE CASTLE, LAW HILL

Start	Ribigill (NC 58440 54670)
Distance	25km (15 miles)
Total ascent	1100m (3600ft)
Difficulty	Contrary to appearances, the ascent is very easy and there is only a very short section of difficult terrain on the descent. However, it would not be a good mountain on which to be lost in bad weather, so the inexperienced would be advised to wait for good visibility.
Time	6hr 50min
Summits	An Caisteal, Ben Loyal (765m, 2506ft)
Maps	OS Landranger 10
Access	From Durness follow the A838 E to Tongue and head S down the minor road past the Ben Loyal Hotel until an estate road goes straight on when the road bends right after 2.3km. There is limited parking by the gate 50m down the estate road.
Note	The easiest and quickest descent would be to descend by the ascent route. The experienced walker could shorten the descent route by heading W of Sgorr Fhionnaich and down to the Allt Lon Malmsgaig, but this route could land you in difficulty if your navigation is poor.

Ben Loyal is the most north-easterly Corbett and gives magnificent views along the N coast of Scotland and across the sea to the Orkney Islands. It is an impressive mountain, especially when viewed from the NW when the buttresses on the W ridges add to the grandeur of the main ridge.

On the descent you will see **Loch Fhionnaich** in a 150m deep gash between Sgor a' Chleirich and Sgorr Fhionnaich on the W ridge of Beinn Bheag. It is very difficult to work out how such an unusual feature could have come into existence. The only explanation seems to be that, during the ice ages, the gap must have been a large S-facing corrie and

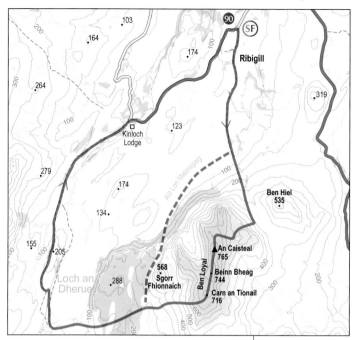

then the big glacier flowing along the line of the Allt
Lon Malmsgaig eroded away the head wall.

Head S down the estate road to **Ribigill Farm** and continue S along a good track through sheep country, ignoring a right fork. The track has deteriorated to a sometimes
boggy path by the time the **Allt Lon Malmsgaig** burn is
reached (45min, 60m, 58080 51570). Ford the burn and
head SSE up the faint path which passes under the steep
crags of Sgor Chaonasaid. You may lose the path (at about
380m, 58760 49710), if so just head WSW up the hill.
The path eventually fades away in a boggy plateau to
the N of Loch na Creige Riabhaich. Head W up to the
N ridge of **An Caisteal** and turn left along the ridge. The
rocky tor of An Caisteal looks daunting, but it is actually

Ben Loyal

very easy to climb to the trig point on the summit from the NW (front right) (2hr 35min, 765m, 57810 48850).

Climb down the tor by the same route then follow the path which is developing around the W side of the summit tor. Continue S to **Beinn Bheag** (744m, 57630 48240) and **Carr an Tionail** (716m, 57600 47670). Continue S for another 200m before turning right, down the W ridge, noting the dramatic Loch Fhionnaich on your right. Continue down to the Allt Fhionnaich and cross it where the burn veers left just below a delightful hidden waterfall (3hr 40min, 250m, 56070 47370). Now head WSW across a mile of surprisingly easy moorland. The final 200m is tougher as you find a way through a line of crags and down to the unnamed burn which feeds the SE corner of **Loch an Dherue**. You need to ensure you are left of the big crags that line the E shore of the loch. You should be able to cross the burn easily unless it is in flood (4hr 15min, 90m, 54280 46730).

There is a good track, not shown on the OS 1:50,000 map, about 100m W of the burn. Turn right along the track and then right at a junction to a bothy at the SW end of the loch. Continue along the track which climbs above the W shore of the loch before turning back N. Follow this track all the way to **Kinloch Lodge** where you follow the tarmac drive down to the public road (5hr 55min, 30m, 55420 52270). Turn right back to the parking area (6hr 50min).

10 SKYE AND HARRIS

Skye and Harris: Bases and facilities

Skye is now normally accessed by the road bridge at the Kyle of Lochalsh which was opened in 1995, but Caledonian MacBrayne still operates vehicle ferries between Mallaig and Armadale.

Base for Routes 91 and 92: Broadford, Skye

Broadford is a large village with excellent facilities for tourists, including a Co-op supermarket.

Broadford SYHA, Isle of Skye, IV49 9AA Tel: 01471 822 442

Broadford Hotel Tel: 01471 822 204 www.broadfordhotel.co.uk

Dunollie Hotel Tel: 08444 146 600

Ashaig Camping and Caravan Site is about 3 miles E of Broadford. Tel: 01471 822 771 www.ashaig-campsite-skye.co.uk

Alternative base for Route 91 and 92: Sligachan

Sligachan Hotel is at the junction of the A87 and A863 NW of Broadford. As well as normal hotel facilities the hotel offers self-catering accommodation, a bunkhouse and a well-equipped camping and caravan site. This old coaching inn has been used as a base for walkers and climbers since it was built in 1830.

The Sligachan Hotel Tel: 01478 650 204 http://sligachan.co.uk

Alternative base for Routes 91 and 92: Kyle of Lochalsh or Kyleakin

You could stay at Kyle of Lochalsh or Kyleakin on either side of the Skye Bridge. Both these villages have good tourist facilities and Kyle of Lochalsh has a Co-op supermarket.

Base for Route 93: Tarbert, Harris

Tarbert is a small village with ferry terminal, several shops, tourist office, several hotels and B&Bs. There is camping and a bunkhouse at Drinishadar on the coast road about 7km S of Tarbert.

Tourist information: VisitScotland, The Pier, Tarbert, Isle of Harris, HS3 3DG Tel: 01859 502 011

Harris Hotel Tel: 01895 502 154 www.harrishotel.com

Hotel Hebrides Tel: 01895 502 578 www.hotel-hebrides.com

Drinishader Hostel offers bunkhouse as well as more luxurious accommodation. Tel: 01895 511 255 www.number5.biz

Minch View Touring Park is also at Drinishader for camping and caravans. Tel: 01895 511 207

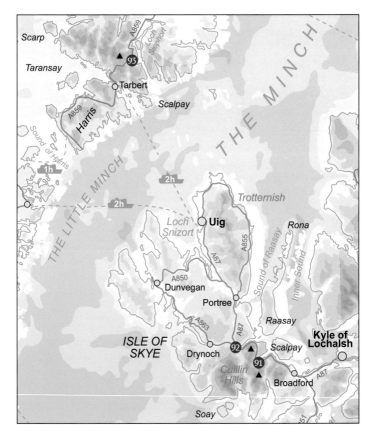

Ciche na Beinne Deirge and Beinn Dearg Mheadhonach from Garbh-bheinn (Route 91)

Access to Harris

Caledonian MacBrayne operates the vehicle ferries to Harris and Lewis with two main routes with 1–2 sailings a day:

- Uig on Skye to Tarbert on Harris with a sailing time of 1hr 40min (no Sunday sailings)
- Ullapool to Stornaway on Lewis with a sailing time of 2hr 45min.

Tel: 0800 066 5000 (UK only) www.calmac.co.uk

The Uig to Tarbert sailing is more convenient since it is only a few miles from the access routes to An Cliseam.

An interesting alternative is take the ferry from Oban to Lochboisdale (6hr 30min) on South Uist and drive, or preferably cycle, to North Uist. Then take the ferry from Berneray to Leverburgh (1hr) and continue to Tarbert to climb An Cliseam and continue to Stornaway for the ferry to Ullapool.

ROUTE 91
Garbh-bheinn ROUGH HILL

Start	Loch Ainort (NG 53450 26730)
Distance	9km (6 miles)
Total ascent	1070m (3500ft)
Difficulty	The ridges are a mixture of crag, boulderfield and scree with boggy moorland on the approach. You need the ability to route-find through the crags. There is easy, but exposed, scrambling high up on Garbh-bheinn, but other crags can be bypassed.
Time	4hr 15min
Summits	Garbh-bheinn (806m, 2649ft), Belig (702m, Graham)
Maps	OS Landranger 32
Access	Head W along the A87 from Broadford and park in a large layby at the head of Loch Ainort
Note	It would be possible to descend from the Bealach na Beiste if you don't want to climb Belig. It would also be possible to combine with the Munro Bla Bheinn, but this would be a much more demanding expedition.

Garbh-bheinn is a fine viewpoint for the Cuillin Hills, the only mountain range in Britain where rock-climbing skills are needed to reach many of the summits. Although geographically in the Red Cuillin, Garbh-bheinn is geologically similar to the Black Cuillin and is an easy, but useful, introduction on the sort of terrain you will meet if you visit the Black Cuillin.

The popularity of the **Cuillins** dates back to the late 19th century. The best known climbers to visit at that time were Norman Collie and Charles Pilkington, often assisted by John MacKenzie, who was born in 1856 at Sconser on Loch Sligachan and was the Cuillin's first and most famous guide. It is believed he climbed Sgurr nan Gillean at the age of 10. Charles Pilkington learnt most of his mountaineering skills in Switzerland and spent a

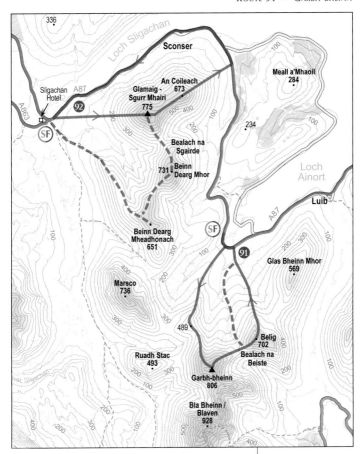

great deal of time on Skye, making successful first climbs of many peaks, with the assistance of John MacKenzie. Collie came to Skye in 1886 and, after two failed attempts to climb Sgurr nan Gillean, also turned to John MacKenzie for help. MacKenzie showed Collie the easiest route to the top, which is now known as 'The Tourist Route'.

Garbh-bheinn

Cross the Allt Coire nam Bruadaran on the road bridge and head roughly SW up one of the faint, boggy and intermittent paths which heads up the Druim Eadar Da Choire ridge. These strands gather into a better path as the ridge becomes better defined. Continue easily to the summit of the ridge (1hr 5min, 489m, 52520 24380). Follow an old fence line down to a saddle (435m) where you notice the change from 'red' rock to 'black' rock and climb easily up the ridge on rock, boulderfield and scree, avoiding difficulties on their right. Head straight up the final broken buttress and along the narrow summit ridge. The scrambling is easy, but exposed. You soon reach the small summit cairn on **Garbh-bheinn** (2hr, 806m, 53130 23230).

Have a look at the ridge between here and Bla Bheinn – this will give you a good impression of some of the difficulties involved in 'walking' in the Black Cuillin.

◄ Head roughly NE along the ridge, with easy but exposed scrambling, staying on or close to the crest of the ridge. As the ridge broadens, the descent continues down scree and boulderfield to a broad saddle, the **Bealach na Beiste**, (2hr 30min, 455m, 53950 23710). You could descend left from here but our route continues NE up Belig. The ridge is a mixture of crag, boulderfield and scree and shouldn't present much difficulty. There is the remains of a solid wall higher up the ridge and you will find it easier to stay left of this wall. There is a small cairn on the summit of **Belig** (3hr, 702m, 54410 24040).

The descent down the N ridge is down easy grass until it steepens above some crags. You will have to work your way carefully through these crags on rock, boulderfield and scree before the descent continues on easy grass. Once you reach the heather moor it is best to veer left so you don't get mixed up in rough terrain close to the burn in Coire Choinnich on your right. Eventually reach the junction of this burn with the Abhainn Ceann Loch Ainort (4hr, 20m, 53820 26250). Cross the left-hand burn and follow it to the road bridge (53810 26520) and turn left back to the parking (4hr 15min).

ROUTE 92

Sgurr Mhairi, Glamaig MARY'S PEAK, GREEDY WOMAN

Start	Sligachan Hotel (NG 48560 29800)
Distance	12km (8 miles)
Total ascent	900m (3000ft)
Difficulty	The ascent route is uncomfortably steep.
Time	4hr 10min
Summits	Sgurr Mhairi, Glamaig (775m, 2542ft), An Coileach (673m)
Maps	OS Landranger 32
Access	Park at or near the Sligachan Hotel on the A87 between Broadford and Portree.
Note	The ascent route is very steep and although it is frequently used in descent, some walkers will find that this is uncomfortably steep, especially in wet conditions. Those who want to avoid long steep slopes should ascend and descend by the descent route. An interesting alternative is to make the steep descent to Bealach na Sgairde, climb steeply to Beinn Dearg Mhor and continue to Beinn Dearg Mheadhonach before descending the easy Druim na Ruaige ridge to Sligachan.

Glamaig is the steep rounded hill, well protected by steep scree slopes, which dominates the view E from Sligachan.

In 1899 a visiting **Ghurkha soldier** called Thapa ran barefoot from the Sligachan Hotel to the top of Glamaig, and back again, in 75 minutes. On being told of this feat, MacLeod of MacLeod, the land-owner, refused to believe it and the luckless Thapa was asked to perform once more. This time he completed the task in just 55 minutes, which remained the official record until the 1980s. A race is now held in July each year and the record time of 44min 41s was set by Mark Rigby in 1997.

See map in Route 91.

From the Sligachan Hotel head about 300m E along the **A87** until just after the Sligachan road sign (48890 30020). Turn right up a faint path which soon passes through a gate and continues as a faint and often boggy path to the foot of **Sgurr Mhairi** (35min, 170m, 50320 30010) where heather gives way to grass. Head straight up the steep slope. It is possible to do a surprisingly large proportion of the ascent on grass rather than scree but this will require good route choice and will not be possible in poor visibility. Eventually you will reach the cairn on the grassy summit ridge (1hr 40min, 775m, 51360 29990).

Sgurr Mhairi, Glamaig

You will see an old fence line as you reach this summit and this can be followed easily ENE down to a saddle (620m) and up the other side to the small cairn on the summit of **An Coileach** (2hr 5min, 673m, 52440 30480). ▶

Continue along the fence line down grassy slopes, avoiding a few crags. At 400m the fence line goes down a nasty rubble chute and it will be easier to descend on grass through the crags to the left of the fence. Lower down the slope a small path is developing to the right of the fence and this eases the descent through rough heather on the lower slopes of the hill. Continue along the fence until you reach the A87 (2hr 50min, 25m, 53650 31430).

Unless you have arranged transport from here it is now a 6.5km road walk back to the Sligachan Hotel (4hr 10min).

You may be lucky enough to see snow buntings on this summit.

ROUTE 93

An Cliseam ROCKY HILL

Start	Abhainn Mharaig (NB 17410 05750)
Distance	14km (9 miles)
Total ascent	1070m (3500ft)
Difficulty	There is boggy terrain on the approaches to the mountain and a little easy scrambling as well as some boulderfield on the summit ridge. This route is not recommended for the inexperienced in poor weather.
Time	5hr
Summits	Mulla-Fo-Dheas (743m), An Cliseam (799m, 2622ft)
Maps	OS Landranger 14
Access	Head N from Tarbert along the A859 and continue to a car park by the Abhainn Mharaig bridge about 3 miles NE of the junction with the B887. It is better to park here than at Bun Abhainn Eadarra where parking is very limited.
Note	The 'peakbagger' may prefer to climb the recommended descent route, but this ascent has little to recommend it.

Famed for its beautiful beaches and intricate, rocky coastline, Harris has some of the finest but least visited mountains in Britain. An Cliseam is the only Corbett on Harris and Lewis. The three nearby Grahams Uisgneabhal Mor, Oireabhal and Tiorga Mor are actually more impressive mountains than the Corbett and you should spend time exploring these mountains during your stay on the island. Mulla-Fo-Dheas doesn't count as a Graham as there is only about 450ft of descent between it and An Cliseam.

Bun Abhainn Eadarra is a **derelict whaling station** which was founded by a Norwegian, Carl Herlofsen, in 1904. The station was operational until 1914 and again from 1918 to 1929. The main product was whale oil, which was used in making soap and margarine as well as for lighting and lubricants.

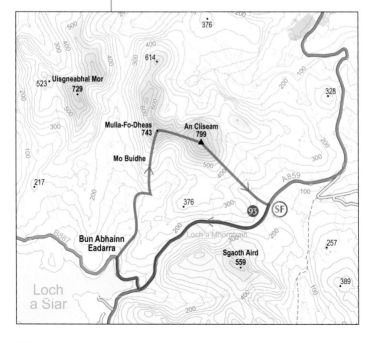

Unless you can arrange transport you start with a 3 mile road walk (or cycle) back to the junction with the **B887**. Turn right and reach **Bun Abhainn Eadarra** in 1 mile. Turn right up the track to the right of the first burn (1hr 20min, 10m, 13130 04270) and left through the rusty gate on a bend and then through the gate at the top of the 'pad-dock'. You can just about follow the boggy remains of the old stalker's path which starts up the right-hand side of the burn, crosses to the left-hand side then veers left away from the burn to pass a small lochan and then drop gen-tly down to reach the Abhainn Thorabraidh (1hr 55min, 80m, 13660 05840). Cross this burn and climb up to the

An Cliseam, Harris's only Corbett

339

left of the waterfalls. Once onto the ridge (at about 165m, 14040 05850) turn N up the broad ridge. The going is easy to **Mo Buidhe** where the slope gets steeper and there is some boulderfield to cross before you reach the summit of **Mulla-Fo-Dheas** which is honoured with two cairns (3hr 15min, 743m, 14320 07620).

Head E down a narrow rocky ridge, veering ESE further down. Care is needed and some use of the hands will be required. It is easiest to bypass the crags at the bottom of the ridge on their left. You will reach a saddle (675m, 14520 07600) and then continue more easily over a minor top (700m) and down to another saddle (605m, 14870 07510). Now climb easily up to a cairn at the NW end of the summit ridge. This ridge is bouldery with rock outcrops and the highest point on **An Cliseam** appears to be a walled enclosure completely surrounding the trig point (4hr, 799m, 15490 07290).

Now head roughly SE directly towards the car park. ◄ There is some boulderfield to cross early on the descent, and then further down the ground can be rather boggy. When you reach the Abhainn Mharaig (at about 250m) you will probably pick up a faint boggy path to the right of the burn which takes you back to the car park (5hr).

There is a bit of a path down the ridge but it isn't obvious where it starts and it seems to be very difficult to follow, so it isn't worth trying to locate.

APPENDIX A

Alphabetical list of Corbetts

Summit	Route no	Page
Ainshval	16	94
Am Bathach	38	159
An Cliseam	93	337
An Dun	Vol 1	
An Stac	9	70
An Ruadh-stac	55	216
An Sidhean	47	188
Aonach Buidhe	43	173
Aonach Shasuinn	45	181
Arkle	87	318
Askival	16	94
Auchnafree Hill	Vol 1	
Bac an Eich	49	194
Baosbheinn	63	242
Beinn Airigh Charr	64	245
Beinn a' Bha'ach Ard	48	191
Beinn a' Bhuiridh	Vol 1	
Beinn a' Chaisgein Mor	73	273
Beinn a' Chaisteil (Auch)	Vol 1	
Beinn a' Chaisteil (Loch Vaich)	67	256
Beinn a' Chlaidheimh	71	267
Beinn a' Choin	Vol 1	
Beinn a' Chrulaiste	Vol 1	

Summit	Route no	Page
Beinn a' Chuallaich	Vol 1	
Beinn an Eoin	62	239
Beinn an Lochain	Vol 1	
Beinn an Oir	Vol 1	
Beinn Bhan (Glen Loy)	18	103
Beinn Bhan (Applecross)	56	219
Beinn Bheula	Vol 1	
Beinn Bhreac	Vol 1	
Beinn Bhreac-liath	Vol 1	
Beinn Bhuidhe	26	123
Beinn Chaorach	Vol 1	
Beinn Chuirn	Vol 1	
Beinn Damh	57	223
Beinn Dearg (Glen Lyon)	Vol 1	
Beinn Dearg (Torridon)	58	226
Beinn Dearg Bheag	72	271
Beinn Dearg Mor	72	271
Beinn Dronaig	51	203
Beinn Each	Vol 1	
Beinn Enaiglair	69	261
Beinn Iaruinn	Vol 1	
Beinn Lair	65	248
Beinn Leoid	83	305

Summit	Route no	Page
Carn Ban	78	289
Carn Chuinneag	77	286
Carn Dearg (Glen Roy)	Vol 1	
Carn Dearg (S of Gleann Eachach)	Vol 1	
Carn Dearg (N of Gleann Eachach)	Vol 1	
Carn Dearg (see Meallan Liath Coire Mhic Dhughaill)		
Carn Dearg Mor	Vol 1	
Carn Ealasaid	Vol 1	
Carn Liath	Vol 1	
Carn Mor (Lecht)	Vol 1	
Carn Mor (Glen Dessarry)	23	116
Carn na Drochaide	Vol 1	
Carn na Nathrach	4	51
Carn na Saobhaidhe	Vol 1	
Cir Mhor	Vol 1	
Clisham (see An Cliseam)		
Conachraig	Vol 1	
Corryhabbie Hill	Vol 1	
Corserine	Vol 1	
Cranstackie	89	323
Creach Bheinn (Loch Creran)	Vol 1	
Creach Bheinn (Loch Linnhe)	2	44
Creag an Dhail Bheag (see Carn Liath)		

Summit	Route no	Page
Creag MacRanaich	Vol 1	
Creag Mhor	Vol 1	
Creag nan Gabhar	Vol 1	
Creag Rainich	70	264
Creag Uchdag	Vol 1	
Creagan na Beinne	Vol 1	
Cruach Innse	Vol 1	
Culardoch	Vol 1	
Cul Beag	75	278
Cul Mor	76	281
Druim nan Cnamh (see Beinn Loinne)		
Dun da Ghaoithe	1	40
Faochaig	42	168
Farragon Hill	Vol 1	
Foinaven	88	320
Fraoch Bheinn	21	112
Fraochaidh	Vol 1	
Fuar Bheinn	2	44
Fuar Tholl	54	213
Ganu Mor (see Foinaven)		
Garbh Bheinn (Loch Leven)	Vol 1	
Garbh Bheinn (Ardgour)	6	57
Garbh-bheinn (Skye)	91	332
Gairbeinn	Vol 1	
Geal Charn (Cairngorms)	Vol 1	
Geal Charn (Loch Arkaig)	19	105

Summit	Route no	Page
Sgurr an Airgid	41	166
Sgurr an Fhuarain	22	113
Sgurr an Utha	11	78
Sgurr Coire Choinnichean	33	145
Sgurr Cos na Breachd-laoigh	22	113
Sgurr Dhomhnuill	5	54
Sgurr Dubh	59	229
Sgurr Gaorsaic	44	176
Sgurr Ghiubhsachain	13	85
Sgurr Innse	Vol 1	
Sgurr Mhairi (see Glamaig)		
Sgurr Mhic Bharraich	40	164
Sgurr Mhurlagain	20	108
Sgurr na Ba Glaise	9	70
Sgurr na Feartaig	53	210
Sgurr nan Ceannaichean	52	207
Sgurr nan Eugallt	29	136

Summit	Route no	Page
Shalloch on Minnoch	Vol 1	
Spidean Coinich (Quinag)	82	302
Sron a' Choire Chnapanich	Vol 1	
Stob a' Bhealach an Sgriodain	12	81
Stob a' Choin	Vol 1	
Stob an Aonaich Mhoir	Vol 1	
Stob Coire a' Chearcaill	8	63
Stob Coire Creagach	Vol 1	
Stob Dubh	Vol 1	
Stob Fear-tomhais	Vol 1	
Streap	14	88
The Brack	Vol 1	
The Cobbler	Vol 1	
The Fara	Vol 1	
The Sow of Atholl	Vol 1	
White Coomb	Vol 1	

APPENDIX B
Sources of information

Corbett and Munro information
The Scottish Mountaineering Club is the custodian of the official list of Corbetts www.smc.org.uk/Corbetts/CorbettsTable

The website www.munromagic.com is a major resource for information on the Munros, Corbetts and Grahams. It gives the pronunciation of the names of the Corbetts and also the English translation used in this guide.

At www.hills-database.co.uk Chris Crocker and Graham Jackson have created a website for those interested in statistics and statistical topics pertaining to the British hills: measurement, classification, lists and data. They have attempted to make accurate measurements of heights of mountains whose status is in doubt and have been responsible for recent demotions of Munros to Corbett status.

Access to Scottish hills
Details of the Scottish Outdoor Access Code and information on stalking can be found at www.outdooraccess-scotland.com.

Mountain weather forecasts
Mountain Weather Information Service www.mwis.org.uk

Met Office www.metoffice.gov.uk/loutdoor/mountainsafety

Sportscotland Avalanche Information Service www.sais.gov.uk

Books
The Corbetts and Other Scottish Hills: Scottish Mountaineering Club Hillwalkers' Guide published by the Scottish Mountaineering Trust: more for home use than use on the hill.

Munro's Tables published by the Scottish Mountaineering Club: the 'official' listing of the Munros and Corbetts.

Climbing the Corbetts by Hamish Brown: Hamish Brown's personal experiences of climbing the Corbetts.

Climb every Mountain by Craig Caldwell: Craig's account of his epic expedition in climbing all the Munros and Corbetts in one self-propelled journey.

Map publishers

Ordnance Survey
OS produce fine maps at 1:50,000 and 1:25,000, covering the whole of Scotland in paper format and digital format for GPS devices and PCs www.ordnancesurvey.co.uk

Harvey
As well as 1:40,000 maps of the most popular areas in Scotland, Harvey have produced a Munro and Corbett Chart that shows and lists all Munros (mountains over 3000ft), Corbetts (over 2500ft), Grahams and Donalds (over 2000ft) www.harveymaps.co.uk

Other organisations
John Muir Trust is the leading wild
land conservation charity in the
UK, protecting 115,000 hectares of
mountain, moorland, rugged coast and
wooded glens across Scotland
www.jmt.org

Scottish Youth Hostel Association Tel:
0845 293 7373 (reservations) Tel:
01786 891 400 (general enquiries)
www.hostellingscotland.com

Scottish Independent Hostels
www.hostel-scotland.co.uk

The Mountain Bothies Association
maintains about 100 bothies in the
Highlands
www.mountainbothies.org.uk

Glenmore Lodge National Outdoor
Training Centre Tel: 01479 861 256
www.glenmorelodge.org.uk

VisitScotland (tourist information)
www.visithighlands.com

The National Trust for Scotland
www.nts.org.uk

Public transport
Map showing rail routes, stations and
ferries in Scotland http://mappery.com/
maps/Scotland-Rail-Map.gif

Scotrail is the train operator in Scotland
www.firstscot.railsaver.co.uk

Most of the ferry services in Scotland
are operated by Caledonian MacBrayne
Tel: 0800 066 5000 www.calmac.co.uk

There are a number of Postbus routes
operated by the Royal Mail in the
Scottish Highlands www.royalmail.com/
you-home/your-community/postbus

Traveline Scotland has links to the
bus operators in Scotland www.
travelinescotland.com then click on the
bus icon

LISTING OF CICERONE GUIDES

Tour of the Oisans: The GR54
Tour of the Queyras
Tour of the Vanoise
Trekking in the Vosges and Jura
Vanoise Ski Touring
Walking in the Auvergne
Walking in the Cathar Region
Walking in the Cevennes
Walking in the Dordogne
Walking in the Haute Savoie
  North & South
Walking in the Languedoc
Walking in the Tarentaise and
  Beaufortain Alps
Walking on Corsica

GERMANY
Germany's Romantic Road
Walking in the Bavarian Alps
Walking the River Rhine Trail

HIMALAYA
8000m
Annapurna
Bhutan: A Trekker's Guide
Everest: A Trekker's Guide
Garhwal and Kumaon: A
  Trekker's and Visitor's Guide
Kangchenjunga: A Trekker's
  Guide
Langtang with Gosainkund and
  Helambu: A Trekker's Guide
Manaslu: A Trekker's Guide
The Mount Kailash Trek
Trekking in Ladakh
Trekking in the Himalaya

ICELAND & GREENLAND
Trekking in Greenland
Walking and Trekking in Iceland

IRELAND
Irish Coastal Walks
The Irish Coast to Coast Walk
The Mountains of Ireland

ITALY
Gran Paradiso
Sibillini National Park
Stelvio National Park
Shorter Walks in the Dolomites
Through the Italian Alps
Trekking in the Apennines
Trekking in the Dolomites
Via Ferratas of the Italian

Dolomites: Vols 1 & 2
Walking in Abruzzo
Walking in Stelvio National Park
Walking in Sardinia
Walking in Sicily
Walking in the Central Italian
  Alps
Walking in the Dolomites
Walking in Tuscany
Walking on the Amalfi Coast
Walking the Italian Lakes

MEDITERRANEAN
Jordan – Walks, Treks, Caves,
  Climbs and Canyons
The Ala Dag
The High Mountains of Crete
The Mountains of Greece
Treks and Climbs in Wadi Rum,
  Jordan
Walking in Malta
Western Crete

NORTH AMERICA
British Columbia
The Grand Canyon
The John Muir Trail
The Pacific Crest Trail

SOUTH AMERICA
Aconcagua and the Southern
  Andes
Hiking and Biking Peru's Inca
  Trails
Torres del Paine

SCANDINAVIA
Walking in Norway

**SLOVENIA, CROATIA AND
MONTENEGRO**
The Julian Alps of Slovenia
The Mountains of Montenegro
Trekking in Slovenia
Walking in Croatia
Walking in Slovenia: The
  Karavanke

SPAIN AND PORTUGAL
Costa Blanca: West
Mountain Walking in Southern
  Catalunya
The Mountains of Central Spain
The Northern Caminos
Trekking through Mallorca
Walking in Madeira

Walking in Mallorca
Walking in the Algarve
Walking in the Cordillera
  Cantabrica
Walking in the Sierra Nevada
Walking on La Gomera and
  El Hierro
Walking on La Palma
Walking on Tenerife
Walking the GR7 in Andalucia
Walks and Climbs in the Picos
  de Europa

SWITZERLAND
Alpine Pass Route
Canyoning in the Alps
Central Switzerland
The Bernese Alps
The Swiss Alps
Tour of the Jungfrau Region
Walking in the Valais
Walking in Ticino
Walks in the Engadine

TECHNIQUES
Geocaching in the UK
Indoor Climbing
Lightweight Camping
Map and Compass
Mountain Weather
Moveable Feasts
Outdoor Photography
Polar Exploration
Rock Climbing
Sport Climbing
The Book of the Bivvy
The Hillwalker's Guide to
  Mountaineering
The Hillwalker's Manual

MINI GUIDES
Avalanche!
Navigating with a GPS
Navigation
Pocket First Aid and Wilderness
  Medicine
Snow

For full information on all
our guides, and to order
books and eBooks, visit our
website:
www.cicerone.co.uk.

Walking – Trekking – Mountaineering – Climbing – Cycling

Over 40 years, Cicerone have built up an outstanding collection of 300 guides, inspiring all sorts of amazing adventures.

Every guide comes from extensive exploration and research by our expert authors, all with a passion for their subjects. They are frequently praised, endorsed and used by clubs, instructors and outdoor organisations.

All our titles can now be bought as **e-books** and many as iPad and Kindle files and we will continue to make all our guides available for these and many other devices.

Our website shows any **new information** we've received since a book was published. Please do let us know if you find anything has changed, so that we can pass on the latest details. On our **website** you'll also find some great ideas and lots of information, including sample chapters, contents lists, reviews, articles and a photo gallery.

It's easy to keep in touch with what's going on at Cicerone, by getting our monthly **free e-newsletter**, which is full of offers, competitions, up-to-date information and topical articles. You can subscribe on our home page and also follow us on **Facebook** and **Twitter**, as well as our **blog**.

Cicerone – the very best guides for exploring the world.

CICERONE

2 Police Square Milnthorpe Cumbria LA7 7PY
Tel: 015395 62069 info@cicerone.co.uk
www.cicerone.co.uk